Imperial print in colonial Calcutta (1780-1820): a realm of early print.
The emergence of heteroglossia in print and society.

TAPATI BHARADWAJ.

IMPERIAL PRINT IN COLONIAL CALCUTTA (1780-1820).

Copyright © 2014 Tapati Bharadwaj.

All rights reserved.

ISBN: 8192875210
ISBN-13: 978-8192875217

DEDICATION

For Ma.

IMPERIAL PRINT IN COLONIAL CALCUTTA (1780-1820).

IMPERIAL PRINT IN COLONIAL CALCUTTA (1780-1820).

CONTENTS

	Acknowledgments	i
1	Introduction. the early realm of print culture in colonial Calcutta; conceptualizing new methodologies.	1
2	When the *sahibs* of the East India Company came: establishing realms of power and the arrival of print, paraphernalia and empire.	30
3	The emergence of early print in colonial Calcutta (1780-1820).	57
4	Reading Histories: The making of imperial diasporic citizens.	86
5	Cheese, wine and colonial Calcutta: the making of an imperial social identity.	115
6	Heteroglossic texts: English-native newspapers in colonial Calcutta.	150
7	Conclusion: the emergence of a larger print public sphere.	176
	Bibliography	180

FIGURES

Figure 1: Title page of a grammar book.	4
Figure 2: Geo-social realms of power.	39
Figure 3: East facing map of Calcutta.	42
Figure 4: Advertisements.	45
Figure 5: Advertisements.	46
Figure 6: Advertisements of a circulating library.	59
Figure 7: Editorial in the *Calcutta Journal*.	95

Figure 8: Summaries from other newspapers. 104

Figure 9: Extracts from State papers. 105

Figure 10: News on wars on the Continent. 107

Figure 11: Extract of letter written by Cornwallis. 109

Figure 12: Treaty between Tipu Sultan and the EIC. 110

Figure 13: Public entry of the captured princes. 111

Figure 14: Advertisements in newspapers. 129

Figure 15: Sailing ships 136

Figure 16: Advertisements for a new publication 140

Figure 17: Advertisements of printed books. 141

Figure 18: Advertisements of books to be printed. 142

Figure 19: Advertisements of vocabulary and grammar books 144

Figure 20: Advertisement of a bilingual translation. 145

Figure 21: Multilingual texts. 151

IMPERIAL PRINT IN COLONIAL CALCUTTA (1780-1820).

IMPERIAL PRINT IN COLONIAL CALCUTTA (1780-1820).

ACKNOWLEDGMENTS

It has been a while since I first started work on the nature of print culture in colonial India. I journeyed across continents, moving baggage and family. I wish to thank all my teachers in the English Department at Loyola University, Chicago, who have been involved in my intellectual growth. I also wish to thank the English Department at Jadavpur University, Calcutta. The people involved in the archives at the National Library, Calcutta were also very kind and helpful.

Printed texts have a life of their own, as they travel around the world, stay hidden from the public eyes for centuries only to emerge and create change. For me, it is always an interesting experience to think that if I were writing in 1780 in India, I might a) not have written at all being a woman in India and not have access to learning and b) have used manuscripts to write what I had to write. A part of who we are is derived from other civilizations and cultures.

IMPERIAL PRINT IN COLONIAL CALCUTTA (1780-1820).

1 INTRODUCTION. THE EARLY REALM OF PRINT CULTURE IN COLONIAL CALCUTTA: CONCEPTUALISING NEW METHODOLOGIES.

Nathaniel Halhed's grammar book, *A Grammar of the Bengal language*,[1] was printed in 1778, and was one of the first printed texts in India. It had a multilingual title page; it had a Bengali subtitle alongside the English title (and the Roman numericals at the bottom), making it undoubtedly a first of its kind. (fig.1) The grammar book was targeting an English readership located both in India and in England. The advent of print in colonial Bengal in the last two decades of the eighteenth century is a story that has its beginnings far away from its source of production. Print technology developed in the western world and was carried across to Calcutta as a byproduct of colonization and the efforts of the East India Company. If the natives were to trust the Britishers, and be complicit partners, they had to believe that the rulers were there for their own good and happiness. A realm of print culture developed that was extremely sophisticated in its use of technology and the manner in which it was conceptualized by the Britishers. Initially, both native and English texts were meant to be consumed by the Britishers, as is evident in the book above, but subsequent native use was implied. Close interaction between the natives and the Englishmen would allow the natives to understand how print worked and they would inevitably want to learn about it.

---

[1] Nathaniel Halhed, *A Grammar of the Bengal Language*, 1778. Reprint, ed. R. C. Alston (England: The Scolar Press, 1969).

Figure 1: Title page of a grammar book.

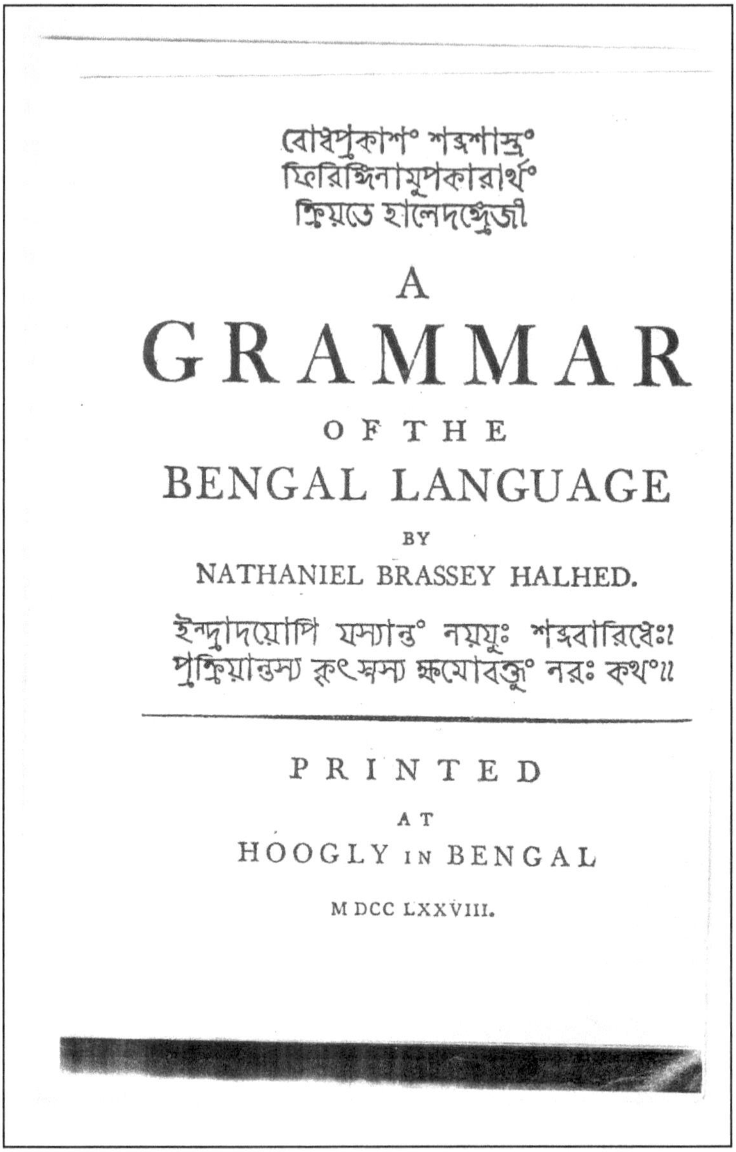

বোধপ্রকাশং শব্দশাস্ত্রং
ফিরিঙ্গিনাযুপকারার্থং
ক্রিয়তে হালেদঞ্জেজী

A
GRAMMAR
OF THE
BENGAL LANGUAGE
BY
NATHANIEL BRASSEY HALHED.

ইন্দ্রাদয়োপি যস্যান্তং নয়যুঃ শব্দবারিধেঃ
পুক্রিয়ান্তস্য রুৎস্নস্য ক্ষমোবক্তুং নরঃ কথং॥

PRINTED
AT
HOOGLY IN BENGAL
M DCC LXXVIII.

IMPERIAL PRINT IN COLONIAL CALCUTTA (1780-1820).

In order to print a multilingual text, native types were needed, and so were printing presses. Charles Wilkins, a twenty eight year old writer with the East India Company, was requested by the then Governor General Warren Hastings to come up with Bengali types which were used to print Halhed's book in Hooghly. I am not sure as to what a printing press would be doing in Hooghly, unless it was an isolated instance of printing being done in a port where British presence would have been inevitable. Printing was not an easy task; for example, in the absence of paper mills, most of the paper was imported; two types of paper were available – Indian hand made paper, also called Patna paper and the more expensive imported paper. William Carey's paper mill was built around 1800 but there were also efforts taken to build paper mills before.[2]

Till as recently as two hundred years ago, India was a manuscript culture meaning that the printed text did not exist. When the transition took place from a manuscript culture to a print one, it seems to have taken place easelessly, implying that the shift was made without much murmurs and complaints from at least the native, elite sections of society. The Britishers, on the other hand, at seeing the beautiful manuscripts in Indian languages, must have been reminded of their pre-print past and a lot of care was taken to ensure that these manuscripts were well kept. When Tipu Sultan lost the Mysore wars (1780-90s), his library was also taken and a concern was raised by the Company soldiers as to how the manuscripts were to be kept safe: "That part of the library of the late Tippoo Sultan, which was presented by the army to the Court of Directors, is lately arrived in Bengal; the Governor-General strongly recommends that the Oriental manuscripts composing this collection, should be deposited in the library of the College of Fort William, and it is his intention to retain the manuscripts accordingly, until he shall receive the orders of the Court upon the subject."[3] There was

---

[2] For more see Graham Shaw, *Printing in Calcutta before 1800* (Oxford: Oxford University Press, 1981), pp. 28-39.

[3] "Introduction," in *The Annals of the College of Fort William, from the Period of its Foundation*. Arranged and Published by Thomas Roebuck, Calcutta (Printed by Philip Periera at the Hindoostanee Press, 1819), pp. i-liii, p. xxv. In *The Annals*, there is also mention on the importance of preserving old manuscripts: "The preservation and augmentation of the Collection of Eastern Manuscripts, afford the only means of arresting the progressive

no rampant erasure of the Indian manuscript past, and in fact, the Company was keen to preserve this aspect of Indian culture.

Were the Indians happy at the advent of print technology and did they understand the epistemic shift that would take place at the introduction of print? When we consider how print did impact what was essentially a manuscript and oral culture, we have to construe and add meaning in narratives written by the Britishers who often would grandly boast about their achievements in India. Even if we hear little from the natives at this time period of print technology in Calcutta, the Britishers were extravagant in their rhetoric when it came to describing the need for print in India: "amidst the numerous blessings which have flowed from it [the rule of England], one of the most important is, the introduction of that mighty engine of improvement to which Europe is itself so highly indebted — the Press."[4] An editorial in a newspaper summarizes the presence of the native press in laudatory terms, as if justifying the good of colonial rule:

> The era of improvement and of civilization has already dawned on this country. The Natives possess a Press of their own, and its operations have commenced with that vigour and effect which warrant the most sanguine expectations. Within the last ten years, native works have been printed by Natives themselves, and sold among the Hindoo population with astonishing rapidity. An unprecedented impulse has been communicated to the inhabitants of Bengal, and the avidity for reading has increased beyond all former example. Before this period, the press had been confined to Europeans, and the only works in the native languages were printed at their expense, and circulated gratis. The natives have now taken the work into their own hands, and the commencement is commensurate with the avarice of native editors, and the rich fund of

---

destruction of Oriental learning. Since the dismemberment of the Muslim, those works have been dispersed over India, and have been exposed to the injuries and hazards of time, accident and neglect. It is worthy of the ambition of this great Empire to employ every effort of its influence in preserving from destruction and decay, these valuable records of Oriental history, Science and Religion." p. 114.

[4] "Art. V. - On the effect of the Native Press in India," *The Friend of India*. Quarterly Series (No. 1): 130-154, pp. 132-133.

wealth enjoyed by the higher class of Hindoos.[5]

As readers situated in the present where print is prolific and an intrinsic element in our lives, we really are unable to comprehend how printed texts would have affected a manuscript culture, and often we are given an interpretation which would have to be partially biased, as it comes from the perspective of the Britishers. The editorial continues in a similar extravagant manner:

> The multiplication of printed works has excited a taste for reading, hitherto unknown in India, which promises to become gradually more extensive and more refined. Compared with preceding years, when manuscripts alone existed, books are now exceedingly common: men of wealth and influence begin already to value themselves on the possession of a library, and on obtaining the earliest intelligence of the operations of the press. Even among the inferior gentry, there are few who do not possess some of the works which the press has created. The country partakes of the same spirit with the metropolis, though in an inferior degree. The encouragement afforded to this incipient plan, has likewise called forth a race of editors.[6]

Within a span of a few decades, the editorial writes, a "body of enlightened natives animated with an unconquerable thirst for knowledge" would emerge. There is a sense that print would allow for the emergence of a new kind of a print-informed native, and large societal changes would enable a realm of print culture to be established, with readers, writers, editors, distributors and so on.

Oftentimes, the enormous justification as to why there was a need to colonize India was transferred onto the natives who were construed as wanting progress from the west. We can only imagine how the print

---

[5] Ibid., p. 133.

[6] Ibid., p. 135.

informed landscape in Calcutta would have changed in the last two decades of the eighteenth century; presses, paper, books, magazines and other print paraphernalia would have arrived as cargo in the ships from England, they would be carted across and stored somewhere and then subsequently bought by printers and booksellers.

Doing archival research.

A central premise upon which this book rests is that book history in India relies on archival research and more needs to be done. Looking from a larger, cross disciplinary perspective makes one conclude that archival research has unearthed a lot of unexplored territories and established new disciplines. For example, a lot of the work that is done on early book history in American studies is based on little used and little read archival material. Book history, of the antebellum period, within American studies often uses minor texts. Matthew Brown's "The Thick Style: steady sellers, textual aesthetics, and early modern devotional reading"[7] in the 2006 January edition of the *PMLA* makes use as primary texts devotional writings that were printed in the early seventeenth century in America. These devotional works comprised of "manuals of piety, guides to conversion, sermon series, and psalm books" alongside scriptures which formed the popular literature of early New England and were written by moderate to radical Reformers and Non conformists.[8] Brown argues that these works are little known texts, but can be construed as defining a "literary culture" of the seventeenth century, helping to substantiate the "scroll-to-codex" analogy."[9] In a similar manner, in *The Letters of the Republic*, Michael Warner argues that a transformation of power took place in eighteenth century America as a result of "an increased volume of print" and also because of how printed texts were construed by the reading public; he uses the examples of legal texts, constitutional tracts, writings of Benjamin Franklin, magazines and newspapers of eighteenth century

---

[7] Matthew P. Brown, "The Thick Style: Steady Sellers, Textual Aesthetics, and Early Modern Devotional Reading." *PMLA*, Vol. 121(1): 67-86.

[8] Ibid.,p. 68.

[9] Ibid., p. 69

America.[10] The development of the discipline of early book history in American studies was dependent on being able to retrieve and access archived texts.

The discipline of black feminist literary criticism is a recent creation and Barbara Christian's works have been seminal in establishing a literary genealogy of black women writers who were erased from the literary imagination; *Black Women Novelists: The Development of a Tradition*[11] looks at the writings of Zora Neale Hurston and Nella Larsen. On a similar note, her work, *Black Feminist Criticism: Perspectives on black women writers*[12] draws attention to the manner in which she was involved in retrieving a forgotten literary tradition of black women writers. The need to retrieve a lost African American literary tradition is elaborated in another essay[13] where she describes how in the August 1974 edition of *Black World*, the most widely read publication on African American literature, culture and politics of that time, a picture of a then little known writer, Zora Neale Hurston, was used as a picture cover. It implied a "literary foremother who had been neglected by Afro-Americanists of the past but who was finally being recognized by her daughters and reinstated as a major figure in the African American literary tradition."[14] Christian writes that it was "virtually impossible to locate either the works of many 19th century writers or those of contemporary writers;"[15] moreover, there was a dearth of secondary material on these writers in the 1970s. Thus, not only was a new discipline formed, through retrieving forgotten writers but there was a focus on the

---

[10] Michael Warner, *Letters of the Republic* (Harvarad, Harvard University Press, 1990).

[11] Barbara Christian, *Black Women Novelists: The Development of a Tradition* (Westport, Connecticut: Greenwood Press, 1980).

[12] Barbara Christian, *Black Feminist Criticism: Perspectives on black women writers* (Teachers College Press, 1985).

[13] Barbara Christian, "But What Do We Think We've Being Doing Anyway: The State of Black Feminist Criticism(s) or My Version of a Little Bit of History" in *New Black Feminist Criticism 1985-2000, Barbara Christian*, eds. Gloria Bowles, M. Giulia Febi and Arlene R. Keizer (Urbana: University of Illinois Press, 2007), pp.5-19.

[14] Ibid., p. 5.

[15] Ibid., p. 9.

need to generate scholarship on how to interpret these texts.

Within the Indian context, there are many writers whom we have forgotten, and who were writing in the late eighteenth and early nineteenth centuries and their works also comprise the first printed texts. The first literary works in India in English were by Englishmen for their personal consumption, and was part of the imperial hegemonic sub public realm of print. That such literary works were locally printed meant the emergence and establishment of a group of editors and literary journals that was conversant with the literary tradition. Eventually, these printed works would allow for and pave the way for natives who would also write in English. Archival research will allow us to figure out the books that were written in the last two decades of the eighteenth century, and a few that we can consider are: *The bevy of Calcutta beauties. A collection of poems*,[16] *The poems of Anna Maria*,[17] *The happy prescription; or, the lady relieved from her lovers: a comedy in rhyme*,[18] *The two connoisseurs; a comedy, in rhyme*,[19] *East India Company. Treaties. Etc*,[20] *Kalidasa. The seasons: A descriptive poem*, by calidas, in the original Sanskrit,[21]. *A collection of poems, written in the East Indies*. With miscellaneous remarks in real life,[22] *A poem, on the capture of Seringapatnam, by a Bengal officer*.[23] In the early nineteenth century, many literary magazines were also printed in Calcutta and notwithstanding the fact that the emergence of print culture was but twenty years old, a sophisticated realm of literature evolved. Retrieving these archived texts will allow us to conceptualize new methodologies and areas of study in early print culture in colonial Calcutta.

---

[16] Published in Calcutta; printed by Daniel Stuart, 1785.

[17] Published in Calcutta; from the press of Thomson and Ferris, 1793.

[18] Written for a private theatre, by William Hayley, Esq. – Calcutta: printed in the year, 1785.

[19] Written for the private theatre, by William Hayley, Esq. – Calcutta; printed in the year, 1785.

[20] Published in Calcutta: printed at the Honourable Company's Press, 1788.

[21] Published in Calcutta; printed at the Honourable Company's Press, 1792.

[22] By John Horsford, Calcutta; printed by Joseph Cooper, Telegraph Press, 1797.

[23] Published in Calcutta; printed at the Telegraph office, 1799.

Shifting the models of analysis in book history: hypothesis and methodology used.

My scholarship is a shift from a model of technological determinism which considers print and the book as affecting systems of thought——scientific, political and aesthetic (amongst others). Such a deterministic approach considers print as having an ontological status, existing prior to culture; for example, the title of Elizabeth Eisenstein's text, *The Printing Press as an Agent of Change,* makes use of such an approach as the emphasis is on how print had introduced epistemic changes affecting the very nature of what comprised knowledge during the early modern period.[24] My scholarship, on the other hand, does not eschew the assumption of the mutual reciprocity between social events and technology—as print in South Asia was introduced under colonization and as a result of the efforts of the East India Company, this social process determines the very nature of how print evolved. Print culture is seen as operating and emerging from within a large socio-literary realm, one which involves native and English bookmakers, publishers, and distributors and a reading audience. Socio-cultural conditions determine, to a very large extent, the logic of how print operates. Undoubtedly, print that had been introduced under a non imperialistic social structure would have operated differently from print that was part and parcel of British colonization. For example, colonization did determine the intervention and perpetuation of English as a language of rule and communication, which needed to be mastered by the Indians. New literary forms and genres were introduced in a manner that would not have occurred in other conditions. A print-induced public sub-sphere was formed, one that soon was conversant with the techniques of print. English print culture was a part of a multilingual sphere of textuality, coexisting alongside oral and scribal cultures, and could be used to address both the imperialists and the natives.

Literary scholars working on print culture use a different methodology and position themselves differently from those who are book

---

[24] Elizabeth Eisenstein, *The Printing Press as an Agent of Change* (Cambridge: Cambridge University Press, 1980).

historians. Even as I am aware of the interdisciplinary nature of my subject matter, I consider my work as a part of cultural studies. My primary material covers newspapers, as I trace the emergence of imperial print and the gradual involvement of natives in the realm of print. I cover a time period of around twenty years and I begin around 1780, when James Hicky set up his printing press in Calcutta and published the first newspaper in India for the white settler community in Calcutta. The scholarship that emerges from within print culture is often of this nature, covering large periods of time, as it traces social changes related to print: Jonathan Rose's *The Intellectual Life of the British Working Class*,[25] Jacqueline Pearson's *Women's Reading in Britain, 1750-1835*[26], David Vincent's *Literacy and Popular Culture: England 1750-1914*[27], Richard Altick's *The English Common Reader: A Social History of the Mass Reading Public, 1800-1900*[28] are a few instances of scholarly texts that examine extensive periods of time to describe the textual practices in the West. My work, moreover, is largely textual and involves archival research.

Most of my research has been conducted at the National Library, Kolkata. It has a repository of the first newspapers that were printed in the late eighteenth century in Calcutta. I examine these newspapers in my book where I look at the nature of print that emerged in the last two decades of the eighteenth century and catered to the needs of the Britishers. I set out with an aim of finding the following newspapers: *Hicky's Bengal Gazette or Calcutta General Advertiser* (1780), *The India Gazette* (1780), *The Calcutta Gazette* (1784), *The Bengal Journal* (1785), *The Asiatic Miscellany* (1785), *The Calcutta Chronicle and General Advertiser* (1786), *The Asiatic Mirror and Commercial Advertiser* (1788), *The Calcutta Monthly Register and India Repository* (1790), *The World* (1791), *The Calcutta Evening Post and The Calcutta Morning Post* (1792), *The Calcutta Monthly Journal* (1794), *The Bengal Harkaru* (1795) and *The Asiatic*

---

[25] Jonathan Rose, *The Intellectual Life of the British Working Classes* (New Haven: Yale University Press, 2001).

[26] Jacqueline Pearson, *Women's Reading in Britain, 1750-1835: A Dangerous Recreation* (Cambridge: Cambridge University Press, 1999).

[27] David Vincent, *Literacy and Popular Culture: England 1750-1914* (Cambridge: Cambridge University Press, 1989).

[28] Richard Daniel Altick, *The English Common Reader: A Social History of the Mass Reading Public, 1800-1900*. 2nd ed. (Columbus: Ohio State UP, 1998).

Magazine (1798). In making my choice of what to focus on in the newspapers, I had in mind certain themes which are central to my study; a few important subjects that I chose are the following: how were these first newspapers being perceived by the English writers who had just arrived from England, how was the newspaper being used within Calcutta, reports of wars, commentaries of social functions being conducted for the Britishers, consumer items being advertised.

Between 1780 and 1800, print was used mostly by the Britishers living in Calcutta, but by the turn of the early eighteenth century, natives picked up the technology of print. Native writers in English who used print and the English language with dexterity were Rammohun Roy and Henry Derozio – whose English works are mentioned in the last chapter. These early moments in the history of English print in India are unique and little explored. The initial realm of print served the needs of the Britishers, but how so easily and within a few decades, the natives picked it up to the point where someone like Rammohun Roy, who had grown up within a manuscript culture, carried out serious theological debate and dashed off pamphlets within India and across the globe, using this realm of print.

So where is this book located? Situating the realm of early print within the domain of existing scholarship.

The scholarship on print culture within the south Asian context is still in its nascent stages. Though there are works like B. S. Kesavan's *The History of Printing and Publishing in India*[29] which does a thorough survey of the early history of Indian printing, its central focus is on literary analysis. To be able to gauge the reading habits and practices of the "natives," and the world of publishers and printers that were involved in the realm of print culture in South Asia, empirical and statistical research is needed, involving archives. Thankappan Nair's *A History of the Calcutta Press*[30] and *Hicky and his Gazette*[31]

---

[29] B.S. Kesavan, *The History of Printing and Publishing in India* (India: National Book Trust, 1984).

[30] Thankappan Nair, *A History of the Calcutta Press* (Calcutta: Firma KLM, 1987).

[31] Thankappan Nair, *Hicky and his Gazette* (Calcutta: S.T. Books, 2001).

examine the nature of British newspapers and periodicals in the last two decades of the eighteenth century in Calcutta; a similar kind of analysis and documentation is also done by Graham Shaw in *Printing in Calcutta to 1800*.[32]

Intensive archival research is evident in Rimi Chatterjee's *Empires of the Mind: A History of Oxford University Press under the Raj*.[33] She examines the history of Oxford University Press between 1880 to 1947, and the people and policies behind the operation of the publishing house. In many ways, the book is a history of Indian scholarly publishing. In a similar fashion, but using statistics, in *In Another Country*, Priya Joshi looks at habits of consumption.[34] She makes use of methods of book history – by looking at publishers' records in England and catalogues of libraries in India – and also literary analyses. Her work covers the nineteenth and the twentieth centuries, spanning the colonial and the postcolonial periods. Textual consumption by the Indian subjects, Priya Joshi writes, can explain the success of the British novel in India and the "processes of cultural transmission."[35] Her aim is to see how ideas were "received, transmogrified, rejected, or refashioned by that small but influential part of the Indian population who ha[d] access to this world of print."[36] First readers and then writers of the English novel, through acts of "cultural interpretations," produced new meaninsg to the "products deployed by the colonizer," thus allowing for the agency of the colonized to be revealed.[37] Ulrike Stark's *An Empire of Books: Naval Kishore Press and the Diffusion of the Printed Word in Colonial India* is a similar study, where she examines Lucknow's Naval Kishor press, the foremost printing unit in nineteenth century north India,

---

[32] Graham Shaw, *Printing in Calcutta to 1800. A description and checklist of printing in late 18th century Calcutta* (London: The Bibliographical Society, 1981).

[33] Rimi B. Chatterjee, *Empires of the Mind: A History of Oxford University Press under the Raj* (New Delhi: Oxford University Press, 2006).

[34] Priya Joshi, *In Another Country. Colonialism, Culture, and the English Novel in India* (New York: Columbia University Press, 2002).

[35] Ibid., p. 4.

[36] Ibid., p. 18.

[37] Ibid., p. 23.

and the coming of the book in Hindi and Urdu.[38] The press was both a commercial enterprise and an intellectual center, functioning within a colonial public sphere.

Incendiary ideas became easily communicable within a print-induced public realm, and the British government passed the Press and Registration Act in 1867, Robert Darnton writes, to keep track of and catalogue all the books that were published in British India.[39] This was a way in which knowledge could be documented and controlled. Priya Joshi argues that despite the measures of control introduced by the British government, there was a limit to the "extent of British authority over Indian print."[40] Social structures also underwent changes. Veena Naregal states that "colonial domination operated by altering the structures and categories of discursive production" and that print was basic to the making of colonial literacy, proposing links between "educational policy, colonial bilingualism and the strategies of the native intelligentsia in Western India to realize their hegemonic aspirations within the sphere of colonial literate politics."[41] The new medium of print created a new discursive space; journals and newspapers created an audience that did not have to be in physical contact with each other in order to engage in debate.

It is equally important to keep in mind the presence of pre-print public spaces. In the colonial Indian context in the nineteenth century, Anindita Ghosh argues, one has to take into account the existence of "significant preprint literate [performance based] communities" which continued to operate in the presence of print as "print sustained earlier reading and writing traditions."[42] Different kinds of public spheres

---

[38] Ulrike Stark, *An Empire of Books: Naval Kishore Press and the Diffusion of the Printed Word in Colonial India* (New Delhi: Permanent Black, 2009).

[39] Robert Darnton, "Literary Surveillance in the British Raj. The Contradictions of Liberal Imperialism." *Book History,* 4(2001): 133-176.

[40] Priya Joshi, "Quantative Method, Literary History," *Book History* 5(2002): 263-274; 266.

[41] Veena Naregal, *Language Politics, Elites and the Public Sphere. Western India Under Colonialism* (London: Anthem Press, 2001), p. 5.

[42] Anindita Ghosh, "An Uncertain 'Coming of the Book'; Early Print Cultures in Colonial

emerged, and these did not necessarily exist in mutual harmony. Often, as Kumkum Sangari has pointed out, there was a constant shift between print and orality. In her examination of the tradition of the *qissa*, a literary technique, she examines on how in the late nineteenth century, it circulated between orality, print and performance.[43] But eventually, as the editors of *India's Literary History* state, it was "printed prose which became the principal vehicle for a literary modernity in colonial India."[44] For example, Stuart Blackburn examines how print affected Tamil prose.[45] In fact, Blackburn argues elsewhere that most printed books in Tamil in the early nineteenth century were collections of folklore, revealing the convergence between print and folklore.[46] As the editors of *Moveable Type* write, the nineteenth and the twentieth centuries saw an "astonishing degree of mobility displayed by writers, booksellers and printers cutting across linguistic and regional divides."[47] It is keeping in mind this vast background tableau of a multilingual print space comprised of Indian languages which emerged in the last two centuries that I position my scholarship which examines English print between 1780 and 1800.[48] My book, therefore, is an

---

India." *Book History* 6(2003): 23-55; 25, 44.

[43] Kumkum Sangari, "Multiple Temporalities, Unsettled Boundaries, Trickster Women. Reading a Nineteenth Century Qissa", in *India's Literary History. Essays on the Nineteenth Century*, ed. Stuart Blackburn and Vasudha Dalmia (New Delhi: Permanent Black, 2004), pp. 213-250.

[44] "Introduction", in *India's Literary History. Essays on the Nineteenth Century*, p. 11.

[45] Stuart Blackburn, "The Burden of Authenticity: Printed Oral Tales in Tamil Literary History.", in *India's Literary History*, pp. 119-145.

[46] Stuart Blackburn, *Print, Folklore and Nationalism in Colonial South India* (New Delhi: Permanent Black, 2003).

[47] "Introduction," in *Moveable Type*, ed. Abhijit Gupta and Swapan Chakvarty (New Delhi: Permanent Black, 2008), p. 2.

[48] The editors of *Print Areas: Book History in India* state that "reading and writing in the English language in this country" was almost two centuries old, and a complex network of publishers, readers, booksellers and authors arose in the nineteenth century"; as works in English were read, natives learnt with this realm of print, and "commented on this new world of knowledge and ideas opened up for them by the English." In the "Introduction," in *Print Areas: Book History in India,* ed. Swapan Chakravarty and Abhijit Gupta (New Delhi: Permanent Black, 2004), p. 14. Also see *Moveable Type: Book History in India II* (New Delhi: Permanent Black, 2008).

intervention in a time period in the history of print in India which has not been explored. The emergence of a realm of English print in colonial Bengal, which was first used by the Britishers and subsequently learnt by the native in the early nineteenth century, is a little examined subject.

Interrogating the notion of hybridity in Postcolonial theory.

British presence in India introduced the technology of print and the English language. Was this cultural engagement a coercive force that silenced the natives and compelled them to accept the technology and the supposedly superior culture of the colonizers? How do we describe Rammohun Roy and Derozio in their acceptance of English culture?

There is a large body of theoretical scholarship that examines the nature of western colonial encounters with the colonies. For the most, postcolonial theory has tended to focus on the engagement between Europe and the colonies they acquired in Asia and Africa. Frantz Fanon (1925-1961), for example, in his works arrives at a disenfranchised Alegrian identity which underwent absolute rupture in the presence of the French colonizer.[49] In *Black Skin, White Mask*, he writes that the black psyche undergoes alienation in the presence of the superior French culture. He describes the black man in the following manner:

> The black man has two dimensions. One with his fellows, the other with the white man. A Negro behaves differently with the white man and with another Negro. That this self division is a direct result of colonialist subjugation is beyond question. ...

> Every colonized people – in other words, every people in whose soul an inferiority complex has been created by the death and burial of its local cultural originality – finds itself face to face with the language of the civilizing nation; that is, with the culture of the

---

[49] His following works are representative of his ideas: *Black Skin, White Mask*, Reprint of *Peau noire, masques blancs* (London: Pluto Press, 1986) and *The Wretched of the Earth*, Reprint of *Les damnes de la terre* (New York: Grove, 1968).

mother country. The colonized is elevated above his jungle status in proportion to his adoption of the mother country's cultural standards. He becomes whiter as he renounces his blackness, his jungle.[50]

For Fanon, European cultural engagement leads to a complete erasure of his black African identity. What we draw from Fanon, who was writing around the 1950s, is but one notion of the hybrid where he describes a socio-psychical situation where the colonial subject was absolutely at the mercy of the colonial powers. This, though, cannot be representative and descriptive of all cultural encounters, as in many ways, it takes away all acts of agency from the perspective of the native. Such a Fanon-ian notion of the hybrid should not be definitive of how we describe cultural encounters and the inevitable give and take of languages, culture and technology.[51] There has to be theoretical means which we make use of in order to describe cultural confrontations and engagements as did take place in the first few decades of colonial presence in Calcutta.

The focus in this book is on a specific moment in time when the Britishers arrived in India; but before the Britishers came, India had always forever constantly negotiated with a vast array of cultural and religious invaders. Pre colonial India was influenced by Islamic culture. Indian culture that emerged under the Mughals would also have been hybrid, in the same manner as it was under the Britishers. So, what exactly is hybridity? Is it a cultural phenomenon, specific to the last few centuries. Helen Tiffin[52] makes such an assumption when she states that postcolonial cultures are

---

[50] "Remembering Fanon, Introduction," in *Black Skin, White Mask*, ed. Homi Bhabha, pp. 17-18.

[51] Postcolonial scholars, like Benita Parry, argue that valorizing ethnic identities allowed for oppressed cultures to survive the onslaught of imperialisms; citing the examples of Cesaire and Fanon, she writes that both "affirmed the invention of an insurgent, unified black self, acknowledged the revolutionary energies released by valorizing the cultures denigrated by colonialism." In Benita Parry, "Resistance Theory/ Theorizing Resistance or Two Cheers for Nativism" in *Contemporary Postcolonial Theory: A Reader*, ed. Padmini Mongia (London: Arnold, 1996), pp. 84-109.

[52] Helen Tiffin, "Postcolonial Literatures and Counter Cultures," in *The Post-colonial Studies Reader*, ed. Bill Ashcroft, Gareth Griffiths and Helen Tiffin (London: Routledge, 1995), pp. 95-98.

"inevitably hybridized, involving a dialectical relationship between European ontology and epistemology and the impulse to create or recreate independent local identity."[53] She goes on to write that decolonization "invokes an ongoing dialectic between hegemonist centrist systems and peripheral subversion of them; between European or British discourses and their post-colonial dis/mantling."[54] Therefore, the project of post-colonial writings is to investigate the means by "which Europe imposed and maintained its codes on the colonial domination of so much of the rest of the world."[55] Tiffin assumes that native cultures were completely overwritten by colonial presence, and that Europeans dictated terms which left little space for natives to maneuver their positions and identities. The colonial culture, therefore, that emerged was hybrid but dominated by the superior European culture.

The image of the passive native is also present in Gauri Viswanath's *Masks of Conquest*, when she writes that the discipline of English was part of the "imperial mission of educating and civilizing colonial subjects in the literature and thought of England, a mission that in the long run served to strengthen Western cultural hegemony in enormously complex ways."[56] According to her, "a great deal of strategic maneuvering went into the creation of a blueprint for social control in the guise of a humanistic program of enlightenment."[57] Infact, the introduction of English literature marks the "effacement of a sordid history of colonialist expropriation, material exploitation, and class and race oppression behind European world dominance" and the English literary text functioned as a surrogate Englishman in his "highest and most perfect state" becoming a "mask for economic exploitation, so successfully camouflaging the material

---

[53] Ibid., p. 95.

[54] Ibid., p. 95.

[55] Ibid., p. 95.

[56] Gauri Viswanathan, *Masks of Conquest. Literary Study and British Rule in India* (New Delhi: Oxford University Press), p. 2.

[57] Ibid., p. 10.

activities of the colonizer."[58] The native, in this instance, was a compliant subject, undergoing drastic cultural changes under British presence.

But this notion of hybridity that emerges only post colonization would not really be of much use in the context of cultures like India where pre colonial India was equally hybrid under Islamic rule. Tracing how the term hybrid has been used within postcolonial theory allows us to gain an understanding of how contentious and challenging a notion it is. Hybrid as a term has been co-opted by postcolonial scholars, across the board. Aijaz Ahmad points out that the term has become a "transhistorical thing, always present and always in process of dissolution in one part of the world or another, so that everyone gets the privilege, ... of being colonizer, colonized and postcolonial - sometimes all at once, in the case of Australia."[59] He writes, in his critique of the hybrid as has been used by postcolonialists:

> The idea of hybridity - which presents itself as a critique of essentialism, partakes of a carnivalesque collapse and play of identities, ... The basic idea that informs the notion of cultural hybridity is in itself simple enough, namely that the traffic among modern cultures is now so brisk that one can hardly speak of discrete national cultures that are not fundamentally transformed by that traffic.[60]

Ahmad's harsh criticism of theory that states that there does not exist "discrete national cultures" is antithetical to what is proposed by Homi Bhabha, who writes in his introduction to *Nation and Narration* that the boundary of national culture is "Janus-faced and the problem of outside/inside must always itself be a process of hybridity, incorporating new 'people' in relation to the body politic, generating other sites of meaning and, inevitably, in the political process...."[61] For Bhabha, hybridity

---

[58] Ibid., p. 20.

[59] Ajaz Ahmad, "The Politics of Literary Postcoloniality," in *Contemporary Postcolonial Theory: A Reader,* pp. 276-293.

[60] Ibid., 286.

[61] Homi Bhabha, "Introduction" to *Nation and Narration* (London: Routledge, 1990), p.3.

is a colonial product, often erasing the agency of the colonized; for him, postcolonial criticism therefore, bears witness to the "unequal and uneven forces of cultural representation" in the contest for socio-political authority in the modern world order.[62] I would, on the other hand, pose the question whether all cultural engagements that have taken place between the natives and the Britishers have been unequal, in the manner as has been described by Bhabha. It is not inevitable, as I will show in my book that the initial moments of contact between the natives and the Britishers was an unequal one; the colonizers would have introduced new systems of culture and technology, but the natives did not use them passively or in ways that were mere acts of Fanon-ian mimicry. The new culture that emerged was hybrid but in ways that showed the natives involved as active agents, deciding how print technology was to be used.

In my book, I argue for a more nuanced notion of hybridity, one which would consider the process of cultural exchange as an ongoing one. It is not that colonial India gave rise to a hybrid notion of identity; Indian culture had always been in a state of being influenced by other cultures and colonial presence was but one more to the many other non-native, foreign presences. Closely examining how the exchange of culture took place in the early years of colonization (1780-1820) – this is the time period I cover in my book - would allow me to arrive at a more complex definition of hybridity. Infact, pre 1850s was a time period when the colonial powers had not become the monolithic institution that it later became, and there was more parity in the relationship between colonizer and colonized. For example, the early years of colonization had seen Warren Hastings' emphasis on Orientalist learning and this eventually gave way to a more interventionist attitude of Charles Grant who wanted a more homogeneous India. Grant was elected to the board of the East India Company in 1794 and to Parliament in 1802 and it was because of his espousal of evangelical ideas of the Clapham sect that the East India Company introduced a pious clause into its charter of 1813. Post 1850s, with Darwin's *On the Origin of the Species* (1859) proposing evolutionary biology as a model of existence,

---

[62] Homi Bhabha, The Postcolonial and the Postmodern, The question of agency," in *The Location of Culture* (London: Routledge, 1994), pp. 245-282, p. 244.

Christianity was no longer a tool that could be used to control the natives and instead, imperialism was used as a religion to control the natives; print became an instrument of the empire.

My scholarship does not solely depend on an Eisensteinian, deterministic model, where print is seen as having an ontological status, prior to culture and affecting all aspects of society. The processes of colonization did affect what books were to be printed, and the use of the English language. The printing press had been introduced in India a long time ago; the Jesuits brought the technology in 1556, but its use was very limited. It was only with the advent of the Britishers, and with the import of printing presses, typesetters and editors from England, that printed texts were printed for large groups of people. This is a significant moment in the history of print in India. Therefore, when Nathaniel Halhed printed his book, *A Grammar of the Bengal Language* in 1778, he was codifying a local, regional language and giving it status by placing it in front of an English readership. That Halhed, who studied in Oxford and had literary ambitions as is evident in that he was familiar with Richard Sheridan, would travel to Calcutta as a writer of the East India Company and bring out a book on Bengali grammar is a fascinating anecdote, and represents the close interaction between England and India. The technology that he used in Calcutta was meant to be used so that printed texts could be distributed for a mass readership. The readers were Englishmen situated in England and in India, and the book was a first in its history. Within a few years, natives would also make use of print technology, and printed books would flood India, catering to the needs of the natives. My book therefore, is a first of its kind as it attempts to examine the nature of the first printed books and texts that were written in English in colonial India. This is a significant moment in the history of print in India. The book was a hybrid result, but how do we describe, or even theorize this notion of the hybrid? I have explained above that existing postcolonial theories of the hybrid fall short and it cannot be a valid theoretical tool in this instance. My book examines the emergence and proliferation of the printed text, but clearly distances itself away from the dominant notion of hybridity and instead argues for hybridity to represent cultural exchange which took place in a manner that allowed the natives more agency in determining how to make use of the technology.

A communication circuit.

As the book examines the emergence of English print in colonial Bengal in the last two decades of the eighteenth century, it can also be described as the "social and cultural history of communication by print"[63] According to Robert Darnton, the purpose of such studies in print culture is to understand how ideas were communicated through print, and how these ideas and books came into contact with society and affected the thoughts of the society they spread in. Darnton's interpretative model informs my study as I trace the formation of the realm of imperial print in colonial Calcutta, determined by the imperatives of the East India Company; books, journals and newspapers were carted across England in ships, printed and distributed amongst the fledgling white community in India and also to a global readership. A print induced public sphere formed. Both natives and Britishers were involved in the establishment of this realm of imperial print where native fonts were also made and grammar books written and printed.

Books, therefore, have very interesting social lifes and Darnton argues that all printed books generally pass through the same "life cycle" which is also a "communications circuit" that runs from the author, to the publisher, the printer, the shipper, the bookseller, and the reader."[64] In "What is the History of Books?" Darnton cites an example to elucidate what such social and cultural histories of the book would look like; he examines the historical conditions under which Voltaire's *Questions sur l'Encyclopedie*, an important work of the Enlightenment, was transmitted. A book historian could study the "circuit of its transmission at any point"— —like bibliographers who study when Voltaire wrote the work to campaign against religious intolerance; or the study of how the book was printed and the numerous editions that came out; or the work of literary historians who use statistical analysis to examine the book's assimilation in libraries.[65]

---

[63] Robert Darnton, "What is the History of Books?" in *The Book History Reader*, ed. David Finkelstein and Alistair McCleery (London and New York: Routledge, 2002), pp. 9-26; p. 9.

[64] Ibid., p. 11.

[65] Ibid., p. 11.

Darnton studies the role of the bookseller Isaac-Pierre Rigaud of Montpellier, who received copies of the book from the printer in Prussia as the pirated editions being published there were cheaper than the original ones from Geneva, where Voltaire's regular printer Gabriel Cramer had his publishing house. The books were carted across the Alps with the aid of a large number of middlemen before Rigaud could receive them. For Voltaire, according to Darnton, the motive for publishing was not economical but to spread the ideas of the Enlightenment and so he often allowed pirated editions of his work to be printed. The social, economic, political and intellectual conditions of that period determined the conditions under which Voltaire wrote, and how his book was transmitted across Europe.

In defining imperial print in the Indian colonial context, I consider the world of the book, and of print, as operating and emerging from within a large heteroglossic socio-literary realm, one which involves native and English bookmakers, publishers, distributors, and a reading audience that was both within India and abroad. Roger Chartier describes it differently when he states: "reading is not already inscribed in the text ... and that, correlatively, a text does not exist except for a reader who gives it significance."[66] How the book is "put to use, by whom, in what circumstances, and to what effect," John Adrian comments, are pertinent questions.[67] And these factors inform how I understand the notion of imperial print, and it is dependent on the following criteria: intended readership, actual audience, content and the effects of the texts on the readership. Readership, to a large extent, depends on the imagined public the writer has in mind, but the actual audience, could be different. Print culture, in Bengal pre-1800 was produced for a non-native audience, that was also located in Europe. The small group of non-native residents in Bengal was connected with Europe and each other through print. The capacity to imagine themselves as part of empire and to define their identity as imperial subjects was made possible through the to-and-fro movement

---

[66] Roger Chartier, "Labourers and Voyagers: From the Text to the Reader" in *The Book History Reader*, ed. David Finkelstein and Alistair McCleery (London and NY: Routledge, 2002), pp. 47-58; p. 47.

[67] Adrian Johns, *The Nature of the Book: Print and Knowledge in the Making* (Chicago: University of Chicago Press, 1998).

IMPERIAL PRINT IN COLONIAL CALCUTTA (1780-1820).

of texts.

In the next two chapters, I discuss how the "communications circuit" in the early phases of print culture in Calcutta, that is pre-1800, catered to the specific needs of the Britishers. That is, prior to the turn of the century, the realm of print culture was a closed circuit—all books, newspapers, gazettes, legal translations, in fact, all printed material had a very specific readership and catered to the practical, aesthetic and intellectual needs of the Europeans. I begin the first chapter by examining certain theoretical issues which underlie my book, namely – how was power established, maintained and perpetuated by the East India company in its establishment of the realm of print? A realm of power was established through print and other socio-cultural formations in colonial Calcutta. What were the reasons as to why there was such an intense engagement with the natives, whereby the whole paraphernalia of British civilization was transported to aid in empire building? Imperial print that emerged was defined by the imperatives of the British empire, and to clarify what I mean by imperial print, I examine the works of Sir William Jones, East India Company sponsored works on India, and Nathaniel Halhed's *A Grammar of the Bengal Language*. All these texts operated on a single premise – territorial control of the colonies would be managed through the realm of print.

In the fourth and fifth chapters, I argue that the print industry in Calcutta in the last two decades of the eighteenth century was dominated by newspapers; examining these newspapers that replicated the realm of print culture in England allows us to understand the processes of textual transmission. I look at the characteristics of print culture that were carried across by the Englishmen who came to Calcutta. The newspapers in the last two decades of the eighteenth century performed a very important function in the very fabric of their existence – allowing those in the metropole in Calcutta to consider themselves as connected to the daily activities of the center, enabling a sense of diasporic imperial citizenry to emerge. A print induced sub public emerged, replete with discourses of empire and colonization. There was an underlying premise that even if Calcutta was a colonial city inhabited with heathen natives, it was almost like living in a far away, newly established town which was beset with difficulties but was in the process of being made livable. The socio-cultural relevance of newspapers in Calcutta becomes clear if we consider how reading was important in the every day lives of people in eighteenth century England.

The last chapter looks at the multilingual newspaper in Calcutta, and argues that it was a comment on the multilingual nature of Indian society. I conclude the chapter by drawing upon the English writings of Rammohun Roy (1772/74-1833) who dominated the realm of English native print in the early nineteenth century. Even though Rammohun was educated within pre-colonial educational systems, he quickly learned about western systems of thinking after he started working for the officials of the East India Company after 1805. Henry Derozio (1809-1831) was another such figure, positioned at the confluences of Indian and British identities, and writing in the early years of the nineteenth century and is considered the first Indian poet writing in English. The realm of early nineteenth century print culture in Calcutta was a heterogeneous one, where natives and colonizers engaged with print in a heteroglossic manner.

Conclusion

By the early nineteenth century, the realm of imperial print worked contiguously with the realm of native print. There was close intimacy between the Britishers and the natives -- an intimacy that did not operate on dislike, oppression or contempt. Natives were involved in the imperial realm of print as compositors, writers, booksellers, printers, teachers and translators, mastering and replicating all aspects of print culture and technology. It was almost as if the Britishers had on display the best of their culture so that the Indians would want to emulate them – which they did. It is not an exaggeration to say that Rammohun Roy was the first native to understand what it meant to participate in the newly established English print communication circuit – by engaging with English printers, starting his own printing house, and mastering the English language and the technology of print culture.

Literary writings and journals sprung up within the realm of imperial print in the late eighteenth century, and a sphere of literary-ness was cultivated within the colonial situation. It was easy for a Britisher raised in England to arrive in India and write literary works which were meant to be read by his fellow citizens in this part of the world. What would it have taken for a native to have access to this literary realm in Calcutta and if so, how would he have been trained? Henry Derozio was the first native who was able to engage with this realm of imperial literary print that had sprung up. While at Hindu College, he would have worked alongside someone like D.L. Richardson, who was also a teacher there, besides being a poet and an editor of the *Bengal Annual* - a yearly collection of poetry and prose that was published seven times between 1830 and 1836. Richardson was an active participant in the realm of imperial literary print, and Derozio would have had access to it through him. Henry Derozio published his first collection called *Poems* in 1827; the Baptist Mission Press in Srirampur was his publishing house. The same press published one of Rammohun Roy's initial works in 1819, *A Second Conference Between an Advocate and an Opponent on the Practice of Burning Widows Alive*. Everybody in the domain of English print knew each other. It was, after all, a small realm of print. The Mission Press was run by a group of European missionaries who were deeply involved with the realm of native print, and involved in printing books that were not meant for proselytisation. Indian pandits (like Ramram Basu, Chandicharan Munshi, Rajiblochan Mukhopadhay) attached to the Baptist Mission Press also printed books of fiction in Bengali, and can thus be described as the first writers in Bengali who had their works printed. A few decades previously, this same group of pandits would have used manuscripts, but now were turning their efforts to print technology, working alongside Christian missionaries and the officials of the East India Company.

In determining the nature of the new work place that was established, we see that there would have been close physical contact between the Britishers and the Indians. Oftentimes, Indians worked as compositors in foundries which printed English works, without knowing the language. John Borthwick Gilchrist in his preface to *A Dictionary English and Hindoostanee*, wrote in 1798 that he was astounded with the "eternal treacherous behavior: of his Bengali assistants, a "posse of unprincipled black knaves."[68] H goes on to write about the "slavish drudgery of

---

[68] John Borthwick Gilchirst, *A Dictionary of English and Hindoostanee*. Printed by Stuart and Cooper, p. xv.

correcting the press ... where the compositors were every one more ignorant than another of the subject they were engaged to[*sic*]."[69] A similar shift occurred in Europe, in the modern period, with the introduction of printing presses where diverse occupational groups worked with each other in the new workshops that were set up by the early printers. Elisabeth Eisenstein describes the numerous processes that were involved: "The advent of printing led to the creation of a new kind of shop structure; to a regrouping which entailed closer contacts among diversely skilled workers and encouraged new forms of cross-cultural interchange." Thus it was not uncommon to find university professors and "former priests among early printers or former abbots serving as editors or correctors," thus, coming into closer contact with metal workers and mechanics.[70] When the printing presses were introduced in Bengal, the hierarchy between the English and the Indians was maintained. The editors and the master printers were Europeans, many of whom were employed from England, while the compositors were Indians.

The development of the realm of print culture in Calcutta and its subsequent use by the natives is an interesting story; as engaging and intriguing as the development of the city itself. The exchange that took place, albeit forced, coerced and under circumstances that were far from agreeable from the perspective of the natives, can also be described as a socio-cultural and technological engagement. For example, a few of the British printers who came to Calcutta had served as apprentices in England. George Gordon was the nephew of one of the most eminent eighteenth century London printers, William Strahan, who was the King's Printer, and a friend of Samuel Johnson and Benjamin Franklin. Most of them, though, were trained in Calcutta and a few can be named: Andrew Bones, Joseph Cooper, Paul Ferris, James Hicky, Thomas Jones, James Leary, Bernard Messink, John Miller, Aaron Upjohn, Charles Wilkins.[71] Eventually, it did

---

[69] Ibid, pp. xv, xii.

[70] Elizabeth Eisenstein, "Defining the Initial Shift: Some Features of Print Culture" in *The Book History Reader*, ed. David Finkelstein and Alistair McCleery (London and New York: Routledge, 2002), pp. 156-157.

[71] For more see Graham Shaw, *Printing in Calcutta to 1800*, pp. 42-71.

not matter. The Europeans settled in India and introduced certain institutions and systems of rule and governance, both for themselves and for the natives. The realm of print was one such institution. Gradually, the Indians learnt it, and replicated all aspects of print. This process of cultural transmission and exchange did not pass through any phase of mimicry. What did matter was that the realm of print allowed both Britishers and the natives to engage with each other and for the natives, to reach out to a global readership.

2 WHEN THE *SAHIBS* OF THE EAST INDIA COMPANY CAME: ESTABLISHING REALMS OF POWER AND THE ARRIVAL OF PRINT, PARAPEHRNALIA AND EMPIRE.

Nathaniel Halhed's *A Grammar of the Bengal Language* (1778) has reasons to be lauded as the first in many ways: most importantly, it was multilingual, involving the efforts of both the English and the natives.[72] For the natives, living within a manuscript culture, to see printed texts emerge, transcribing and documenting Bengali words and their English synonyms, would have been a unique experience. The book was printed in Hooghly, made its way to England and was sold in London by Elmsley. In 1783, a review in an English journal, *The English Review*, succinctly pointed to the numerous aspects of ingenuity in the book:[73]

> The work now before us (the first perhaps printed in Hindostan) has many circumstances of novelty, as well as of utility to recommend it to public attention.
> One gentleman presents us with the elements of a language

---

[72] Nathaniel Brassey Halhed, *A Grammar of the Bengal Language*. 1778. Reprint, ed. R. C. Alston (England: The Scolar Press, 1969).

[73] Review of "A Grammar of the Bengal Language," *The English Review, or, An Abstract of English and Foreign Literature* Vol. I (1783): 5-14.

hitherto disregarded, and almost unknown in Europe. Another gentleman employs the extraordinary efforts of a singular and persevering genius in the fabrication of types of a very novel and difficult construction: while we find a Governor General, (unlike every description of public men in Britain) amidst all the busy scenes of war and state affairs, cultivating the arts of peace; advising, soliciting, animating men of ability to undertake, to persevere, and to accomplish pursuits so laudable in themselves, and so strongly pointed to attest and extend the India Company's most essential interests in Bengal.[74]

The review drew upon an easy equation between the study of Indian languages and its use in maintaining the British empire in India. The argument that was made was an interesting one: the aim of the British government was "to establish an empire over the minds as well as over the country of the natives," and grammar books were needed to allow for an "easy" intercourse with the "native" as no people could "cheerfully submit to rulers" they did not understand."[75] The central assumption within eighteenth century British print culture, where print technology was seen at the apex of communication forms, was transferred onto the colonies by the East India Company. Such was the realm of print that evolved in Calcutta in the last two decades of the twentieth century to serve the needs of the empire.

At the turn of the century, books made their way into Indian society and began to displace a manuscript culture. Natives started to read, make use of and negotiate their lives through printed texts. Moreover, the press initiated a shift in the very nature of how texts were to be written, preserved and disseminated. In fact, it initiated a shift in the very method of writing, a shift that involved cultural habits – Indians would sit on the floor and write, unlike Europeans who used tables and chairs. Nathaniel Halhed describes it in the following manner: "As they have neither chairs nor

---

[74] Ibid., p. 12. Print actually began in 'Hindostan' in 1556 when the Jesuits established the first printing press in Goa.

[75] Ibid., p. 5.

tables, their posture in writing is very different from ours: they sit upon their heels, or sometimes upon their hams, while their left hand held open serves as a desk whereon to lay the paper on which they write, which is kept in its place by the thumb: so that they never write on a large sheet of paper without folding it down to a very small surface."[76] It is fascinating to conjecture as to how exactly the change to print took place. As more and more natives had access to printed texts, that which had been the privilege of a particular class of people, now became democratized. Now, a large canvas of Indian society had access to printed books. How did it feel to be able to touch printed paper and read, and be aware that many others across the land were also reading the same text? Indians closely interacted with the Britishers and learnt their social manners, learning how the technology worked. They also learnt the different uses that print could come into.

I begin this chapter by examining certain theoretical issues which underlie my book, namely – how was power established, maintained and perpetuated by the East India Company in its establishment of the realm of print? What were the reasons as to why there was such an intense engagement with the natives, whereby the whole paraphernalia of British civilization was transported to aid in empire building? Imperial identity is an imaginary construct, made possible in the colonial context. By performing into the cultural and the social norms that were imported from England, the diasporic community established imperial identity, separate from the natives. By the end of the eighteenth century, the Britishers had cultivated and established new realms of institutional power in the colonies and I have examined a few of the important geo-spatial cultural realms later on in this chapter —the development of Calcutta as a westernized city, cartography and the use of maps by the East India Company, and lastly, western habits of consumption in the colonies. The emergent print communication circuit was one such realm that existed in conjunction with the other institutional and disciplinary realms.

Empire making: how print served the East India Company.

Founded in 1600, the East India Company first obtained trading permission

---

[76] Nathaniel Halhed, *A Grammar of the Bengal Language*, p. 2.

from the Mughal ruler Jahangir (1605-27) in 1619. Initially, its presence was limited to a few coastal factories, but by the eighteenth century the English had superseded the other European trading powers, mainly the Portuguese, in becoming the leading European traders in India. Internal contradictions in the politics and economy of India in the late eighteenth century provided the East India Company with ample opportunities to intervene in the politics of the country. Undoubtedly, European trading imperatives was one of the reasons why the EIC, under Robert Clive, became rulers of a country they once traded with. For example, Indian textiles accounted for the most profitable of the goods that were imported by the Company, payment for which was made in silver. The drain of silver from Europe into India was immense, and a solution was reached when it was decided that Indian revenues had to be controlled by the Britishers. In 1765, after wars against the rulers of Bengal, the Company obtained *diwani*, that is the right to collect revenue from Bengal which nearly amounted to three million pounds; the revenue was used to purchase goods from Bengal that was sold at a profit in markets abroad. In order to carry out the administrative and political functions of the EIC, British settlements were established in Calcutta, a trading port in Bengal; the city would grow to become the capital of the British Empire. A white society emerged in Calcutta that carried with it all the civic and socio-cultural institutions of Britishness, and by doing so, defined its imperial identity through racial and geo-spatial/cultural separation from the Indians.

The East India Company's need to colonize India developed slowly and was highly contested from within; the colonies served to define British national identity and more importantly, they were needed for reasons of trade. In the last two decades of the eighteenth century, a realm of print culture evolved in Calcutta serving the needs of empire. The East India Company used this realm——which printed news, gossip, Oriental scholarship, literary journals——to establish and maintain its control over the territories. Moreover, the printed scholarship of the scholar-administrators of the East India Company reveals their belief that print technology was a step into modernity, a move away from Indian scribal culture. Print culture, in Bengal pre-1800 was produced for a non-native audience, that was also located in Europe. As content determines how interpretations take place, I have argued that the white settlers read in order to create a sense of imperial identity and thus, print technology in the colonial context was never innocent. The realm of readership was local and also global. The small group of non-native residents in Bengal was connected with Europe and each other through print. The capacity to imagine themselves as part of empire and to define their identity as imperial subjects was made possible through the to-and-fro movement of texts.

Such a notion of a realm that is invested with power and made possible by print borrows from concepts of cartography. Maps portray a sense of space that is never value-free. Maps do not depict reality with scientific accuracy and objectivity. Brian Harley writes that "cartography is primarily a form of political discourse concerned with the acquisition and maintenance of power."[77] According to Harley:

> Compilation, generalization, classification, formation into hierarchies, and standardization of geographical data, far from being mere "neutral" technical activities, involve power-knowledge relations at work. Just as the disciplinary institutions described by Foucault—prisons, schools, armies, factories—serve to normalize human beings, so too the workshop of the map-maker can be seen as normalizing the phenomena of place and territory in creating a sketch of a made world that society desired.[78]

Maps are "preeminently a language of power, not of protest"[79] and this is most aptly evident in those maps that portray imperial conquest as British cartographers drew maps that reiterated British power. Ian Barrow makes a similar argument when he writes that during the British colonial period, maps were the most effective resources the British had in order to legitimize their roles as a colonial power.[80] The territories they colonized

---

[77] Brian Harley, *The New Nature of Maps; Essays in the History of Cartography* (Baltimore: John Hopkins University Press, 2002), p. 57.

[78] Ibid., p. 22.

[79] Ibid., p. 5.

[80] Ian Barrow, *Making History, Drawing Territory. British Mapping in India, c. 1756-1905* (New Delhi, Oxford University Press, 2003).

were portrayed as inevitably British, and intrinsic to the British empire. For example, John Tallis' *Illustrated Atlas and Modern History of the World* included maps of British India that were accompanied by a text that explained how British power was established over the colony.[81] Maps mimetically represented geographical territory alongside a rendition of a history of how the space was colonized. The power of maps lies in the fact that they can recreate territory in a particular manner through elisions; for example, a map of Calcutta in the 1800s depicted all Indians as peasants or servants and established the land as meant for the English. Maps, thus, portrayed the existing ideologies that were inflected with a sense of imperial legitimacy. And like maps, the realm of printed texts that emerged in the first phase of colonial print, that is pre-1800, reiterated a similar notion of colonial superiority whereby the introduction of print technology was construed as an inevitable move towards modernity and progress.

Colonization and the need for trade.

The eighteenth century saw Europe come into contact with the rest of the world on a scale not seen before. According to Linda Colley, British national identity emerged partially out of its eighteenth century imperialist ventures.[82] In fact, metropolitan elites in the eighteenth century funded imperial expansions in such a manner that overseas trade "acted as a major agent of change within Britain itself."[83] The East India Company established its territorial power through various means, which gave rise to British settlements in Bengal. The colonies were intrinsic to England for reasons of trade, and gradually, British trading-settlements emerged in Bengal. By the end of the eighteenth century, realms of institutional power were established in the colonies and in the process, British imperial identity was formed that was intrinsic to maintaining colonial territories.

---

[81] John Tallis, *Illustrated Atlas and Modern History of the World* (New York: J. &F. Tallis, 1851).

[82] Linda Colley, *Britons: Forging the Nation, 1707-1837* (Yale: Yale University Press, 2005).

[83] H.V. Bowen, *The Business of Empire: The East India Company and Imperial Britain, 1756-1833* (Cambridge: Cambridge University Press, 2006), p. 13.

Initially, the concern of the East India Company was to control the ports, like all other traders. A reason that was used by the EIC and Clive to account for the vast colonies and their explorations, post 1857 and the Battle of Plassey, was that increased trade would satiate the needs of a burgeoning industrial society. The British Empire, created out of a fiscal-military state, depended on commerce and colonial production that, as Adam Smith stated, was needed to satisfy a nation of customers. This was the Whig side of the argument, for whom the empire was always an experiment in social engineering. The empire was seen as inevitable and intrinsic to Britain, and a mercantilist, libertarian notion of empire was disseminated in eighteenth century England through pamphlets, essays, newspapers, articles and Parliamentary speeches. On the other hand, the other, 'Tory' side didn't want to have anything to do with these colonies. Economically, conquering Bengal only fortuitously proved to be a good move when England changed from a consuming to a producing country, courtesy the Industrial Revolution. The resources of the world had to be colonized by England for national power and prosperity, and this could only be achieved through the acquisition of a monopoly on international trade. Kathleen Wilson argues that visions of imperial greatness were embedded in Georgian domestic culture and politics, where the British empire was construed as made up of commercially viable and prosperous colonies, populated by British subjects who served as strongholds of "trade, prosperity, naval strength, and political virtue" of the metropole.[84] This was only true post 1767. Travelogues described the material abundance of the colonies; in 1820, Walter Hamilton wrote about the trading plenitude in Bengal, saying that there was "seldom less than one million sterling in cloths belonging to native merchants" and "every other species of merchandise in an equal proportion."[85] The lure of colonial goods was immense, and not surprisingly, many European trading companies struggled for the monopoly of trading rights in South Asia. By 1763, after the end of the Seven Year War in Europe, England emerged as the major western power in the Indian subcontinent and extended her trading empire there,

---

[84] Kathleen Wilson, "The Good, the Bad, and the Impotent: Imperialism and the Politics of Identity in Georgian England," in *The Consumption of Culture,* ed. Ann Bermingham and John Brewer (New York: Routledge, 1995), pp. 237-262; p. 239.

[85] Walter Hamilton, "Calcutta in 1820," in *Calcutta in the Nineteenth Century,* ed. Thankappan Nair (Calcutta: Firma KLM, 1999), pp. 220-244; p 227.

affecting the very nature of the Indian social structure.[86]

Though trading relations between the two nations had existed since the sixteenth century (the East India Company was set up in 1600 and obtained trading permission from the Indian Mughal ruler Jahangir [1526-1856] in 1619), it was only towards the end of the eighteenth century when the East India Company was granted the right to collect revenue from Bengal (diwani) that the Company intervened in India to include governmental matters in its operations, setting up legal courts and institutions of learning that compelled and enabled both the Indians and the British to negotiate and learn from each other.[87] Though traders, the East India Company was not, as Edmund Burke succinctly commented, "merely a Company formed for the extension of British commerce, but in reality a delegation of the whole power and sovereignty of this [British] kingdom sent to the East."[88] Even in the absence of direct rule of the British government, the East was seen as part of the British nation-empire, and narratives of the colonies percolated through the everyday experiences of the metropole to become an important part of the "European [Enlightenment's] repertoire of ideas, images, hopes and feelings."[89] Print culture facilitated cross cultural encounters that took place within a global context, and became an intrinsic part of the everyday experiences of ordinary Europeans.

Western travel narratives of the eighteenth century describe British traders, settled in the coastal-commercial factories of India, living in

---

[86] This sustained contact with the Indians for reasons of trade was very different from the contact between European ships and Pacific islanders that were occurring at the same time. For more, see Dorinda Outram, "Cross Cultural Encounters in the Enlightenment," in *The Enlightenment World*. ed. Martin Fitzpatrick, Peter Jones et al (New York: Routledge, 2004).

[87] See Kapil Raj, "Refashioning Civilities, Engineering Trust: William Jones, Indian Intermediaries and the Production of Reliable Legal Knowledge in late Eighteenth Century Bengal" *Studies in History* 17 (2001): 23-47.

[88] Quoted in William Kuiters, *The British in Bengal 1756-1773. A Society in Transition Seen through the Biography of a Rebel: William Bolts (1739-1808)* (Paris: Les Indes Savante, 2002), p. 53.

[89] Outram, "Cross Cultural Encounters", p. 561.

sybaritic luxury they could not have afforded or even dreamed of in Britain. As early as 1708, Alexander Hamilton, a Scottish trader and traveler,[90] wrote about the everyday living habits of the traders who had settled in Calcutta, an important trading port of the East India Company. He described a life of leisure and ease, saying that most "Gentlemen and Ladies in Bengal live both splendidly and pleasantly, the Fore-noons being dedicated to Business, and after Dinner to Rest, and in the Evening to recreate themselves in Chaises or Palankins in the Fields, or to Gardens, or by Water in their Budgeroes."[91] By the end of the eighteenth century the city grew to accommodate a sizeable British population. By 1798 the British population, though small in comparison to the native population, totaled around 4300.[92]

The non native population of rulers could live by identifying themselves as separate from the natives; by the end of the eighteenth century, realms of institutional power were established in the colonies and in the process, imperial identity was formed intrinsic to maintaining a territory. Print culture was one such import that made colonial control possible. The realm of print was both spatial (through acts of reading) and a

---

[90] Alexander Hamilton, "Travelogue" in *Calcutta in the Eighteenth Century*. ed. Thankappan Nair (Calcutta: KLM Firma, 1984).The full title of the book was: "A New Account of the East Indies, Being the Observations and Remarks of Captain Alexander Hamilton Who Spent his Time There from the Year 1688-1723 Trading and Travelling, by the Sea and Land, to Most of the Countries and Islands of Commerce and Navigation, between the Cape of Good-hope and the Island of Japan."

[91] Ibid., p. 7. We see similar accounts in most travel narratives where the European's life is seen as one of luxury; where the average household would have numerous people working as scribes and domestic help. Admiral Stavorinus wrote in 1768: "Europeans lead, in Bengal, a very easy life; the men, who are almost all in the service of the Company, ... this mode of life naturally occasions an enormous expenditure.-... The dearness of provisions which are brought from Europe, contributes hereto; but perhaps the greatest cause may be traced in the excessive expense which the ladies incur, in the articles of dress and appearance. Domestic peace and tranquility must be purchased, by a shower of jewels, a wardrobe of the richest clothes, and a kingly parade of plate upon the sideboard; ... The women generally rise between eight and nine o clock. The forenoon is spent in paying visits to their friends, or in lolling upon a sofa, with their arms across. Dinner is ready at half past one; they go to sleep till half past four or five; they then dress in form; and the evening and part of the might is spent in company, or at dancing parties, which are frequent, during the colder season." In *Calcutta in the Eighteenth Century,* pp. 165-166.

[92] Alexander Hamilton, "Travelogue", p. 228.

geo-physical domain (the realm of printers and type foundries). This was akin to many other realms that emerged in the last two decades of the eighteenth century, and I have examined a few important socio-cultural realms in the following section—the development of Calcutta as a westernized city, cartography and the use of maps by the East India Company, and lastly, western habits of consumption in the colonies. The print induced communication circuit was one such realm which existed in conjunction with the other institutional and disciplinary realms.(fig. 2)

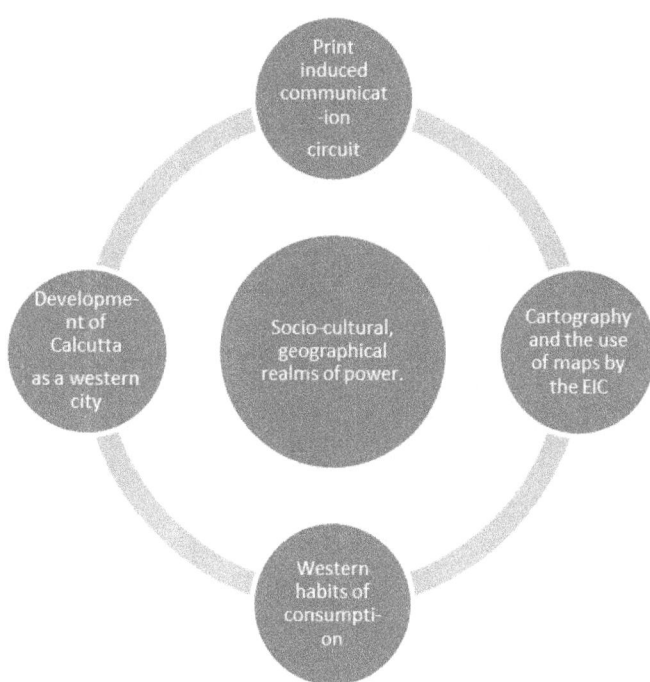

Figure 2: Geo-social realms of power.

The three realms of power: establishing imperial identity.
i. The realm of a western city/ architecture.

The servants of the East India Company and other European trading companies lived in semi-independent enclaves in the commercial parts of seventeenth century India. By the end of the eighteenth century, trade from

Bengal comprised a large percentage of the goods sent to Europe and Calcutta as its port grew in importance to become the commercial and administrative center of the British empire. As the white residents had very little contact with the natives, could not own land outside Calcutta, and lived under the strict control of the Company, a semi-isolated colonial realm-city was created. All the civic, socio-architectural and cultural institutions of England were imported and in the process, the architectural landscape of the city was changed.[93] Writing in the early nineteenth century, Viscount George Valentia described Calcutta as "well worthy of being the seat of our Eastern Government, both from its size, and from the magnificent buildings which decorate the part of it inhabited by Europeans."[94]

Colonial territorial power was made evident through a visual display of spectacle where the architectural presence of buildings created an aura of imperial separation, wealth and British superiority. The realm of a western city created and enabled the establishment of a socio-imperial identity in Calcutta, intrinsic to maintaining a colonial territory. Western travel writings describe the construction of a magnificent city that would be an appropriate capital of the British Empire. Within a time span of a hundred years, Walter Hamilton wrote in his travelogue in 1820, Calcutta had grown from villages to become a "magnificent" city, with "elegant villas on each side of the river," botanic gardens, and the "spires of the churches, temples and minarets."[95] Palatial houses were needed, the Viscount George Valentia commented, as such displays of Oriental splendor were appropriate rebuttals to European (mostly French) criticism about the mercantile spirit of the English; India was "to be ruled from a palace, not from a countinghouse; with the ideas of a Prince, not with those [of a] retail

---

[93] William Kuiters, *The British in Bengal*, pp. 23-62.

[94] Viscount George Valencia, "Calcutta in 1803." in *Calcutta in the Nineteenth Century*. ed. Thankappan Nair (Calcutta: Firma KLM, 1999), pp. 1-35; p. 11. He goes on to say: "The sums expended upon [the city] have been considered as extravagant by those who carry European ideas and European economy into Asia; but they ought to remember, that India, is a country of splendor, of extravagance, and of outward appearances: that the Head of a mighty empire ought to conform himself to the prejudices of the country he rules over." p. 12.

[95] Walter Hamilton, "Calcutta in 1820," p. 220.

dealer in muslins and indigo."[96] By the latter part of the eighteenth century, a sense of imperial identity had been established through the realm of architecture that created socio-spatial separation between the English and the natives. The realm of architecture was European, and was construed as a source of power. This realm, in many ways, was representative of the technological domain of print culture. In its early stages, only the Europeans had mastery over print, and knew how to operate the presses and foundries.

ii. The realm of maps.

The spatial characteristics of print culture can be best explained by looking at the realm of cartography, another disciplinary institution that made it possible to legitimize British rule. The architectural non-indigenous characteristics of Calcutta implied power and this was portrayed in the maps that were drawn by the East India Company. Cartography demarcated the European-ness of the city. A close look at the map of Calcutta (fig.3) reveals that the city was built in such a manner that it had two distinct sections; there was the white part of the town where the Europeans lived and the area outside it where the natives lived.[97] Maps like these were meant to be used by the officials of the East India Company and other Europeans who lived in the city or wanted to reside there and enabled them to identify power. The named spaces on the map represented legitimate, European identities, while the empty unnamed spaces referred to the vast stretches inhabited by the natives, outside the living quarters of the whites.

---

[96] Viscount George Valencia, "Calcutta in 1803," p. 12.

[97] Tropes of the imperial city, where the Britishers lived, recur in many travel narratives of this time. And the natives, when they feature in the texts, are at times referred to as "blacks." Writing in 1767, Mrs. Nathaniel Kindersley commented on the native part of the city, where "the most like a street is the Buzar, the name they call every place by where any thing is to be sold"; "the Buzar," she continues, "is full of little shabby-looking shops, ... kept by black people." The "black town" was meant for the "the servants of the English to reside in. See Nathaniel Kindersley, *Letters from the Island of Tenerisse, Brazil, the Cape of God Hope, and the East Indies,* in *Calcutta in the 18th Century,* ed. P. Thankappan Nair (Calcutta: Firma KLM, 1984), pp. 138-152.

Figure 3. East Facing map of Calcutta.

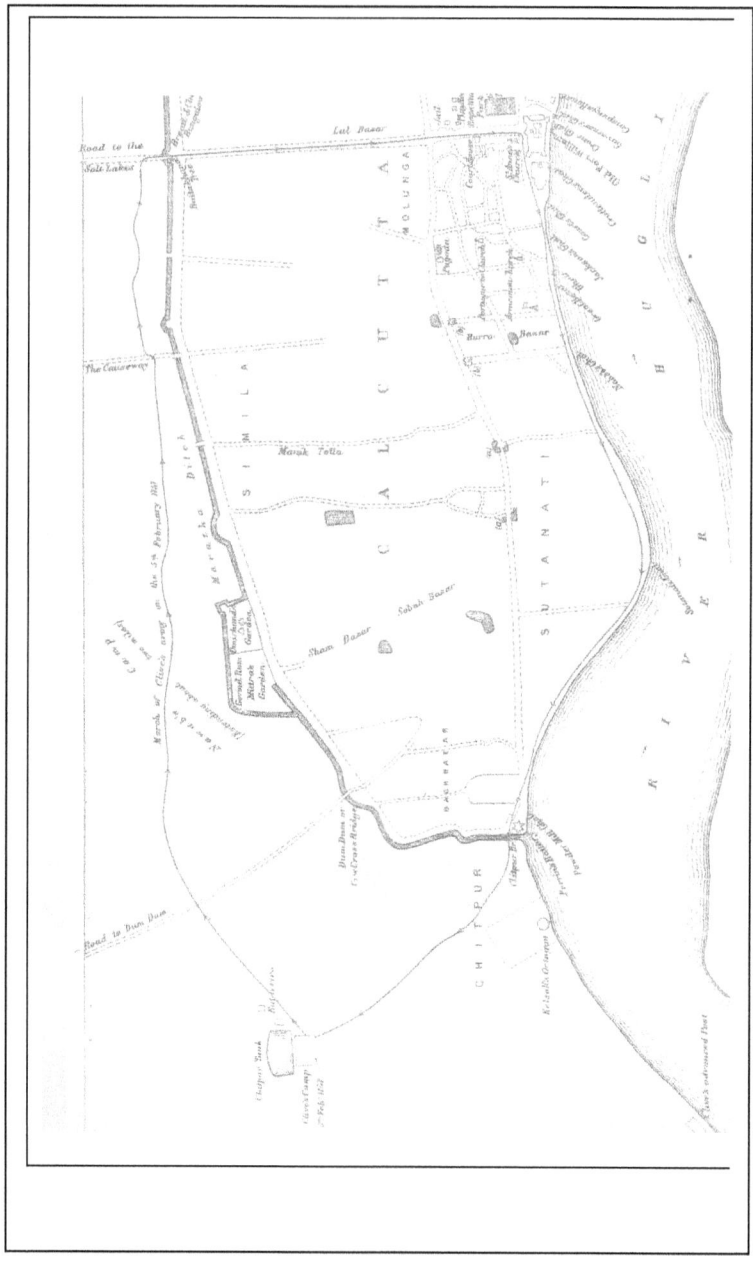

IMPERIAL PRINT IN COLONIAL CALCUTTA (1780-1820).

The history of the cartography of Calcutta, Keya Dasgupta argues, since the beginning of the eighteenth century, reflects the "requirements of the colonial power."[98] Early maps, drawn by Company officers and engineers, were needed for reasons of defense and as the city of Calcutta grew in commercial and administrative activity, attracting a large civilian population, map making concerned itself with issues of revenue and civil administration.[99] Interpreting maps within a social context allows us to reflect that imperial identity was established through disciplinary institutions like cartography that re-imagined space, doing away with the neutrality of spatial portrayal.

iii. The realm of consumption

The maps drawn and used by the East India Company reiterated the realm of colonial power by its portrayal of social reality, i.e., the geo-spatial separation of whites and natives. The depiction of such a realm reminds us that the diasporic community was knitted together not only through their racial identification as whites, but also through their British cultural habits. The realm of consumption - of fashions and foods – serves as an explanatory model to throw light on the importance of print culture in the lives of this community. New printing ventures would crop up, implying the never ending need for print. The white community was bound by their desire for print, in the same way that they were bound by their cultural habits.

London in the mid-eighteenth century was the "epicenter of public fashion and consumption,"[100] where tastes were cultivated that were dependent on Asian goods and commodities. These habits were in turn

---

[98] Keya Dasgupta. "A City Away from Home: The Mapping of Calcutta." In *Texts of Power. Emerging Disciplines in Colonial Bengal*, ed. Partha Chatterjee (Minneapolis, U of Minneapolic Press, 1995), p. 146.

[99] Ibid., p. 146.

[100] James Walvin, *Fruits of Empire. Exotic produce and British taste. 1660-1800* (New York: NY Press, 1997), p. 155.

carried over to the colonies by the traders. In examining the historical origins of seventeenth and eighteenth century British social and domestic habits of "food, clothing and habitat," James Walvin argues that British well being at home was a result of global trade and imperial settlement" abroad.[101] Before 1500, as a result of indirect trade, the rich and wealthy of Europe had access to the all the commodities of the East. Post-1500, European nations gained direct trading access and became maritime powers. As European traders came in contact with distant regions, they remade these regions to "serve their broader self interest" and plants and commodities were transmuted into "major instruments of profit, public taste and global expansion."[102] The social and personal tastes that were developed by the British were a result of the "specific course of British imperial and commercial history" and cut across all classes of people.[103] The development of such profit based global market systems implied a reliance on goods, and reflects the kind of commodity fetishism through which social and cultural relations and habits were formed. To a significant degree, eighteenth century British identity that emerged in the colonies depended on commodity consumption.

Commodity fetishism was a British import in India; there was no desire for European goods in Bengal. European traders had to pay in specie as the market of European goods in Bengal, before the East India Company became rulers, was very limited. For the white settlers, having access to all the material and cultural habits of Englishness was a requirement that made it possible for them to settle in India and differentiate themselves as rulers. In the English newspapers that were published for the settlers, a large section was devoted to advertisement (figs. 4 and 5), and in the third chapter, I will look at the role of newspapers and advertisements at greater lengths to argue that objects and goods, in the colonial context, assumed a role greater than themselves, providing a sense of identity to a group of people, and allowing for social connection and community. The performative aspect of imperial identity made it possible

---

[101] Ibid., p. ix.

[102] Ibid., p. x, xii.

[103] Ibid., p. 194.

IMPERIAL PRINT IN COLONIAL CALCUTTA (1780-1820).

Figure 4. Advertisements in the Calcutta Gazette, 1800.

Figure 5. Advertisements in the Calcutta Gazette, 1800.

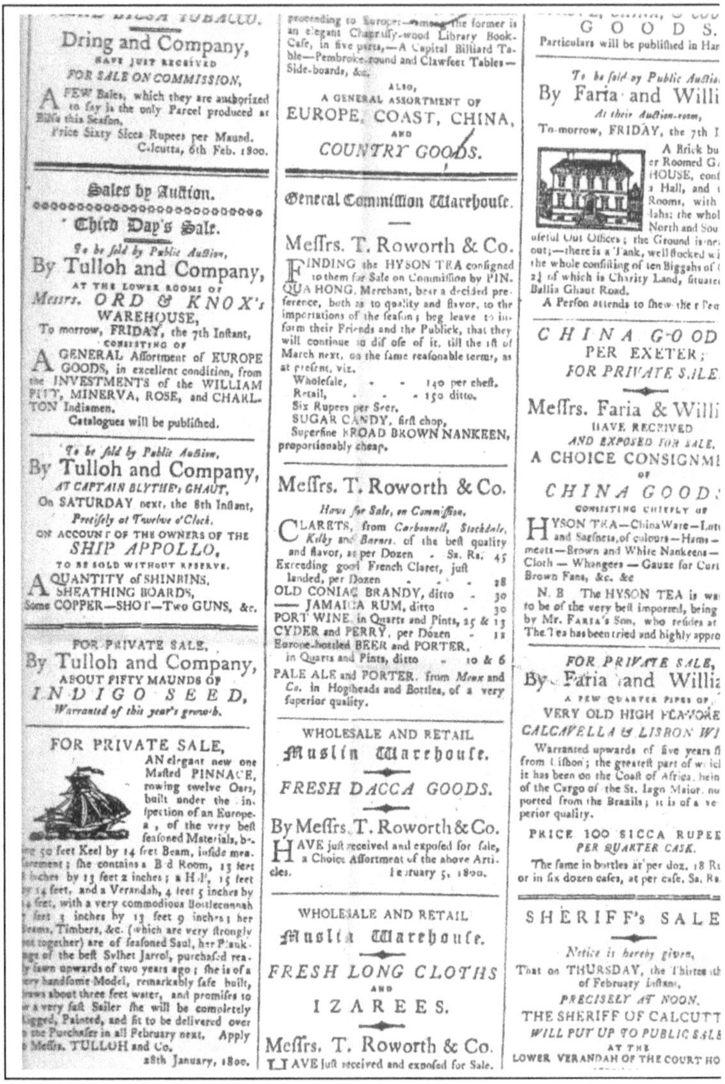

Dring and Company,
HAVE JUST RECEIVED
FOR SALE ON COMMISSION,
A FEW Bales, which they are authorized to say is the only Parcel produced at Bilsa this Season,
Price Sixty Sicca Rupees per Maund.
Calcutta, 6th Feb. 1800.

Sales by Auction.

Third Day's Sale.

To be sold by Public Auction,
By Tulloh and Company,
AT THE LOWER ROOMS OF
Messrs. ORD & KNOX's
WAREHOUSE,
To morrow, FRIDAY, the 7th Instant,
CONSISTING OF
A GENERAL Assortment of EUROPE GOODS, in excellent condition, from the INVESTMENTS of the WILLIAM PITT, MINERVA, ROSE, and CHARLTON Indiamen.
Catalogues will be published.

To be sold by Public Auction,
By Tulloh and Company,
AT CAPTAIN BLYTHE's GHAUT,
On SATURDAY next, the 8th Instant,
Precisely at Twelve o'Clock,
ON ACCOUNT OF THE OWNERS OF THE
SHIP APPOLLO,
TO BE SOLD WITHOUT RESERVE.
A QUANTITY of SHINBINS,
SHEATHING BOARDS,
Some COPPER—SHOT—Two GUNS, &c.

FOR PRIVATE SALE,
By Tulloh and Company,
ABOUT FIFTY MAUNDS OF
INDIGO SEED,
Warranted of this year's growth.

FOR PRIVATE SALE,
AN elegant new one Masted PINNACE, rowing twelve Oars, built under the inspection of an Europe-a, of the very best seasoned Materials, being 50 feet Keel by 14 feet Beam, inside measurement; she contains a Bed Room, 13 feet inches by 13 feet 2 inches; a Hall, 15 feet by 14 feet, and a Verandah, 4 feet 5 inches by 14 feet, with a very commodious Boutleconnah feet 3 inches by 13 feet 9 inches; her Beams, Timbers, &c. (which are very strongly put together) are of seasoned Saul, her Plank-ings of the best Sylhet Jarrol, purchased ready sawn upwards of two years ago; she is of a very handsome Model, remarkably safe built, draws about three feet water, and promises to be a very fast Sailer she will be completely Rigged, Painted, and fit to be delivered over to the Purchaser in all February next. Apply to Messrs. TULLOH and Co.
28th January, 1800.

proceeding to Europe—among the former is an elegant Chaprassy-wood Library Book-Case, in five parts,—A Capital Billiard Table—Pembroke-round and Clawfeet Tables—Side-boards, &c.
ALSO,
A GENERAL ASSORTMENT OF
EUROPE, COAST, CHINA,
AND
COUNTRY GOODS.

General Commission Warehouse.

Messrs. T. Roworth & Co.
FINDING the HYSON TEA consigned to them for Sale on Commission by PINQUA HONG, Merchant, bear a decided preference, both as to quality and flavor, to the importations of the season; beg leave to inform their Friends and the Publick, that they will continue to dispose of it, till the 1st of March next, on the same reasonable terms, as at present, viz.
Wholesale, - - 140 per chest.
Retail, - - - 150 ditto.
Six Rupees per Seer.
SUGAR CANDY, first chop,
Superfine BROAD BROWN NANKEEN, proportionably cheap.

Messrs. T. Roworth & Co.
Have for Sale, on Commission,

CLARETS, from *Carbonnell, Stockdale, Kilby* and *Barnet*, of the best quality and flavor, at per Dozen - Ss. Rs.	45
Exceeding good French Claret, just landed, per Dozen	18
OLD CONIAC BRANDY, ditto	30
—— JAMAICA RUM, ditto	30
PORT WINE in Quarts and Pints, 25 &	13
CYDER and PERRY, per Dozen	12
Europe-bottled BEER and PORTER, in Quarts and Pints, ditto	10 & 6

PALE ALE and PORTER, from *Meux* and *Co.* in Hogsheads and Bottles, of a very superior quality.

WHOLESALE AND RETAIL
Muslin Warehouse.
FRESH DACCA GOODS.
By Messrs. T. Roworth & Co.
HAVE just received and exposed for sale, a Choice Assortment of the above Articles.
February 5, 1800.

WHOLESALE AND RETAIL
Muslin Warehouse.
FRESH LONG CLOTHS
AND
IZAREES.
Messrs. T. Roworth & Co.
HAVE just received and exposed for Sale.

GOODS.
Particulars will be published in Har

To be sold by Public Auctio
By Faria and Willi
At their Auction-room,
To-morrow, FRIDAY, the 7th I
A Brick bu er Roomed G HOUSE, cons a Hall, and Rooms, with lahs; the whol North and Sou useful Out Offices; the Ground is ne out;—there is a Tank, well stocked wi the whole consisting of ten Biggahs of 2½ of which is Charity Land, situate Ballia Ghaut Road.
A Person attends to shew the Pr

CHINA GOOD
PER EXETER;
FOR PRIVATE SALE.

Messrs. Faria & Willi
HAVE RECEIVED
AND EXPOSED FOR SALE,
A CHOICE CONSIGNM
OF
CHINA GOOD
CONSISTING CHIEFLY OF
HYSON TEA—China Ware—Lut and Sarsnets, of colours—Hams—meats—Brown and White Nankeens—Cloth—Whangees—Gauze for Curt Brown Fans, &c. &c
N. B The HYSON TEA is wa to be of the very best imported, being by Mr. FARIA's Son, who resides at The Tea has been tried and highly appro

FOR PRIVATE SALE,
By Faria and Willi
A FEW QUARTER PIPES OF
VERY OLD HIGH FLAVORE
CALCAVELLA & LISBON WI
Warranted upwards of five years fr from Lisbon; the greatest part of which it has been on the Coast of Africa, bein of the Cargo of the St. Iago Maior, no ported from the Brazils; it is of a ve perior quality.
PRICE 100 SICCA RUPEE
PER QUARTER CASK.
The same in bottles at per doz. 18 Rs or in six dozen cases, at per case, Sa. Rs.

SHERIFF's SALE
Notice is hereby given,
That on THURSDAY, the Thirteenth of February instant,
PRECISELY AT NOON,
THE SHERIFF OF CALCUTT
WILL PUT UP TO PUBLIC SALE
AT THE
LOWER VERANDAH OF THE COURT HO

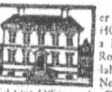

for those in the colonies to participate in the cultural and the social norms that were imported from England—through the city that was built architecturally, and the disciplinary and social institutions that were British— and establish a diasporic community, separate from the natives.

Metropole and center: the realm of print and empire making.
The specifics of the realm of print.

The realm of print was a complicit partner in the processes of empire making. When we consider how print was intrinsic to the formation of a colony by the East India Company, we are given a different perspective on the nature of how print entered India. In *Indian Ink, Script and Print in the Making of the English East India Company*,[104] Miles Ogborn looks at the importance of different modes of writing to the English East India Company in the seventeenth and eighteenth centuries, arguing that the company's world was "one made on paper as well as on land and sea."[105] Central to the book is the assumption that the "complexities of the exertion of power and the making of knowledge and profit in these mercantile and imperial worlds" are made evident in how different forms of writing were developed and deployed by the Company; thereby examining these texts can give us an insight in the connections between power and knowledge.[106] For example, the correspondence of Robert Boyle,[107] the scientist who was also a member of the Court of Committees that managed the Company's operations, reveals that his world was also the "world of the English East

---

[104] Miles Ogborn, *India Ink, Script and Print in the making of the English East India Company* (Chicago: University of Chicago Press, 1997).

[105] Ibid., p. xvii. What Ogborn wants to demonstrate is a way to look at the interconnections between imperial spaces, knowledge and power through "recent histories of reading, writing, and publishing." He goes on to argue that the operations and workings of power are found in the "concrete processes of the making, distribution, and use of texts as material objects." (pp. 5-6).

[106] Ibid., p. xxi.

[107] Robert Boyle owned East India stocks, and used his position in the Company to find jobs for those who used his patronage.

India Company."[108] The leading scientific figures of England were involved in the processes of empire making (despite denying their monetary involvements), thus shifting the dynamics of how colonization took place – it was not a mere event of brutal force and gunpowder but the intellectual elite of England were involved and seemingly quite keen to disseminate knowledge.

The use of print in the colonies was not inevitable as manuscripts were used as well as handwritten notices and circulars. Initially print was seen as a threat and many printers who attempted to print were deported to Europe. The works of Orientalist scholars are well known, but what need was there for grammar books and dictionaries to be printed and publicized and what part did the dissemination of printed material play in the debate of empire building in Bengal? Government patronage did determine the nature of print in the early years and for the publication of works on philology and grammar.[109] Patterns of dissemination and distribution were also determined by government finance.[110] Printed texts were circulated, enabling an imperial sphere of 'social communication' to be constructed that included readers and writers in India and in England, but this cannot necessarily be assumed to be a "consensual interpretative community"[111] for natives were not equal collaborators in this enterprise. These grammar books, legal texts and translations of religious texts were printed, placing them within an "imperial circuit" of production, dissemination and reception.[112] Moreover, the needs of empire building determined why grammar books were printed, and did not necessarily reflect the needs of the natives. Subsequently, these grammar books – meant to aid in standardizing Indian languages -- did become the definitive norm in India.

---

[108] Ibid., p. xvii. Boyle, though, was keen to emphasis that his involvement with the company was out of the desire for knowledge and not profit. Ogborn writes that historians of science consider Boyle's involvement in the seventeenth century scientific revolution and the foundation of the Royal Society to argue for a "conception of scientific knowledge that understands it as an engagement with political concerns that are inseparable from matters of practice." p.xxi.

[109] Ibid., p. 220.

[110] Ibid., p. 221.

[111] Ibid., p. 223.

[112] Ibid., p. 225.

IMPERIAL PRINT IN COLONIAL CALCUTTA (1780-1820).

When examining the nature of how grammar books emerged in Calcutta, written on the same lines as grammar books in England, and the complicated logic behind them, it would be relevant to understand how grammar books evolved in England in a completely different context – or for that matter, how the emergence of the printing press helped in standardizing the English language. When William Caxton set up his printing press around 1476, it was about fifty years since the Chancery English had been adopted as the standard, based on the London and the East Midland dialect. Caxton's press aided in making this dialect of English as the norm. Caxton set up his printing press in Westminister close to Parliament, and decided to print in the vernacular, realizing the economic prospects of the new venture. This was a smart move, as there had been other printers who had set up presses on Oxford and St. Albans, and had failed. These printers had published academic books in Latin, not realizing that such books could easily be available through trade with the Continent.[113]

It was largely for economic reasons that Caxton was searching for a "relatively stable language variety that could serve a superregional function to speakers of different dialects."[114] He used a dialect that was the most widely accepted written variety, and used by the literate segments of society, which constituted his own intended audience. By the end of the fifteenth century, "economic motivations contributed significantly to earlier linguistic and political ones in the standardization of the language."[115] Writing dictionaries and grammar books were some of the processes that were involved in standardizing a language. The first dictionaries were written in the early eighteenth century and were meant to include new, unfamiliar words that had entered the English language over the centuries; dictionaries were needed to explain these words to the common user or to the well

---

[113] Norman Blake, *Caxton and his World* (London: Andre Deutsch,1969).

[114] Terttu Nevalainen and Ingrid Tieken-Boon van Ostade. "Standardisation," in *A History of the English Language*. eds. Richard Hogg and David Denison (Cambridge: Cambridge University Press, 1992), pp. 271-311; p. 278.

[115] Ibid., p. 278.

educated[116] and did not include those words that were in everyday use. Nathan Bailey's *Dictionarium Britannicum*, that was written in 1730, was the first dictionary to include all words and was subsequently used as a source for Johnson's *Dictionary of the English Language* (1755).[117] Early grammarians resorted to Latin grammar to provide them with a model and English grammar was not considered as an object worthy of study for its own sake till 1653 with the publication of Wallis's *Grammatica Linguae Anglicanae*. English grammar was treated like Latin, and emphasis was given to its morphology. Grammarians of the eighteenth century wanted to fix the language, only to realize that a living language could not be fixed. Lindley Murray's grammar book (first published in 1795) came to be looked upon as a handbook of English grammar. English grammar books were taken as a model for grammar books on native languages and the need to write such books were driven by the needs of empire and the East India Company.

The nature of how these grammar books in the colonial context came to be written is symptomatic of Tony Ballantyne's argument that imperial knowledge was often disembodied from the socio-traditional context from within which they emerged. Ballantyne argues that colonial states gathered knowledge from a wide range of sources about the colonies and printing was crucial to the systematization and dissemination of colonial knowledge.[118] This form of codified knowledge was the basis of the day to day operation of colonial power, but "the processes by which they were created profoundly altered the knowledge they recorded, disembodying these traditions, wrenching them free of the traditional social contexts of knowledge transmissions to revalue them as an aid to the operation of imperial authority."[119] Recent histories of empire look at the connections between the role of colonial knowledge and the establishment of colonial authority.[120]

---

[116] Ibid., p. 283.

[117] Ibid., p. 284.

[118] Tony Ballantyne, "What Difference does Colonialism Make? Reassessing Print and Social Change in an age of global imperialism," in *Agent of Change: Print Culture Studies After Elizabeth L Eisenstein*, eds. Sabrina Baron, Eric Lindquist and Eleanor Shevlin (Amherst: University of Massachusetts Press, 2007).

[119] Ibid., p. 345.

[120] As printing was "central" to the working of the modern colonial state, it has "become an

IMPERIAL PRINT IN COLONIAL CALCUTTA (1780-1820).

Even as colonial authorities used print to exercise power, what is not very clear is the nature of power? It is easy to write off colonial power as being absolute but power in this instance – as the preceding analysis has shown – was far from being totalitarian. Colonial authority did not operate in a binary of absolute coercion and pliant submission and the natives – for that matter, the intellectual elites in many instances – participated in the dissemination of colonial authority. Those who were being ruled allowed themselves to be a part of this process of technological exchange, even as it was used to make them subordinates.

Homi Bhabha and Mimicry:[121] of books, men and pale imitations.

The closer we get to see how these processes of socio-cultural exchange took place, we can understand that it was not a simple matter of give and take; it was also not absolute coercion from the side of the Britishers and complicit acceptance by the natives.[122] Infact, the dissemination of colonial authority was quite a nuanced phenomenon. And more importantly and inevitably, like the grammar books on Indian languages, the emergence of colonial print itself was a result of exchange and transformation. In theoretical terms, postcolonial scholars use the concept of mimicry to describe these processes of engagement and exchange and the question to ask is whether this term comprehensively describes the particular phenomenon of how natives learnt about print technology. Homi Bhabha's theoretical analysis on mimicry and hybridization are often used as iconic

---

important point of debate in the scholarship on modern empire building"; print was an important tool for "colonial administrators, missionaries and social reformers" and was reconceptualized in the colonial situation. Ibid., p. 343.

[121] Homi Bhabha, *The Location of Culture* (London and New York: Routledge, 1994).

[122] If we consider the motives behind which a lot of postcolonial theory emerges from, we can understand what determines its fundamental premises of alienation; and this is best and most succinctly commented upon when Bhaba describes his sense of acute marginalization on arriving in England: "I do not mean, in any sense, to glorify margins and peripheries. However, I do want to make graphic what it means to survive, to produce and to create, within a world-system whose major economic impulse and cultural investments are pointed in a direction away from you, your country or your people. Such neglect can be a deeply negating experience, oppressive and exclusionary, and it spurs you resist the polarities of power and prejudice, to reach beyond and behind the invidious narratives of center and periphery." Ibid., p. xi.

and definitive descriptions of native-colonial engagements. These initial moments, when colonial presence interacts with the natives, have been construed as terrifying and Bhabha aptly describes this sense of horror:

> ...then colonial mimicry is the desire for a reformed, recognizable Other, *as a subject of a difference that is almost the same, but not quite.* Which is to say, that the discourse of mimicry is constructed around an ambivalence; in order to be effective, mimicry must continually produce its slippage, its excess, its difference....[123]

Mimicry, therefore, is a replication that can never be the same as the original, and this "slippage" causes a sense a sense of disturbing ambivalence "on the authority of colonial discourse." Bhabha goes on to write:

> It is from this area between mimicry and mockery, where the reforming, civilizing mission is threatened by the displacing gaze of its disciplining double, that my instances of colonial imitation come. What they all share is a discursive process by which the excess or slippage produced by the ambivalence of mimicry (almost the same, but not quite) does not merely 'rupture' the discourse, but becomes transformed into an uncertainty which fixes the colonial subject as a 'partial' presence. ...[124]

According to Bhabha, when the natives replicate the British, it becomes an act of mimicry and the native becomes a subject who is nearly the same as the master – but as the subject can never exactly be the same as the origin, s/he is always caught within an "excess, or a "difference." The colonial subject becomes a "partial presence" caused by the fact the there is always ambivalence in the "reforming, civilizing mission" of the colonial authority and the "mockery" of the disciplined double. In this chapter and in the subsequent chapters, what I draw attention to is that in many instances, this particular definition of mimicry becomes problematic - was it mimicry when the natives used print, or even for that matter, can it describe the

---

[123] Ibid., pp. 122-123.
[124] Ibid., pp. 122-123.

process by which the Britishers involved the natives to introduce print for their own needs? To what extent was the authority of "colonial discourse" of the Britishers disturbed by the mimicry of the natives as they interacted with them and learnt about print? In the process of "mimicking" the Europeans, the native did not really become partial subjects, almost the same as the rulers but not so.

For Bhabha, a central notion that describes these moments of socio-cultural exchanges is hybridity, or *mettisage*, which means being in a state of in-between-ness. He urges for moving beyond monolithic, conceptual categories of class and gender, and to "think beyond the narratives of originary and initial subjectivities and to focus on those moments or processes that are produced in the articulation of cultural difference."[125] Bhabha writes that these in-between spaces "provide the terrain for elaborating "strategies of selfhood."[126] Frantz Fanon is used as an example by Bhabha who argues that even though Fanon recognizes the importance for marginalized societies of "asserting their indigenous cultural traditions and retrieving their repressed histories," he is aware of the dangers that is involved in fetishizing calcified "colonial cultures" or in "homogenizing the history of the past" or in celebrations of the past.[127] Moreover, cultural engagement is produced "performatively" and "from the minority perspective, is a complex on-going negotiation that seeks to authorize cultural hybridities that emerge in moments of historical transformation."[128] Hybridity as a concept is best explained in Bhabha's essay, "Signs Taken for Wonders" where he defines this term more comprehensively:

> Produced through the strategy of disavowal, the reference of discrimination is always to a process of splitting as the condition of subjection: a discrimination between the mother culture and its bastards, the self and its doubles, where the trace of what is

---

[125] Ibid., p. 2.

[126] Ibid., p.2

[127] Ibid., p. 131.

[128] Ibid., p. 3.

avowed is not repressed but repeated as something different – a mutation, a hybrid. It is such a partial and double force that is more than the mimetic but less than the symbolic, that disturbs the visibility of the colonial presence and makes the recognition of its authority problematic.[129]

Therefore, Bhabha argues, the native culture that replicated the socio-technological aspects of the mother culture became bastardized in the process of doing so; as a result, the native psyche splits up and its presence disturbs and problematises the authority of the colonial masters. As I unravel some aspects of how print entered Calcutta between 1780 and the early nineteenth century, I would consider Bhabha's description of how the colonial psyche transmuted itself on encountering the colonial other as partially explanatory of how print entered Bengal. These dominant narratives of postcolonial theory cannot be considered as absolute overarching grand theories which explain all the processes that accompanied colonization. It goes without saying but this assumption is the unstated underbelly of my book, as I examine the early moments of the "communication circuit" as it emerged in Calcutta in the late eighteenth century.

Conclusion.

A basic fundamental question that keeps on arising over and over again is on how the realm of print in colonial Bengal (between 1780 and 1800) perpetuated and embodied power? Was it such a simple process of shifting ship loads of people and technology across the oceans and settling them down in Calcutta? What was it that motivated people to move themselves from England, apart from the obvious monetary attraction? Examining a few moments (and a few people involved) in the process of technological exchange will allow us a more nuanced understanding of what is usually written off as mere mimicry by most postcolonial theorists.

George Gordon was one of the printers who came and started a printing press in Calcutta; he was also the only printer who was

---
[129] Ibid., p. 159.

professionally trained as a printer before his departure from England.[130] Gordon was the nephew of one of the most eminent eighteenth century London printers, William Strahan, who was also the king's printer, and a friend of Samuel Johnson and Benjamin Franklin. He was recommended by his uncle to the Court of Directors of the East India Company and was the only licensed printer by the Company. Another well known printer was Charles Wilkins who joined the East India Company in 1770 as a writer; he was well versed in Persian and Bengali and made the earliest known types in Bengali.[131] He was also invited to establish a printing press for the Company so that it could print its own official documents. He was appointed as the first superintendent of the Honourable Company's Press in Decemebr 1778. The press was in Malda where the Company's factories were located, and Wilkins was also the supervisor of these factories. Here Wilkins made a set of Persian types. The Company's press was removed to Calcutta in 1781 where Wilkins was transferred as the Persian and Bengali translator to the Committee of Revenue. The first work to be printed here was his own *A Translation of a royal grant of land by one of the ancient Rajaas of Hindostan*; Francis Gladwin's translation of *Ayeen Akbari* was the last work to be printed under his supervision in 1783. After Wilkins left for Benaras in December 1783, Gladwin succeeded him as the superintendent of the press in January of 1784. All of these people were involved in the process of empire making, meticulously learning the languages and the habits of the natives. Some of them carried with them the best of British civilization and imparted it to the natives.

It would therefore be a more meaningful discussion if we understood power as operating in a more sophisticated manner rather than simply being imposed upon others in a binary fashion. Those Britishers who traveled to India were people who were part and parcel of the Juggernaut of empire making and they were blood and flesh people and not necessarily heinously mean or cruel. The intellectual brahminical elite allowed themselves to be participants in this process, only because they

---

[130] For more see Graham Shaw, *Printing in Calcutta before 1800* (Oxford: Oxford University Press, 1981), pp. 48-50.

[131] For more see Shaw, pp. 69-71.

were involved in a new epistemic shift; the tradeoff must have been fair. It is rather simplistic to construe the natives as being overpowered or incapable of resistance of any sort. The sheer fascination with the new-ness of the social and technological aspects of print culture might have been, after all, irresistible.

3 THE EMERGENCE OF EARLY PRINT IN COLONIAL CALCUTTA (1780-1820).

Introduction

The early realm of print in Calcutta comprised of a wide variety of printed texts; from historical accounts like Francis Gladwin's *A dictionary of religious ceremonies of the eastern nations* (1787), William Hunter's *A Concise account of the kingdom of Pegu*,[132] to grammar books like John Gilchrist's *A dictionary, English and Hindoostanee*, and literary endeavors like *The bevy of Calcutta beauties. A collection of poems*,[133] *The poems of Anna Maria*,[134] *The happy prescription; or, the lady relieved from her lovers: a comedy in rhyme*.[135] Official documents were also a part of this wide spectrum of printed material: like the East India Company *Treaties*,[136] Jonathan Duncan's *Bengal, Governor and Council. Translation of the regulations for the administration of justice in the Courts of Dewanny Adawlut*,[137] alongside historical narratives like Francis Gladwin's translation

---

[132] Printed by John Hay, 1785.

[133] Published in Calcutta; printed by Daniel Stuart, 1785.

[134] Published in Calcutta: from the press of Thomson and Ferris, 1793.

[135] Written for a private theatre, by William Hayley, Esq. – Calcutta: printed in the year, 1785.

[136] Published in Calcutta: printed at the Honourable Company's Press, 1788.

[137] Printed at the Honourable Company's Press, 1784.

of Abu al-Fazl ib Mubarak's *Ayeen Akbery* and *The History of Hindostan, during the reigns of Jehangir, Shahejhan and Aurungzebe*.[138] Literary translations like *Kalidasa. The seasons: A descriptive poem, by Calidas, in the original Sanskrit*,[139] Joseph Champion's translations of *The Poems of Firdosi*,[140] medical treatises like Francis Balfour's *A treatise on the influence of the moon in fevers*,[141] travel narratives like Henry Abbott's *A journal with occasional remarks, made on a trip from Aleppo to Bussora*[142] were also part of this large spectrum of printed texts.

    The emergence of print culture in colonial Bengal, under the East India Company, is largely an untold story. Calcutta would become the capital of the British empire, and the realm of print culture played an important role in maintaining and perpetuating British rights to this colonial territory. The history of how this realm of print culture evolved in Calcutta is central to this chapter. Ships that sailed from England carried books; printing presses were brought all the way from Europe and with the help of Indians, print workshops were set up. Many fortune seekers who traveled to India in the hope of making money through printing ventures, set up printing presses and published newspapers. Sadly, many such ventures failed. Economic losses implied the absence of a readership. The focus was, unreasonably so, on being able to use print technology even when there was no readership. Catalogues were published in Calcutta which advertised the books that had been imported from England which were auctioned on arrival like any other ships' cargoes. Printers mostly bought these imported books which were sold on to the public. Circulating libraries cropped up which needed imported books; an advertisement in the *Calcutta Gazette* in 1787 refers to the opening of a new library which stocked imported books (fig.6): "Mr. Shakell [who succeeds John Hay as the printer of the *India Gazette*] having now arranged his late purchases by the last ships, and completed his Catalogue, presumes to assure the public that they will find

---

[138] From the press of Stuart and Cooper, 1788.

[139] Calcutta; printed at the Honourable Company's Press, 1792.

[140] Printed by John Hay, 1785.

[141] Printed by George Gordon, 1784.

[142] From the press of Joseph Cooper, 1789

IMPERIAL PRINT IN COLONIAL CALCUTTA (1780-1820).

Figure 6: Advertisement of a circulating library.

his Circulating Library, well worthy of their patronage."[143] Tabloid-like gossip was also printed in newspapers. Oriental scholars had their works printed in Calcutta, the best known being Sir William Jones who also published journals on the proceedings of the Asiatic Society. Nonetheless, the reading public in Calcutta was small. In many ways, this realm of print enabled the community to imagine itself to be a part of the British imperialist project, and bound it with the metropolis.

It is slightly ironic that the first book to be printed in Bengal, India, Nathaniel Halhed's *A Grammar of the Bengal Language* (1778), was under the patronage of the East India Company and meant for a British readership.[144] The book was printed in Hooghly, made its way to England and sold in London by Elmsley. In 1783, a review in an English journal, *A New Review*, described the book as "classical" and of much use to those Britishers who traveled to India to work in "public departments," allowing for better "correspondence" between the natives and the rulers.[145] The need for communication was but one of the reasons why the book was praised; the Bengali "characters" are "beautiful," the reviewer wrote, and would arouse the curiosity of the British reader. Letterpress technology had captured the "exotic" beauty of the Bengali script, revealing the apparent mastery of western print mechanization over scribal manuscripts. The central assumption within eighteenth century British print culture, where print technology was seen at the apex of communication forms, was transferred to the colonies by the East India Company. Such was the realm of early print that evolved in Calcutta, in the last two decades of the eighteenth century, serving the needs of the empire.

In this chapter, I look at the "communications circuit" in the early phases of print culture in Calcutta, that is pre-1800, and how it catered to the specific needs of the Britishers. The booksellers, writers and printers were English. That is, prior to the turn of the century, the realm of print culture was a closed circuit—all books, newspapers, gazettes, legal

---

[143] *Calcutta Gazette*, August 29, 1787.

[144] Nathaniel Brassey Halhed, *A Grammar of the Bengal Language*. Hooghly in Bengal, 1778. Reprint. ed. R. C. Alston (Menston, England: Scolar Press, 1969).

[145] "Review of *A Grammar of the Bengal Language*," *A New Review* 3(1783): 156-157.

translations, in fact, all printed material had a very specific readership and catered to the practical, aesthetic and intellectual needs of the Europeans. Interestingly enough, the newspapers also occasionally had news items in native languages (see above fig. 6). One wonders, who would have been the readers of news in Bengali in a newspaper that catered to the Britishers? Would the English readers be expected to know enough of the language, barely nine years after Halhed's Bengali grammar book was published? I have mentioned earlier that as the grammar book was meant to both educate those Britishers who traveled to India for work, and also to impress the non-native readers about the beauty of the Bengali fonts, the multilingual newspaper was printed on similar lines. The polyphonic nature of the newspaper at this early stage of print in colonial Calcutta is remarkable.

In the first section of this chapter, I examine the nature of the "communications circuit" that evolved in Calcutta, drawing attention to the interrelationship between technology, print culture and imperial knowledge-making. The motives behind how the "circuit" of printers and writers operated are examined in the second section. The realm of print culture in Bengal was defined by the imperatives of empire; it would not have emerged the way it did if it had not been for the economic support of the East India Company. To clarify what I mean by imperial print, I examine the works of Sir William Jones and the Company Orientalists, a body of scholarship that emerged under the auspices of the East India Company. For Sir William Jones, steeped in the culture of print, the technology of print had the power to transform a pre-modern, Indian scribal culture into western modernity. The last section in my chapter examines Nathaniel Halhed's *A Grammar of the Bengal Language*, and defines 1778, the year of its publication, as a watershed moment in the history of print as it entrenches British colonial print culture in Calcutta which was transparent about its motives and origins. Halhed has to be seen as working within the existing ideological notions of empire making, where Britain defined itself as civilized and modern by characterizing India and its languages as primitive. The author draws attention to the mechanical aspects of print technology; the natives are emasculated and deviant, awaiting British colonization for progress, and in a similar manner, archaic Indian scribal culture would undergo modern change through print technology. In order to maintain order and control the colonies, it was essential to learn the languages of the Indians—the underlying assumption was that the territorial domain of the colonies could be managed through the realm of print.

Pre-1800 print culture: the establishment of imperial print.

The "communications circuit" in the initial phases of print culture, that is pre-1800, was meant solely for the Britishers. Print intervened in a realm of scribal and oral cultures in India; the availability of scribes alleviated any sense of urgency for the East India Company government to introduce print for trade or for commerce.[146] The Company was concerned in maintaining a trading monopoly that prevented independent merchants from conducting business and was aware that print could be used to initiate critical discussion within the settler community against the trading policies of the East India Company. It is not surprising to note that the lack of print before the advent of print technology was commented upon by the early traders. A public notice was set up in 1768 in a commercial area of Calcutta, by one William Bolts, addressed to the Public: "Mr Bolts takes this method of informing the public that the want of a printing press in this city being of great disadvantage in business, and making it extremely difficult to communicate such intelligence to the community as is of the utmost importance to every British subject."[147] The "community" was British, and so was the "public" – and Bolts' efforts to initiate a printing press landed him in trouble with the authorities (even though there is little evidence to show that he had any English or Bengali fonts) and he was subsequently deported.[148] The early printers were self-taught, and it was only later, by the

---

[146] On 7th April, 1781, a letter to the editor of the *India Gazette* makes this clear: "Not many months ago, before the fear of printing in Bengal was somewhat abated, the discerning humourists of the colony were not infrequently entertained with manuscript advertisements, hand bills, and other manuals of advice, with divers and sundry further literary productions; either hawked about, like state minutes in circulation; or else nailed up against military barriers, ecclesiastic porticoes, judicial piazzas, or other angular places of diurectic resort." Cited in Graham Shaw, *Printing in Calcutta to 1800* (London: The Bibliographical Society, 1981), p. 1.

[147] Quoted in Thankappan Nair, *A History of the Calcutta Press* (Calcutta: Firma KLM, 1987), p. 1.

[148] Ibid., pp. 1-15.

middle 1780s that professionally trained printers from England came to India to ply their trade. The printing presses that cropped up, pre-1800, were run by Europeans.

In *Printing in Calcutta to 1800*, Graham Shaw documents the number of presses that were in operation till 1800.[149] From 1780 to 1790, there were between three and five presses continually in operation, and from 1791 to 1799, between seven and ten active in each year. The presses were mostly concerned with the printing of newspapers, and the increase reflects the opening of newspaper offices in Calcutta in 1791-2. All the newspapers were meant to be read by the British residents. (These newspapers, I argue in my next chapter, enabled the formation of imperial identity.) When we try to recover the nature of readership from these early printed texts, we have to look at the historical context within which these newspapers were written. The diasporic community was the targeted readers, and the locale of readership meant that these texts were read by a select audience. For the small fledgling community of British traders and administrators, print was a medium of communication with the metropoles, and between themselves. In the first issue of *The World*, on 15 October 1791, William Duane wrote with great aplomb that the "civilized world affords no similar instance in the rise and culture of the arts, and to such perfection as Calcutta this day affords – the mechanical arts, which depend on the luxuries of society, and the tangibility of fashion, are arrived to the summit of perfection."[150] And he continued in a laudatory note that "in no respects can she [Calcutta] appear so eminently so, as in her publications … If in Europe, the number of publications give the grounds to ratiocinate the learning and refinement of particular cities, we may place Calcutta in rank above Vienna, Copenhagen, Petersburg, Madrid, Venice, Turin, Naples, or even Rome."[151] Print culture played an important role in the lives of this expatriate community of diasporic residents who carried with them the culture of print from eighteenth century England, that was still in a state of transit as it shifted away from oral and manuscript cultures.

---

[149] Graham Shaw, *Printing in Calcutta to 1800* (London: The Bibliographical Society, 1981).

[150] Quoted in Shaw, *Printing in Calcutta*, p. 4.

[151] Ibid., p. 4.

By the end of the eighteenth century, the number of titles that had appeared in England multiplied ten times when compared to what it was a hundred and fifty years ago. In England, about 6000 titles had appeared during the 1620s; that number climbed to almost 21,000 during the 1710s and to over 56,000 by the 1790s.[152] Print culture gained legitimacy in eighteenth century England, and even as the diasporic residents imported the technology leading to a proliferation of printing presses in Calcutta, not all presses were profit making institutions. Often, many presses were shut down due to debt and the owners were put into debtors' prisons.[153] For printing ventures to be economically viable, there had to be a kind of symmetrical harmony within the "communications circuit"—that is, between the readers, writers, publishers and the booksellers. Local printing was expensive and often, many authors preferred to send their work to be published in England. (This stopped after 1840.) Many books were printed by publishers in London; Graham Shaw mentions that some printers like Debrett and Stockdale specialized in publishing books meant for the India market.[154] The initial realm of print culture in Calcutta was still in its nascent stages of establishing a perfect harmony within the "communications circuit" of the readers, printer-booksellers and the writers.

The small group of white residents in Bengal was connected with Europe and within themselves through print. English newspapers and books made their way to Calcutta as cargo of ships; likewise books that were printed in Calcutta also had a readership in England. The capacity to imagine themselves as part of empire and to define their identity as imperial subjects was made possible through the to-and-fro movement of texts. The culture of print in Calcutta enabled the production of Orientalist

---

[152] Such changes were not only specific to England but happened all across Europe; rising literacy rates explain the dramatic increase in publishing and printing.

[153] Shaw, *Printing in Calcutta*, pp. 23-27.

[154] There are numerous advertisements by London publishers in the Calcutta weeklies of this time; the following is an example from the *Calcutta Gazette* (1785): "Messrs. Cooper and Becket, of London, beg leave to inform the Settlement, that they have, by the advice of certain Gentlemen, long resident in India, undertaken a new Periodical Publication, entitled, *The Intelligencer for India, a Monthly Compendium of Public Events*." Quoted in Shaw, *Printing in Calcutta*, p. 20.

scholarship in the eighteenth century and gradually spread across Europe, aiding in establishing imperial identity and enabling imperial power. One can ask: would the empire have been formed in the way it did without print, as print helped in developing a sphere of readership that stretched across continents? Company Orientalism, a body of scholarship that emerged as a result of the contact between England and India, enabled the empire to perpetuate itself. Imperial knowledge, and imperial print, produced under the patronage of the East India Company, informed British practices of commerce and trade and finance, disseminated notions of Aryanism within Europe, and most importantly, helped the white diasporic community to define itself as members of the empire on a day-to-day basis. The business of empire-making was not only a geo-territorial event, but also a geo-spatial and textual act. Print culture was intrinsic to the making of imperial identity and being-ness, as it bound together those of the white community within themselves and also with the metropoles.

East India Company Orientalism: the reasons behind the emergence of imperial print.

i. Economic imperatives and the East India Company
The realm of early print culture in Bengal was defined by the imperatives of empire and it would not have emerged the way it did if it had not been but for the economic support of the East India Company. We have to take into account the socio-historical and economic imperatives that determined the emergence of print culture in colonial Bengal. What are the socio-historical factors that determine how the "communications circuit" operated? In addition to the "communications circuit" that involves the author, the publisher, the shipper, the bookseller and the reader, we have to consider their relation within the larger socio-historical and economic contexts. In this section, I examine the impetus behind the formation of imperial print and East India Company-sponsored scholarship, to argue that this body of work was created in order to sustain the empire.

The realm of early print before 1800, in Calcutta, still in its burgeoning stages and was meant primarily for the white settlers. 1800 marks a shift in the domain of print in Bengal as the year saw the establishment of two institutions, the Srirampur Missionary Press and the college of Fort William, where books, intended for the native population, were published under the auspices and patronage of the British government and Baptist missionaries. Disseminating books among the Indians would create an indigenous sphere of print culture, allowing the natives to engage with the materiality of the text, establish a reading public, and imbibe habits of reading, factors that would eventually enable the English to transmit European culture and ideas. Prior to the turn of the century, the realm of print culture was a closed circuit: all books, newspapers, gazettes, legal translations, in fact, all printed material had a very specific readership and catered to the practical, aesthetic and intellectual needs of the Europeans.

Tabulating the books that were printed before 1800, Graham Shaw categorizes the subjects that were dealt with: translations from Persian and Sanskrit, literary and historical works, dictionaries, art works, travelogues, maps, Indian economics, works on religion, law, and military regulations. To a certain extent, this body of printed work written about India can be seen as contributing to a larger body of work that would become Orientalist scholarship, which according to Edward Said, was a "corporate institution dealing with the Orient."[155] For Said, the Orient came into being as a result of the printed narratives that were written about the East and filtered into the consciousness of Europe; these narratives were discursive constructs and distorted the material realities that they portrayed. A complete description of the "communications circuit" of printers, authors and booksellers remains incomplete if we fail to address the fact that it was partially driven by the needs of British empire. For example, a review of Nathaniel Halhed's *Grammar of the Bengal Language* in the *English Review* in 1783 makes an easy equation between the study of Indian languages and its use in maintaining the British Empire in India.[156] The argument that is posited in the review is quite relevant in the present context: the aim of the British government was "to establish an empire over the minds as well as over the country of the natives," and grammar books were needed to allow for an "easy" intercourse with the "native." The review states that the

---

[155] Edward Said, *Orientalism* (New York: Vintage, 1979).

[156] "Review of Halhed's *Grammar of the Bengal Langauage*," *The English Review or An Abstract of Foreign and English Literature* 1(1783): 5-14.

"languages of India" have been "totally disregarded by the Parliament and the Ministers of Britain; and they have been nearly as much neglected by the East India Direction"; it was because of the "literary zeal" of a "few private men" that progress was made in such studies and "Mr. Jones led the way" with his *Persian Grammar,* his *Poesis Asiatica Commentarii,* and other publications of erudition and elegance," followed by Mr. Richardson who also wrote "several works of ingenuity and research" particularly the *Dictionary of the Persian, Arabic, and English languages.*[157]

In fact, even the realm of print culture in Europe was partially determined by the institutions of empire and imperialism, as the public imagination of Georgian England was prolific with portrayals of imperial greatness and the colonies. Kathleen Wilson argues that images of empire permeated all aspects of domestic culture and politics.[158] Newspapers and periodical presses, even those that were the most apolitical, alongside with histories and topographies of the colonies "supported British superiority and power, fed the growing enthusiasm for the exotic and the primitive, and legitimated British domination in terms comprehensible to the empire's domestic consumers [in England]."[159] The nature of the epistemological model that informed these portrayals of the empire is debatable; for Said, these representations of the Orient were fictive renditions of the Other and the writer-observers had little face-to-face interaction with the natives, while I would argue against such an assumption.

There was a sustained effort undertaken by the East India Company to ensure that there evolved a realm of print culture that contributed to imperial knowledge-making. The process of imperial knowledge-making did operate outside a dichotomous relationship of European active observer and native passive observed, and recent scholarship draws attention to such a model of analysis. Imperial

---

[157] Ibid., pp. 5-6.

[158] Kathleen Wilson. "The Good, the Bad, and the Impotent: Imperialism and the Politics of Identity in Georgian England", in *The Consumption of Culture,* ed. Ann Bermingham and John Brewer (New York: Routledge, 1995), pp. 237-262.

[159] Ibid., p. 242.

knowledge-making, in fact, involved both natives and British scholars. Sir William Jones, referred to as the father of scientific linguistics and comparative philology, is a perfect example of a scholar who worked outside the Orientalist knowledge-making framework. He was also steeped in the culture of eighteenth century British print and had an immense trust in the veracity of printed texts. An employee of the East India Company, Jones examined Indian languages in order to make linguistic connections with European languages, drawing attention to the complexities of the local culture while also placing it on a "pattern of human history at a global level."[160] In his annual address to the Asiatic Society in Calcutta, which he founded, in February 1789, Jones described the Sanskrit language within a global context, stating; that "the Sanskrit language, whatever be its antiquity, is of a wonderful structure; [it is] more perfect than the Greek, more copious than the Latin, and more exquisitely refined than either, yet bearing to both of them a stronger affinity."[161] Jones had a very clear idea of how the Asiatic Society would operate, revealing an awareness that the process of Company-sponsored Orientalist knowledge construction would have to involve the natives. Jones makes it clear when he says:

> Much may ... be expected from the communications of learned natives, whether lawyers, physicians, or private scholars, who should eagerly, on the first invitation, send us their ... [works] on a variety of subjects.... With a view to avail ourselves of this disposition, and to bring their latent science under our inspection, it might be advisable to print and circulate a short memorial, in Persian and Hindi ... [advertising] the design of our institution. ... To instruct others is the prescribed duty of learned Brahmans, and, if they be men of substance, without reward; ... and the Mahomedans have not only the permission, but the positive commands, of their law giver, to search for learning even in the remotest parts of the globe.[162]

---

[160] Kapil Raj. "Refashioning Civilities, Engineering Trust: William Jones, Indian Intermediaries and the Production of Reliable Legal Knowledge in Late Eighteenth Century Bengal," *Studies in History* 17(2001): 23-47, 29.

[161] William Jones, *The Collected Works of Sir William Jones. 3 Vols.* (New York: New York University Press, 1993), *Vol. 3*, p. 34.

[162] Jones, *Collected Works, Vol. 3,* pp. 21-22.

IMPERIAL PRINT IN COLONIAL CALCUTTA (1780-1820).

In his address to the white diasporic community in Calcutta comprising scholar-administrators, Sir William Jones encourages them to be involved in the apparatuses of knowledge-gathering, laying out specific instructions as to how they were to work. They were to "contribute a succinct description of such manuscripts" as had been "perused or inspected, with their dates and the names of their owners, and to propose for solution such questions as had occurred to him concerning Asiatik Art, Science, and History, natural or civil"; subsequently, the Asiatic Society would "possess without labour, ... a fuller catalogue of Oriental books."[163] It was through a collaborative process, dependant on a relationship between the scholar and natives, that a catalogue of Oriental books could be established. Jones was implementing the strictures of British eighteenth century print culture, evident in his valorization of print technology as against manuscript culture.

In order to contribute to this realm of print culture, there were specific methods and methodologies that informed how the books were to be printed and written. A zone of contact was to be created so that the natives would trust the East India Company scholars and impart their knowledge; this process of imperial knowledge making was an act of intellectual engagement. In many ways, William Jones displays an attitude in keeping with the notion of gentlemanly etiquette that marked the European seventeenth century scientific community on how experiments were to be conducted. Drawing upon the arguments of Steven Shapin that notions of "trust" and civility" were dominant attitudes that defined the nature of scientific experiments in seventeenth century England, Kapil Raj arrives at a similar conclusion in his examination of the works of William Jones, stating that it was a "new, hybrid regime of knowledge, organizing and disciplining both Indian and British functionaries" and introduced a sense of "security, loyalty, and hierarchy."[164] I would shy away from describing this new colonial "hybrid" system of imperial knowledge-making as operating within benevolent spaces of intellectual engagement. Even when face-to-face

---

[163] Ibid., pp. 21-22.

[164] Raj, "Refashioning Civilities," p. 20.

contact took place between the white rulers and the natives, there was an uneven structure of power that marked these encounters despite the element of civility. In most instances, with changes in the local, native patronages, where local rulers suffered under the political interventions of the East India Company-state, disrupting indigenous institutions of learning, the educated natives were compelled to impart knowledge to the white scholar-administrators of the East India Company in order to survive. There was a fracture between William Jones' private affinity, admiration and loyalty to Asiatic culture and his inevitable public role as intelligencer, surveyor and enumerator of the Raj.

The scholarship of Sir William Jones can be considered Company Orientalism and emerged only after 1780. Sanskrit, as a language, was till then, an enigma and remained elusive to Europeans. Sanskrit was seen as having the keys to a vast store of Indian knowledge, but there were very few who would help the Britishers learn the language. Most educated Hindus were hesitant to engage with Europeans and communicate to them any aspects of their own religion. But towards the end of the eighteenth century, with the rise of the East India Company as rulers, Orientalist scholarship as a disciplinary institution came into being under the patronage of the scholar-administrators of the Company. The East India Company substituted for native patronages of learning, and with the decline of the native aristocracies, many Brahmin scholars became destitute and gradually had to accept positions imparting knowledge to the new rulers.[165] For Sir William Jones, native scholars were to be used, but were never to be considered as intrinsic to the mission. For example, Jones wanted to admit natives into the Asiatic society but was unsure as to how his proposal would be received by the other Britishers. He compiled translations of Hindu and Muslim Laws in order to aid the "benevolent intentions of the legislature of Great Britain,"[166] using the knowledge of the "most learned Hindus and Mohammedans."[167] There was little "amusement" in working on these translations, except the belief and desire of "rendering his knowledge useful

---

[165] Tony Ballantyne, *Orientalism and Race: Aryanism in the British Empire* (New York: Palgrave, 2002), pp. 1-55.

[166] Jones, *Complete Works, Vol. 3*, p. vi.

[167] Ibid., p. vii.

to his nation, and beneficial to the inhabitants of these provinces."[168] Company Orientalism, unlike Said's Foucault-inspired version of Orientalism, emerged as a result of the close interaction between the natives and the Europeans and can be described as a detailed and organized body of knowledge fashioned by the East India Company in the late eighteenth century.[169]

The power of this realm of print culture is evident in the fact that it enabled to maintain control over the colonial territories. As early as 1783, a review appeared in an English journal, which when describing the need for grammar books and language books on the natives said that "without an easy and general intercourse with the natives, through the medium of language, no system of regulation ... can promote any solid, rational or permanent establishment of authority and power" as no people could "cheerfully submit to rulers" they did not understand."[170] More importantly, the cultivation of this kind of imperial print was a sustained effort and in keeping with the East India Company policies; the Company's trading success was a result of the scientific revolution of the seventeenth century and the EIC had eminent scientists of the Royal Society, like Robert Boyle, Isaac Newton, Joseph Banks as its directors or major shareholders. Not surprisingly, Company Orientalism had a small but influential readership, a sphere of print communication that informed the practices of empire

---

[168] Ibid., p. vii.

[169] Central to Company Orientalism was a Sanskrito-centric vision of India that celebrated Sanskrit and the ancient past, but decried contemporary culture as debased. This attitude was in keeping with the eighteenth century fascination with the classical languages and literatures making the British believe that the ancient Hindus, like the Greeks and the Romans, had created a culture that was lost as a result of the medieval dark ages. Jones was much aware of the dichotomy within which he was operating, as he wrote, "Whoever travels in Asia, especially if he conversant with the literature of the countries through which he passes, must naturally remark on the superiority of European talents" (Jones, *Complete Works, Vol. 3*, p. 12). As "minute geographical knowledge "was needed" so was the knowledge of the "natural productions of these territories, especially in the vegetable and mineral systems" as these were "momentous objects of research to an imperial" and "commercial people" (Ibid., pp. 13-14).

[170] "Review of Halhed's Grammar Book," *The English Review, or, An Abstract of English and Foreign Literature* 1(1783): 5-14, 5.

formation. The body of Orientalist work that emerged from India in the late eighteenth century and influenced European notions of the colonies was a result of print capital. The works of the Calcutta based Orientalists were widely disseminated in Europe as a result of Jones' letter writing and print culture.[171] The "communications circuit" was immense, spreading across continents. A single author, located in India, had books printed in India and England and these were translated and read by a European audience.

ii. The characteristics of Western print.

Empire making was made possible through the realm of print culture. Not only was the technology transferred, but so were the socially ascribed characteristics of print. Sir William Jones, operating within the ideology of eighteenth century print culture that associated print with truth, assumed that the technology of print had the power to transform a pre-modern, Indian scribal culture into western modernity. But this equation between print and truth was not intrinsic to letterpress technology as till the early decades of the eighteenth century there was a suspicion of the printed word. In *The Nature of the Book: Print and Knowledge in the Making*, Adrian Johns draws attention to assumptions about print culture, stating that what we "often regard as essential elements and necessary concomitants of print are in fact rather more contingent than generally acknowledged. Veracity in particular is … extrinsic to the press itself, and has had to be grafted onto it."[172] A printed book could never be trusted to be what it claimed. Johns claims that in the seventeenth century, piracy and plagiarism were dominant fears. It was a matter of routine that books could be considered dubious; therefore, it was impossible to trust any printed report. Pirate editions of Shakespeare, Donne and Sir Thomas Browne were liable to egregious errors, and so was Sir Isaac Newton's unauthorized publication of *Principia* and the first scientific journal, the *Philosophical Transactions*. It was only in 1760 that the first book was printed without any errors.

Not surprisingly, till early in the eighteenth century, print was seen

---

[171] Ballantyne, *Orientalism and Race*, pp. 1-55.

[172] Adrian Johns, *The Nature of the Book: Print and Knowledge in the Making* (Chicago: University of Chicago Press, 2000), p. 2.

as suspect, without any intrinsic characteristic of truth. Printers, booksellers and authors, who gained the most commercially, put forward the notion of the truth and superiority of print in contrast to manuscripts. If print culture was to be a viable economical institution, a "communications circuit" involving the author, publisher, the printer, the shipper, the book-seller, and the reader had to be in harmonious coexistence, with the reader believing in the veracity of print. Writers were often propagandists of print, as much as theorists, and this is how Paula McDowell describes Daniel Defoe, the eighteenth century's "most prolific printed author," who wrote in his *Essay upon Literature* (1726), "The Printing Art has out-run the Pen, and may pass for the greatest improvement of its Kind in the World."[173] All of Defoe's writings imply that the oral past should be, but is not, cut off from the print-oriented present and future. Regarding Defoe's historical fiction, *A Journal of the Plague Year* (1772), McDowell points out that the text moves diachronically in time as the present modern age of print was a move away from the backward past associated with oral culture. Defoe also moves "synchronically across different communicative modes that in reality are coexisting and interdependent" but are represented as parts of a "linear, progressive development."[174] Defoe's printed books contribute to an "emergent model of a hierarchy of forms of communication with print at its apex"[175] as the writer attempts to draw an equation, not existing before, between print and "enhanced fidelity, reliability, and truth."[176] In this process, orality is relegated to the realm of old wives tales.

By the time of Sir William Jones, England had become an increasingly print-oriented society, shifting away from its oral past. This explains Jones' feverish desire to transcribe every manuscript into print, as the process would lend an element of fixity to unstable scribal texts. In an advertisement in *The Calcutta Gazette*, in 1789, Sir William Jones wrote:

---

[173] Paula McDowell, "Defoe and the Contagion of the Oral: Modeling Media Shift in A Journal of the Plague Year," *PMLA* 121(1): 87-106.

[174] Ibid., p. 88.

[175] Ibid., p. 89.

[176] Johns, *The Nature of the Book*, p. 5.

> The correctness of modern Arabian and Persian Books is truly deplorable, nothing can preserve them in any degree of accuracy but the art of printing; and if Asiatic literature should ever be general, it must diffuse itself, as Greek learning was diffused in Italy after the taking of Constantinople, by mere impressions of the best manuscripts without versions or comments, which future scholars would add at their leisure to future editions: but no printer should engage in so expensive a business without the patronage and the purse of monarchs of states, or society of wealthy individuals or at least without a large public subscription.[177]

Jones was extremely conscious of entering a realm of scribal culture in Bengal, and this is reflected in his desire to constantly transfer manuscripts into printed texts. In a way, by transferring written texts into print, his central aim was to codify knowledge, and in the process allow for control of what was disseminated about India. In 1768, before Jones sailed for India, he wrote to Count Revicski, the Imperial Minister of Warsaw, describing the difficulties that were present when trying to locate a single meaning in manuscripts; it was "impossible to find two manuscripts [of Oriental literature] without error," he wrote, and "it was "absolutely necessary … to possess two copies of every one" which he would read so that "faults of the one" would be "corrected by the other."[178] In many of his letters, Jones voices a similar concern, where he reveals an intense desire to transcribe everything that he reads into print. Writing to one Dr. Patrick Russel in 1786, he said, "I congratulate you on the completion of your two works, but exhort you to publish them."[179] Jones goes on to say, "think how much fame Koenig lost by delaying his publications" and even if printing is "dear at Calcutta," if "government" printed Russel's works, he would "cheerfully superintend commas and colons."[180] A year later, Jones voices a similar

---

[177] William Jones, *The Calcutta Gazette*, October 29, 1789.

[178] Jones, *Complete Works*, *Vol. 1*, p. 101.

[179] Jones, *Complete Works*, *Vol. 2*, p. 99.

concern in another letter,

> I have just read a very old book on that art [of music] in Sanskrit. I hope to present the world with the substance of it, as soon as the transactions of our society [The Asiatic Society] can be printed; but we go slowly, since the press is often engaged by government; ... The *Asiatik Miscellany*, to which you allude, is not the publication of our society, who mean to print no scraps, nor any *mere* translations. It was the undertaking of a private gentleman, and will certainly be of use in diffusing Oriental literature, though it has [not?] been so correctly printed as I could wish.[181]

Manuscripts are seen as being less than perfect while printed texts allow for true, correct knowledge to emerge. Print technology is invested with a kind of truth power that is denied to manuscripts. Power resides in the capacity to be able to use print, and in the process, to make it accessible to larger groups of people. Mechanical reproducibility, made possible as a result of letterpress technology, would make knowledge more reproducible but also more authentic. The realm of print spread across continents, and made it possible to control the colonial territories.

The East India Company was interested in documenting all forms of knowledge that it could lay its hands on and supported many such works; all grammar books and translations were justified as they could help in empire building. Translations of historical and administrative works were seen as essential in carrying out the operations of the Company, and often, these works were partially subscribed and recommended by the East India Company. For example, Francis Gladwin's translation of Abu al-Fazl Ibn Mubarak's *Ayeen Akbery* was published in 1783, and seen as an endeavor that would serve the company as the "work comprehends the original constitution of the Mogul Empire, described under the immediate inspection of its founder; and will serve to assist the judgment of the Court

---

[180] Ibid., pp. 100-101.

[181] Ibid., pp. 123-124.

of Directors."[182] In the introduction to the translation, there is a lengthy explanation of how the text would be beneficial to the company: "It will show where the measures of their administration approach to the first principles, which perhaps will be found superior to any that have been built on their ruins, and certainly most easy, as the most familiar to the minds of the people, and when any deviation from them may be likely to counteract, or to assimilate with them."[183] The third volume contained a "full account of the religion of the Hindoos; their books and the subjects of them: their several sects and the points in which they differ."[184] There were astronomical notes which were provided by Reuben Burrow, who applied with "great diligence to the study of the Sanskrit language" and also made a "perfect knowledge of Hindoo astronomy."[185] The Governor General and Council recommended to the Court of Director the purchase of one hundred and fifty copies of the first edition of the *Ayeen Akbery*; this was, after all, a "work which may prove of the utmost utility to the Company, as it contains the original Institutes of the Sultan Akber, the founder of the empire."[186] Company patronage did provide a much needed monetary impetus for native types to be developed and these were subsequently used by the natives.

Grammar Books and print culture

Grammar books on Indian languages were meant to aid the East India Company. In order to maintain order in the colonies, it was essential to learn the languages of the Indians; this territorial domain of the colonies could be controlled by mastering the realm of native languages and codifying them in grammar books. Grammar books like Francis Gladwin's *The Persian Moonshe* (1795), *A Vocabulary, Persian, Arabic, and English* (1797),

---

[182] *Ayeen Akbery: or The Institutes of the Emperor Akber*, Vol. I. trans. by Francis Gladwin, pp. xi-xii. 1783.

[183] Ibid., p. xi-xii.

[184] The "Preface" to *Ayeen Akbery*, Vol. III. trans. by Francis Gladwin. Printed by William Mackay, Calcutta Gazette Press, 1786.

[185] Ibid.

[186] *Fort William-India House Correspondence, vol. IX, 1782-85*, edited by B.A. Saletore, Delhi, 1959. Also Gladwin's "Preface" to *Ayeen Akbery*, Vol. II, p. iii.

which aided the British to learn Persian and Bengali, were printed by English printing presses to cater to the needs of the administrators of the Company. This realm of texts was specific to the English community in Calcutta, and was meant to aid in trade and rule. Such texts play a similar role as that of colonial cartography in the processes of British empire building. As Ian Barrow argues, the mapping of India and the creation of colonial territory helped to build British national identity.[187] Colonial cartography depicted histories of British territorial possession and these histories helped the British to remake themselves as legitimate rulers while also reinforcing the notion of a British national identity. Grammar books, for the most, made colonial possession more legitimate. One of the first books to be written was Nathaniel Halhed's *A Grammar of the Bengal Language*, in 1778. In 1783, a reviewer in *The English Review* wrote that the "settlements in the East" deserve the "chief attention" of Britain. A printed grammar book would draw public attention to the language spoken by "millions of industrious British subjects" and would also aid in the "proper management of the commercial, military and revenue departments in Bengal."[188]

Printing a grammar book would allow for better communication between the government and the natives, enabling benevolent rule. Print was an extension of the state and the state defined itself through print. For Halhed:

> The wisdom of the British Parliament has within these few years taken a decisive part in the internal policy and civil administration of its Asiatic territories…. Much however still remains for the completion of this grand work; and we may reasonably presume, that one of its most important desiderata is the cultivation of a right understanding and of a general medium of intercourse between Government, and its subjects; between the natives of Europe who are to

---

[187] Ian Barrow, *Making History, Drawing Territory. British Mapping in India, c. 1756-1905* (New Delhi: Oxford University Press, 2003).

[188] "Review of Halhed's *A Grammar of the Bengal Language*", *The English Review*, p. 5-14.

rule, and the Inhabitants of India who are to obey.[189]

If the British were to rule, then print would play an important function in making that rule possible. Halhed draws a comparison between the present British conquest of Bengal and the colonial desire to learn the language of the natives with a historical antecedent, when the Romans, " a people of little learning and less taste, [who] had no sooner conquered Greece than they applied themselves to the study of Greek."[190] Learning the language of Bengal would allow the rulers to explain the benevolent principles of that Legislation whose decrees they enforce[d]"; the desire was to "convince" and persuade the natives" while they commanded.[191] The economic imperatives were enormous and would be no less beneficial to the Revenue Department.[192] In all respects, the printed grammar book was a means of inevitable social progress in the colonies.

Territorial control was possible because of the scientific and technological advancement of England. A similar argument is made in *Mapping an Empire: The Geographical Construction of British India, 1765-1843*, where Matthew Edney argues that that the extensive trigonometrical surveys conducted in southern and central India in the nineteenth century encouraged many Britishers to believe that they knew the real India.[193] Trigonometrical surveys had the power to depict land in a precise manner and the ideal of scientific, rational depiction was a contrast to the ineffectual and non-rational Indians and the non-elite sections of British society who were caricatured as ineffectual and not capable of sustained rational thought. The power of trigonometrical mapping, with its seemingly objective and scientific nature, permitted the British administrators to believe that these cartographic portrayals could capture the real India, and demonstrate the superiority of the British. The maps portrayed more than

---

[189] Halhed, *A Grammar*, pp. i-ii

[190] Ibid., p. 1.

[191] Ibid., pp. i-ii.

[192] Ibid., p. xv.

[193] Matthew Edney, *Mapping an Empire. The Geographical Construction of British India, 1765-1843* (Chicago: University of Chicago Press, 1999).

land; they depicted totalizing power and knowledge. The belief behind print technology was that the Western disciplinary institutions could control the colonies.

By the latter part of the eighteenth century, print culture was seen as being superior to other forms of communication. The move was towards codifying into print all the existing knowledge systems documented in a scribal-manuscript culture and this was construed as a shift into inevitable progress. Halhed draws attention to the mechanical aspects of print technology. The book, he writes, was to be seen as "extraordinary" and an "instance of mechanic abilities" and meant for the British public whose "curiosity" would be "strongly excited by the beautiful characters" that were displayed in the text.[194] Making Bengali fonts was not easy as the Bengali letters were "very difficult to be imitated in steel." Halhed erroneously credits Mr. Wilkins, an employee of the East India Company as being successful by undertaking the various occupations of "Metallurgist, the Engraver, the Founder and the Printer,"[195] and completely misrepresents the fact that natives were also involved; in fact, Panchanan Karmakar played an important role along with Wilkins. The process that was involved, of creating types in steel, of transferring and establishing clarity to the illegible, handwritten manuscripts—where the "inaccuracy of their writings" frequently deviated from their original forms—imparted a sense of authenticity and fixity to the act of writing.[196] Technology is celebrated as it has the capacity to represent even the most difficult of languages. Print technology made pure the existing state of social affairs; the various "impositions and forgeries with which Bengal at present abounds," Halhed wrote, would be done away with.[197]

Halhed has to be seen as working within the existing ideological notions of empire-making. Britain defined itself as civilized and modern by

---

[194] Halhed, *A Grammar*, p. xxiii.

[195] Ibid., p. xxiv.

[196] Ibid., p .3.

[197] Ibid., p. xxiv.

characterizing India and its languages as primitive. British rule was conceived as benevolent, a system of government, made possible and facilitated through print unlike scribal culture. The British nation was interested in "marking the progress of her conquests by a liberal communication of Arts and Sciences, rather than by the effusion of blood."[198] The "poorer classes of people" were oppressed in a "country still fluctuating between the relics of former despotic dominion, and the liberal spirit of its present legislature."[199] To "enforce stability" in the British empire and in order for the administration to gain in "popularity," the "discouraged husbandman, the neglected artist, and oppressed laborer" would seek "asylum" in British "territories."[200] Print technology possessed all the rational and benevolent characteristics of the English government; the "vigour" and "impartiality" that marked the operations of the government were seen in the printed grammar book. Moreover, Halhed defines how the Bengali language was to be, and attempts to cleanse it, by doing away with "foreign" influences[201] and by presenting the Bengali language as "derived from its parent the Sanskrit";[202] words that were not "natives of the country are not a part of his text and he has only selected the "most authentic and ancient compositions."[203] The study of the language, Halhed argued, was made difficult due to the "carelessness and ignorance of the people"; it had many "anomalous characters" and deviations from the "original forms" giving rise to spurious characters.[204] The existing state of Bengali, as a language, was representative of the natives: lacking a sense of coherence and uniformity. Language and culture were imbued with the characteristics of a nation; the natives were emasculated and deviant, awaiting British colonization, akin to the fact that this scribal culture awaited print culture for progress. The spatial realm of

---

[198] Ibid., p. xxv.

[199] Ibid., p. xvi.

[200] Ibid., p. xvi.

[201] Ibid., p. xx.

[202] Ibid., p. xxi.

[203] Ibid., p. xxii.

[204] Ibid., p. 3.

the communications circuit mimicked and replicated the ideologies of the political.²⁰⁵

Halhed was operating within existing Western ideologies where the British nation was construed as masculine in contrast to the effeminate colonies. Mrinalini Sinha makes a similar argument in *Colonial Masculinity: The "Manly Englishman" and the "Effeminate Bengali" in the Late Nineteenth Century*, when she states that the social constructs of the manly Englishman and the effeminate Bengali in nineteenth-century India were a result of the emerging dynamics between colonial and nationalist politics and "is best captured in the logic of colonial masculinity."²⁰⁶ The contours of colonial masculinity were shaped in the context of an "imperial social formation that included both Britain and India."²⁰⁷ The figures of the "manly Englishman" and the "effeminate Bengali *babu*," according to Sinha, "were produced by, and helped to shape, the shifts in the political economy of colonialism in the late nineteenth century."²⁰⁸ Though Sinha analyses nineteenth century colonial Bengal, the ideological contrasts of British masculinity and colonial effeminacy can be traced back to a hundred years ago, as Halhed makes clear.

There is nothing intrinsic to print for the technology to be considered as masculine and rational in comparison to manuscript texts. The characteristics of masculinity were socially ascribed to printed texts. In the early modern period in England, for example, writers were hesitant to see their works being printed, or to be seen ideologically and physically as involved in the marketplace of printers and publication. For the female writer, Jody Greene argues, publication was akin to prostitution, while the male writers shared this anxiety more acutely.²⁰⁹ The act of publication, that

---

²⁰⁵ Vidyasagar was to echo this criticism fifty years later.

²⁰⁶ Mrinalini Sinha, *Colonial Masculinity: The 'Manly Englishman' and the 'Effeminate Bengali' in the Late Nineteenth Century* (New York: St. Martin's Press, 1995), p. 1.

²⁰⁷ Ibid., p. 2.

²⁰⁸ Ibid., p. 3.

²⁰⁹ Jody Greene, "Francis Kirkman's Counterfeit Authority: Autobiography, Subjectivity,

is, submitting one's works to the press, made the writer vulnerable to charges of sexual deviance and indecent exposure. "The male writer," according to Wendy Wall, "always trades on his vulnerability when he agrees to play the female role and be 'pressed' for the public."[210] By the seventeenth century, in England, increased literacy, the growth of cities and the flow of international capital improved print technology, and authors were more willing to make public works that would have a century ago been limited to private consumption. This caused an explosion in the number of printed books, doing away with how print was conceived. In eighteenth century England, print was seen at the apex of the communication system. For Halhed, writing in 1783, print was imbued with all the characteristics of the British nation and construed as vigorous, rational and truthful.

Scribal-manuscript culture, on the other hand, was defined as archaic and not very reliable. Halhed represents these elements of inauthenticity as inherent in the behavioural habits of the natives, stating that it was with "obstinate and inviolable obscurity the Jentoos conceal … the Mysteries of their faith."[211] This particular grammar text, like other books printed by the scholar-administrators of the East India Company, would undo by making public the concealment, "obscurity" and archaic-ness of scribal knowledge. Halhed was engaged in revealing the knowledge systems that were "shut up in the libraries of Brahmins,"[212] and in undoing the "impenetrable reserve" of the Hindus.[213] While describing the efforts that were taken to write the grammar book, he says that he followed a very clear "set of rules" and in as "comprehensive" a manner as he could "devise" but the "task was rendered very laborious by the great multiplicity of observations" that he had collected.[214] For Halhed, modern print capitalism would give "a new fixity to language" allowing for a sense of

---

Print," *PMLA* 121(1): 17-32.

[210] Wendy Wall, *The Imprint of Gender: Authority and Publication in the English Renaissance* (Ithaca, Cornell UP, 1993), p. 182.

[211] Halhed, *A Grammar*, p. x.

[212] Ibid., p. iii.

[213] Ibid., p. xi.

[214] Ibid., pp. xviii-xix.

"antiquity" of language" central to the formation of a modern consciousness.[215] Therefore, the realm of print culture mimics the ideological realm of the political, making colonial rule possible.

Conclusion.

Even when print is imported to aid in colonization, it never follows the same trajectory in different colonies. Print as a technology never exists in a state of isolation but in a social context; the socio-historical elements determine the nature of print. The central impetus in the colonial Indian context was to learn about the Indians, and through print communication be able to control their land. A point of contrast is seen in the processes of colonization in North America, where the history of print followed a different trajectory, when the Puritans migrated to New England in the 1620s and 1630. Even if New England society was an extremely literate one, its central focus was on creating devotion among the people. The realm of print culture that evolved was one that defined itself through religion.

A lot of migrants from Europe moved to New England in the early seventeenth century for religious reasons. Literacy meant the ability to read the Bible and other religious texts; if reading defined their identity, then, a religious identity was definitive of New England. Even schoolbooks were meant to instill piety. Surviving library catalogues and booksellers records in Puritan New England reveal that religious books outnumber all kinds of books.[216] Most of what was published in Cambridge and Boston were also religious texts: sermons, catechisms, prayer books.[217] Imperial identity of this settler society was established through a sense of religious sameness; they were bound to each other through piety and devotion. When the New

---

[215] Benedict Anderson. *Imagined Communities. Imagined Communities: Reflections on the Origin and Spread of Nationalism* (New York: Verso, 1991), p. 44.

[216] Jilll Lepore, "Literacy and Reading in Puritan New England," In *Perspectives on American Book History,* ed. Scott Jasper, Joanne Chaison and Jeffrey Groves (Amherst: University of Massachusetts Press, 2002), pp. 17-46, pp. 17, 38-40.

[217] Ibid., p. 41.

Englanders found themselves in contact with the indigenous people—the Wampanoags, Narragansetts, Nipmucks, Pequots, and other Algonquian peoples – their main concern was in trying to acquire Indian land, and in the process, bring order to the barbarians, and Christianize them—all of which was possible through sheer physical force. In the 1640s, the Puritan minister, John Eliot learned the Massachusetts language and subsequently, translated the Bible into Massachusetts in the early seventeenth century. He also printed a primer and a book of Psalms in Massachusetts, and used these religious books to teach the Algonquians to read and write. The realm of print culture, in all its aspects, within Puritan New England, aimed towards creating a sense of devotion and piety. The "communications circuit" of authors, booksellers, printers and publishers were all devoted towards creating a domain of religion.

But print culture has a life of its own which is dependent and determined by the larger social life around it, and the emergence of certain aspects of the "communications circuit" of printers, readers, booksellers, shippers, publishers in the colonial Indian context was determined by the imperatives of empire, giving gave rise to a body of work that is known as imperial knowledge. I have argued that the body of Orientalist work that emerged from India in the late eighteenth century and influenced European thought was a result of print capital. Aryanism, emerging from Orientalist scholarship, determined European notions of the colonies, and was made possible through the dissemination of print culture.

I have also posed the following question: how do we determine the nature of readership by looking at the artifact of the book? A similar query is posited by Seth Lehrer,[218] in the special edition of the *PMLA*, when he writes, "How can the history of reading be recovered from the traces of the text?"[219] The "status and interpretation of a word depends on material considerations … [and] the meaning is always produced in a historical setting … [as a result of] the different readings assigned to it by historical,

---

[218] Seth Lehrer, "Epilogue: Falling Asleep over the History of the Book," *PMLA* 121(1): 229-234.

[219] Ibid., p. 231.

rather than ideal, readers."[220] When we try to recover the readership from the traces of the printed text, we have to look at the historical context within which the text was written. In this chapter, in defining the nature of imperial print, I have argued that print culture that emerged in the last two decades of the eighteenth century in colonial Bengal targeted a particular audience. Imperial print culture aided in establishing and perpetuating a sense of imperial identity that made it possible for the British Empire to sustain itself.

---

[220] L. Bishop, "Book History" *The John Hopkins Guide to Literary Theory and Criticism,* ed. Michael Groden, Martin Kreiswirth, and Imre Szeman, 2nd Ed. (Baltimore: John Hopkins UP, 2005), pp. 131-136, p. 131.

4 READING HISTORIES: THE MAKING OF IMPERIAL DIASPORIC CITIZENS.

It is a lovely narrative to tell - the story of how printing presses were set up in the early years of print culture in Calcutta and is both within and outside the narrative of empire making. Tony Ballantyne makes the argument that print in an age of rapid empire building "became a crucial instrument for colonial administrators, missionaries, and social reformers, indigenous leaders and pioneering nationalists, and the members of international scientific, humanitarian, and political communities."[221] But any story that involves the printing press and its agents cannot only be about power and knowledge making that would abet and aid empire building, but has to involve a narrative that also looks at the many people who came and established the realm of print; the story of empire making can be but a part of it. These were Englishmen who carried their trade along with them -- there was George Gordon, who was the only printer, apart from James Hicky, to be professionally trained as a printer before arriving in India and started

---

[221] Tony Ballantyne, "What Difference Does Colonialism Make? Reassessing Print and Social Change in an age of Global Imperialism" in *Agent of Change: Print Culture Studies After Elizabeth L Eisenstein*, eds. Sabrina Baron, Eric Lindquist and Eleanor Shevlin (Amherst: University of Massachusets Press, 2007).

working at the India Gazette office in 1783, and there were others like B Messink, Manuel Canthoper, Jospeh Cooper who were amateurs and learnt the art of printing in India.[222]

The initial realm of print culture in Calcutta not only featured Orientalist scholarship and grammar books, but a large percentage of printed material was of a non-literary kind—stationery, handbills, advertisements, catalogues, legal and mercantile blank forms, calendars and almanacs. The print industry, though, was dominated by newspapers; it was "around the production of weekly newspapers that the whole commercial printing-trade in eighteenth century Calcutta was organized."[223] Twenty four weekly and monthly newspapers were published in the last two decades of the eighteenth century. For a publication to be successful, the patronage of the East India Company was essential.[224] Most of the newspapers were unable to continue beyond a few years and yet this did not prevent the publication of new newspapers. An editorial comment in the *Calcutta Chronicle* put it most succinctly:

> The proprietors of the *Calcutta Chronicle*, in consequence of the large amount of the bills now due to them, (many of them, of several years standing), request these Gentlemen indebted to the Office, will have the goodness to direct the payment of their bills, when presented either to themselves or agents. The aggregate amount of the bills, now outstanding is near 60,000 rupees, the bare interest of so large a sum, amounts to a considerable sum monthly, and as the proprietors have suffered much inconvenience and great loss, from so large an amount being outstanding, they beg to give notice that all bills, &. which remain unpaid on the 31st December next, will, on the 1st of January 1793, be put into the hands of an attorney, to

---

[222] Shaw, *Printing in Calcutta*, pp. 1-9.

[223] Ibid., p. 3.

[224] Ibid., p. 26.

recover by a legal course.[225]

Before 1800, all the printing presses were run by Europeans, and staffed by natives. According to Hadjee Mustapha, who was writing around 1790: "There are but four Printing Offices at Calcutta, amongst which one only is worked by Europeans, that of Cooper's: the three others, although inspected by an European, are worked by natives, who print in a Printing Office, just as they copy in a Counting House, without understanding the language."[226] Native Brahmins, blacksmiths and Englishmen worked side by side in these printing houses, participating in a technological and intellectual exchange that was revolutionary in most ways. The printing house also became a heterogeneous social space.

The unaccounted growth of English newspapers in the last two decades of the eighteenth century was curtailed when censorship was clamped down in 1799, only to be removed in 1818. It was only around this period that newspapers in Indian languages emerged; the first Bengali journal *Digdarshan*, subtitled the *Indian Youth Magazine*, was issued by the Srirampur Mission Press and contained educational information. The Calcutta School Book Society subscribed to a thousand copies of it for its Bengali schools. It was followed by the publication of *Samachar Darpan*, which can theoretically be described as the first newspaper in Bengali. It is circumspect to state that native usage is evident post-1800. Rammohun Roy was able to articulate socio-religious dissent and carry out critical exchange amongst the Indians and the English through his use of pamphlets, newspapers, and journals. Examining the English newspapers of the period—1780 to 1800—allows us to understand the processes of textual transmission. The focus in this chapter is not on native usage of newspapers and print but on the origins of the technology and the genre in England, and how it was carried across to India. What was the realm of print culture like in England, and considering that the colonies were thought of as suburban growths of the metropole, how was print imported to Calcutta by the English?

---

[225] *Calcutta Chronicle*. 1 Jan, 1793, vii, 363, 2.

[226] Quoted in Shaw, *Printing in Calcutta*, p. 3.

IMPERIAL PRINT IN COLONIAL CALCUTTA (1780-1820).

If we go in search of the origins of the newspaper in Calcutta, we go all the way to eighteenth-century England, if not earlier, and this is a fascinating thought: that a printed text that is so intrinsic to our everyday lives in India has its origins in a foreign country, and was carried across and established by the English in the city for their own specific needs. As printing presses and editors were imported from England, it is not surprising that the very format, structure and content of newspapers in Calcutta are replicas of those of English newspapers. Hence, when discussing the evolution of newspapers in Calcutta, we have to consider the nature of the newspaper in England, and how newsbooks of the seventeenth century became printed newspapers by the end of the century. In the first part of this chapter, I look at the characteristics of print culture that were carried across by the Englishmen who came to Calcutta. The second section looks at newspapers that were printed in Calcutta in the last two decades of the eighteenth century, performing a very important function in the very fabric of their existence – allowing those in the metropole in Calcutta to consider themselves as connected to the daily activities of the center. A print induced sub public emerged, replete with discourses of empire and colonization. I also examine the diasporic nature of imperial citizenship that was formed as a result of the consumption of newspapers.

From handwritten newsbooks to printed texts: newspapers in seventeenth and eighteenth century England.

i. Seventeenth century newsbooks.

The history of newspapers in England is a recent one, for printed news emerged in England only towards the early eighteenth century; Ian Atherton writes that till then, manuscripts were the most important form of written news as it was more accurate, less censored, and regarded as more authoritative.[227] For the historians also manuscripts usually make a better

---

[227] Ian Atherton, "The Itch grown a disease: Manuscript Transmission of News in the Seventeenth Century" in *News, Newspaper and Society in Early Modern Britain*, ed. Joan Raymond (London: Frank Cass, 1999), pp. 39-65. p. 40.

"form of historical evidence."[228] Most news of the seventeenth century in England spread through word of mouth and this time period also saw an increase in political news. All forms of written news – newsbook and newspapers, pamphlets, newsletters, sermons, plays, and ballads -- depended heavily on oral news, and the last four were at the "interface between the oral and the written."[229] Interestingly enough, most of the news that was conveyed was foreign; as in the 1620s and 1630s it was illegal to print domestic news in England, making censorship of manuscript news lighter, it was inevitable that the handwritten newsletters would be popular.[230] The writing of newsletters was an accomplishment that the gentry were expected to possess.[231] A central literary issue in the seventeenth century was the relationship between fact and fiction, and the development of the English newspaper has to be seen within this context where there was an "epistemological barrier" between knowledge and opinion.[232]

There were social factors that determined who had access to what kinds of news: printed news – a product of the English Revolution -- was for the masses while newsletters, were for the elite.[233] Moreover, newsbook circulation was broad and socially diverse, "crossing barriers of social distinction where newsletters had not [done so]"; newsbooks were in the public sphere, whereas newsletters belonged to the more private world of correspondence. Mass production and sale by booksellers or hawkers of printed news did away with the more direct relationship between the writer and reader of the newsletters. Often, printed newsbooks were mouthpieces of the ruling political parties[234] and by the 1680s, the "genres of the newsletters [impartial manuscript news] and the newspaper had virtually converged."[235] The circulation of news was also seen as an act that, through

---

[228] Ibid., p. 40.
[229] Ibid., p. 39.
[230] Ibid., p. 42.
[231] Ibid., p. 44.
[232] Ibid., p. 48.
[233] Ibid., p. 52.
[234] Ibid., p. 53.
[235] Ibid., p. 55.

its democratizing effect, spread to the vulgar, and state matters once accessible only to a select readership based on education and birth, had become a part of the common discourse of the masses.[236]

ii. Newspapers and British Imperial Identity

The newspaper print culture in eighteenth century England was able to bind the people within the frame of imperial citizenry, and even those in the provinces identified with the political processes of the state, nation and empire. Most newspapers carried news of war, trade and imperial expansion, shaping the readers notions of the nation and the empire, and British national identity rested on incorporating the colonies within the national imaginary. The print-induced English sub-public was replete with images of the colonies where the British Empire spread across continents. For example, a review of Nathaniel Halhed's *Grammar of the Bengal Language* in the *English Review* in 1783 makes an easy equation between the study of Indian languages and their use in maintaining the British empire in India; "... we shall confine our observations to strictures on the history and usefulness of a language of very high antiquity, spoken by millions of industrious British subjects."[237] For Halhed, the British Empire embraced the newly formed native subjects into becoming "industrious British subjects."

Kathleen Wilson, in her examination of the role of print in the eighteenth century, traces the spread of print culture from urban centres to the provinces, and argues that it played an important role in shaping and disseminating political values and attitudes regarding the nation and state.[238] London, the first centre of newspaper publishing, by the mid-century had

---

[236] Ibid. p. 56.

[237] "Review of Halhed's *Grammar of the Bengal Language,*" *The English Review, or, An Abstract of English and Foreign Literature* 1(1783): 5-14.

[238] Kathleen Wilson, *The Sense of the People, Politics, Culture and Imperialism. 1715-1785* (Cambridge: Cambridge University Press, 1995), and "The Good, the Bad, and the Impotent: Imperialism and the Politics of Identity in Georgian England", in *The Consumption of Culture 1600-1800: Image, Object, Text,* ed. Ann Bermingham and John Brewer (London and New York: Routledge, 1995), pp. 237-262.

numerous daily, fortnightly and monthly newspapers that were also available in the provinces. Most provincial towns had three or more printers and booksellers by 1730 and the number grew. Over a century, newspapers spread across the provinces, structured the national political imaginary and allowed individuals to "participate imaginatively as well as materially in the processes of domestic and imperial government."[239] Newspapers produced "highly mediated national belonging"; cultivating a universal ideal. The significance of the larger polity was made evident, where the aspirations and ideologies of the state were made comprehensible to the citizens.[240]

Newspapers were instruments in the social production of information. By the 1740s and the 1750s, most periodicals had sections called "American Affairs" or "British Plantations" that included current affairs and also had histories and settlement patterns of individual colonies.[241] Such texts "welded the national and imperial interest" while erasing the crueler aspects of colonization.[242] The Empire permeated all aspects of Georgian culture. A mercantilist libertarian view of Empire, Kathleen Wilson argues, was disseminated through commercial printing, in particular the newspapers, establishing a "militaristic" characteristic and English citizenship was equated with colonial aggressiveness. Discourses of patriotism were complicit with those of imperialism, and contained within the grander scheme of colonization. Empire entered the public consciousness in such a manner that it was seen as a birthright, not an end in itself, but enabling a greater good to emerge; it became a national symbol which all, disregarding social inequalities and domestic strife, could participate in. Wilson writes that from mid-century, newspapers in London

---

[239] Wilson, "The Good, the Bad, and The impotent," p. 240.

[240] The role of eighteenth century print is best exemplified by looking at the role of newspapers and periodicals. By the end of the sixteenth century, London publishers printed news pamphlets, and for the most, they were theological. Newspaper publishing took on a modern form in Europe; the first newspaper, *Mercurius Gallobelgicus* was in Latin, and dealt with European military news of the previous six years, was printed in 1594, in Cologne. The origins of newspapers lie in Dutch gazettes of the late seventeenth century, and it became a category of printed matter only after 1700. See Febvre, Lucien and Henri-Jean Martin, *The Coming of the Book: The Impact of Printing. 1450-1800* (London: NLB, 1976), p. 197.

[241] Wilson, "The Good, the Bad, and The impotent," p. 240.

[242] Ibid., pp. 239-240.

and the provinces mirrored such a world view:

> in which trade and the accumulation of wealth appear to be of the highest national and individual good. The progress of war in Europe, America, Africa, and the East Indies, and the prizes taken in battle; the comings and goings of merchant ships, often with lengthy lists of products…; prices, stocks, and bullion values; and advertisements for luxury goods from international and colonial markets … together … account for one third of the contents of individual issues. … [Eighteenth century newspapers] also evinced a widespread interest in the processes of colonial acquisition."[243]

For example, the *Gentleman's Magazine*, which described itself as an unbiased and judicious chronicler of general news and cultural events, concerned itself specifically with imperial matters, as the issues of 1750 make clear. In 1756, the periodical had full accounts of the loss of Minorca, public reactions to it across England, reminiscences of British historical escapades, where Raleigh and Drake were featured alongside recent events like Vernon's siege of Porto Bello in 1739. Such narratives re-established a sense of British imperial supremacy, and citizenry was imagined within a global framework. A regular section in the periodical was the "Journal of American Affairs," also containing anecdotal accounts of the horrific aggression of the French, Spanish and Indians against the brave British. Periodicals like these, recounted colonial events so as to cast the British as superior and morally right, and cultivated and established a sense of legitimacy in the processes of Empire formation. Not surprisingly, those who came to India shared this ideology.

Establishing print and a public culture in India

When the English came to India, they carried certain notions of how print was to be, and how it was to operate, despite the fact that the socio-

---

[243] Ibid., p. 240.

economic conditions that had given rise to such a notion of print in England were absent in India. Newspapers and journals were printed in India, but they addressed a very specific readership, and they were comprehensible mostly to readers who were intellectually and socially connected to England. Though newspapers were being printed around the 1780s in India, it does seem strange that within three decades, there could be immense validation of print, a glorification of its rational and argumentative characteristics. In the *Calcutta Journal,* in 1819, the editorial states (fig. 7):

> We have indeed been accused ... of giving too free utterance to sentiments which it has not been the custom to disseminate through the medium of the Indian press. In India, we have no hesitation in saying that the different Journals published in the country, are, for more than half the British population who are immured in the interior of the country and to whom new books are most inaccessible, the only medium through which they can keep up the knowledge either of literary productions, or scientific discoveries; and those who do not read them, must necessarily remain ignorant of a thousand truths interesting to philosophy and humanity, as marking the rapid strides with which the present age is advancing towards the perfection in both.
>
> England, as we have said before, owes her superiority to other nations, chiefly to the freedom of her press, and the wide diffusion of information, among her people. ... in India, every heart that boasts of being animated by British feelings must not only rejoice in this distinction, but feel a veneration for its causes. ... The Newspaper press has become a more powerful engine by which to promulgate opinions and govern intellect than ever before existed;

Figure 7: Editorial in the Calcutta Journal.

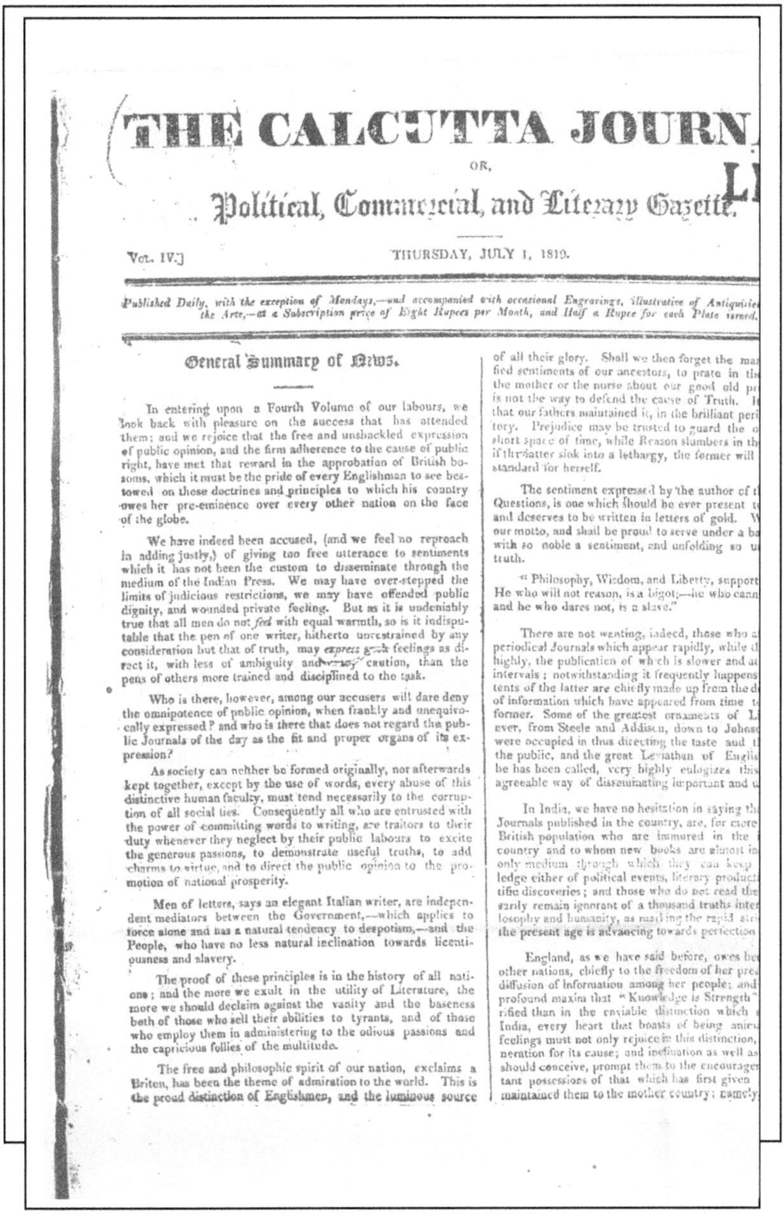

THE CALCUTTA JOURN

OR,

Political, Commercial, and Literary Gazette.

VOL. IV.] THURSDAY, JULY 1, 1819.

Published Daily, with the exception of Mondays,—and accompanied with occasional Engravings, illustrative of Antiquitie[s] the Arts,—at a Subscription price of Eight Rupees per Month, and Half a Rupee for each Plate issued.

General Summary of News.

In entering upon a Fourth Volume of our labours, we look back with pleasure on the success that has attended them; and we rejoice that the free and unshackled expression of public opinion, and the firm adherence to the cause of public right, have met that reward in the approbation of British bosoms, which it must be the pride of every Englishman to see bestowed on these doctrines and principles to which his country owes her pre-eminence over every other nation on the face of the globe.

We have indeed been accused, (and we feel no reproach in adding justly,) of giving too free utterance to sentiments which it has not been the custom to disseminate through the medium of the Indian Press. We may have over-stepped the limits of judicious restrictions, we may have offended public dignity, and wounded private feeling. But as it is undeniably true that all men do not *feel* with equal warmth, so is it indisputable that the pen of one writer, hitherto unrestrained by any consideration but that of truth, may *express* such feelings as direct it, with less of ambiguity and [illegible] caution, than the pens of others more trained and disciplined to the task.

Who is there, however, among our accusers will dare deny the omnipotence of public opinion, when frankly and unequivocally expressed? and who is there that does not regard the public Journals of the day as the fit and proper organs of its expression?

As society can neither be formed originally, nor afterwards kept together, except by the use of words, every abuse of this distinctive human faculty, must tend necessarily to the corruption of all social ties. Consequently all who are entrusted with the power of committing words to writing, are traitors to their duty whenever they neglect by their public labours to excite the generous passions, to demonstrate useful truths, to add charms to virtue, and to direct the public opinion to the promotion of national prosperity.

Men of letters, says an elegant Italian writer, are independent mediators between the Government,—which applies to force alone and has a natural tendency to despotism,—and the People, who have no less natural inclination towards licentiousness and slavery.

The proof of these principles is in the history of all nations; and the more we exult in the utility of Literature, the more we should declaim against the vanity and the baseness both of those who sell their abilities to tyrants, and of those who employ them in administering to the odious passions and the capricious follies of the multitude.

The free and philosophic spirit of our nation, exclaims a Briton, has been the theme of admiration to the world. This is the proud distinction of Englishmen, and the luminous source of all their glory. Shall we then forget the ma[...]
fied sentiments of our ancestors, to prate in th[...]
the mother or the nurse about our good old p[...]
is not the way to defend the cause of Truth. I[...]
that our fathers maintained it, in the brilliant peri[...]
tory. Prejudice may be trusted to guard the o[...]
short space of time, while Reason slumbers in th[...]
if the latter sink into a lethargy, the former will [...]
standard for herself.

The sentiment expressed by the author of t[...]
Questions, is one which should be ever present t[...]
and deserves to be written in letters of gold. W[...]
our motto, and shall be proud to serve under a ba[...]
with so noble a sentiment, and unfolding so u[...]
truth.

"Philosophy, Wisdom, and Liberty, support[...]
He who will not reason, is a bigot;—he who cann[...]
and he who dares not, is a slave."

There are not wanting, indeed, those who a[...]
periodical Journals which appear rapidly, while t[...]
highly, the publication of which is slower and at[...]
intervals; notwithstanding it frequently happens[...]
tents of the latter are chiefly made up from the d[...]
of information which have appeared from time t[...]
former. Some of the greatest ornaments of Li[...]
ever, from Steele and Addison, down to Johns[...]
were occupied in thus directing the taste and t[...]
the public, and the great Leviathan of Englis[...]
he has been called, very highly eulogizes this[...]
agreeable way of disseminating important and u[...]

In India, we have no hesitation in saying th[...]
Journals published in the country, are, for more[...]
British population who are immured in the [...]
country and to whom new books are almost in[...]
only medium through which they can keep [...]
ledge either of political events, literary producti[...]
tific discoveries; and those who do not read the[...]
sarily remain ignorant of a thousand truths inter[...]
losophy and humanity, as marking the rapid str[...]
the present age is advancing towards perfection [...]

England, as we have said before, owes he[...]
other nations, chiefly to the freedom of her pre[...]
diffusion of information among her people; and [...]
profound maxim that "Knowledge is Strength" [...]
rified than in the enviable distinction which [...]
India, every heart that boasts of being anim[...]
feelings must not only rejoice in this distinction, [...]
neration for its cause; and inclination as well as[...]
should conceive, prompt them to the encourage[...]
tant possessions of that which has first given [...]
maintained them to the mother country; namely[...]

than could have been anticipated by any former age; or than can be conceived by foreigners who do not understand, or by natives who have not studied its economy.[244]

The small group of white residents were connected to each other through print, locally and globally, and it was through print that they established a public space. Narratives that emerged from within the realm of print, bound the English residents to form a notion of imperial identity. The plethora of print culture in the form of newspapers, journals and books formed a print-induced sub-public sphere.

Print emerged in Bengal under colonial rule, and this historical event determines how we theorize about the evolution of a print-induced eighteenth century imperial public sphere. I refer to this public sphere as "imperial" as it was specific to the English reading audience, who used print to communicate within themselves in India and across continents, for both social and professional reasons. The print culture that developed, though circumscribed within a small English community as has been described in the preceding sections, was highly sophisticated. This colonial, imperial public sphere is distinct from the European concept of the public sphere, which came into being in the eighteenth century in England as a result of the gradual breakdown of the feudal structure and operated, as Júrgen Habermas argues, separate from the state and civil society, allowing "private people [to] come together as a public"—in order to engage in criticism of the State, and in the process, promoting democratic participation.[245] A central premise in this Habermasian theory was that the identities of the participants were irrelevant as a group of individuals were willing to come together in order to exchange in critical debate. This very act of doing away with the particularities of the individuals is an impossible endeavor, specifically in the colonial context as we cannot homogenize the Indian reading public.[246]

---

[244] *Calcutta Journal.* July 1, No.123 (1819): 1-2.

[245] Jurgen Habermas, *The Structural Transformation of the Public Sphere*, trans. Thomas Burger (Cambridge: MIT Press, 1989), p. 27.

[246] Not surprisingly, such a position, however emancipatory in theory, has received a lot of

IMPERIAL PRINT IN COLONIAL CALCUTTA (1780-1820).

The print-induced public sphere, established in India by the colonial settlers, cannot be gauged on a Habermasian model as it was not a public sphere that emerged as a result of socio-structural changes. The Europeans in India carried print, and assumed that the associated socio-civic characteristics would come into being in the Indian sub-public sphere. The public sphere that was created by the British, through print, has to be seen as hegemonic, disseminating and perpetuating imperial identity. Those who were living in India, albeit for short periods of time, engaged with the politics of England and the colonies through print. They could navigate through vast geographical distances and remain connected with England because of print, and the constant mobility of ships; England, after all, was a maritime power. A diasporic national imaginary was created through these narratives that emerged in the public sphere.[247] The public imagination both in the metropole and the colonies was replete with images of colonization and the Empire, thus undoing the notion of a static, monolithic British identity that emerged from within.

Recent revisionist studies in 18th century studies of British history have made a theoretical move towards including concepts of the empire in

---

negative critical attention. (After all, the print reading public in India in the last two decades of the eighteenth century could not have been but those who knew how to read English!) *The Black Public Sphere* (ed. The Black Public Sphere Collective, Chicago: University of Chicago Press, 1995) argues for the impossibility of conceptualizing the emergence and presence of African American public spaces within the Habermas-ian model, and instead re-articulates the very premises of what constitutes the black public sphere. Feminist critiques target the Habermas-ian notion of the "internally coherent, homogeneous civil public space" as it attains its unity by "banishing its own particularity" and instead, what is proposed is the presence of "multiple" public spheres. Nancy Fraser's post-bourgeois notions of the public sphere state that civil society was constructed through the exclusion of women, and instead she theorizes on the possibility of multiple public spaces co-existing; *Unruly Practices: Power, Discourse, and Gender in Contemporary Social Theory* (Minneapolis: University of Minnesota Press, 1989) and *Justice Interruptus* (New York: Routledge, 1997); as does Michael Warner in *Publics/Counterpublics* (Cambridge: Zone Books, 2003).

[247] This was only possible at this moment, with the constant to and fro movement of ships, and of print culture. It is akin to the present, where a globalized world order exists. Scholars like Arjun Appadurai and Anthony Giddens comment on how national narratives "think" and "feel" beyond the nation to create a "pluralized world-political" community. Such narratives operate in global public spaces, made possible not only through print, but new technologies of the internet, and constant mobility. See Appadurai's *Modernity at Large: Cultural Dimensions of Globalization* (Minneapolis: University of Minnesota Press, 1996).

how the British past is visualized; this has meant reconceptualizing notions of Englishness and Britishness. Kathleen Wilson writes that between 1660 and 1840, the "taxonomic projects of ethnography, natural history" as well as the notion of civilization influenced British politics and territorial conquests. Notions of national belonging were redefined and altered to suit "new international and imperial circumstances" resulting in a precarious sense of self.[248] Therefore, those who traveled across continents into the colonies were able to identify with the metropole, establishing a sense of diasporic citizenhip, which was made possible as a result of the to-and-fro movement of print.

Diasporic Citizenship.

This early realm of print newspapers played an important role in allowing those in the colonies to imagine themselves as always connected with the metropole, thus establishing and maintaining a sense of diasporic citizenship within the imagination of the readers. For an English reader, situated in Bengal, it would have been meaningful for him to be reading news about England, and global affairs, despite being disconnected socially and culturally from his immediate surroundings in Calcutta. Even though he was reading news about wars being fought on the continent and social events of the royal family which were six months old (the time it took for a ship to sail from Britain to India), it allowed the reader to participate in the public functioning of the Empire. Print technology, thus, enabled the far flung colonies to be brought under the umbrella of empire building, paving the way for a notion of diasporic citizenship to be cultivated. A proper system of printing newspapers was established, and so was a postal order which distributed these newspapers in the districts.[249]

There is a correlation between the fact that this realm of print culture, that was imported to India by the English and was an aid in establishing and perpetuating a sense of diasporic citizenship, occurred at a time period where there was a movement of people across the globe who also used print to articulate their desires to be citizens of multiple worlds. It

---

[248] Kathleen Wilson, *The Sense of the People*, pp.1-2.

[249] For more, see Mrinal Kanti Chanda, *The History of the English Press in* Bengal (Calcutta: K.P. Bagchi, 1988), pp. 452-465.

is not a stretch of the imagination to argue that such notions of being imperial citizens – despite being away from the center of power in England – has to be seen as part of this phenomenon of diasporic citizenship being articulated by other communities in this time period, and reflects a sense of self reflexivity. For example, and in a completely different socio-geographical context very unlike those of the English colonizers, there exists a large body of writings by African American from the early 1800s which talk about such concepts of diasporic citizenship.

Written in 1830 in antebellum America, David Walker's "Our Wretchedness in Consequence of the Colonizing Plan"[250] refuses to allow the African American to simply belong to Africa; this text is an outright rejection of the plans of the American Colonization Society, which was formed in 1817 to enable the emigration of free African-Americans to Liberia, and reveals a refusal to establish a pure African identity. It is not possible to arrive at a reductive notion of racial solidarity and we cannot make an easy equation between the African-American and the African and for Walker, the African American is always caught between multiple identities. Walker also refers to the English as African American's greatest friends, and simultaneously aligns himself with Haiti where a revolution against the French had taken place in 1791 (and ended in 1803).[251] For a disenfranchised African American of the antebellum period, the processes of belonging were never stable, as Walker makes clear and cannot be limited to either the United States or to Africa, but have to be seen as being in a state of constant disjuncture, where the diasporic imagination exists in un-home like spaces. Even before the Colonization Society voiced plans of re-settling free blacks into Liberia, a similar concern had been expressed by a group of "Free Africans" led by Prince Hall who wrote a petition to the General Court of Massachusetts in 1787 with a plan to resettle in Africa, due to their "disagreeable and disadvantageous circumstances" in the United States; in Africa they would be living among equals. The emergence

---

[250] David Walker, "Our Wretchedness in Consequence of the Colonizing Plan" in *David Walker's Appeal to the Coloured Citizens of the World*, ed. Peter P. Hinks (University Park: Penn State Press, 2000), pp. 47-82.

[251] Ibid., p. 58.

of a diasporic condition was a result of certain socio-legal conditions that the African Americans faced in the United States, and a heightened sense of self reflexivity.

A similar argument is made by Paul Gilroy in *The Black Atlantic*, where he draws attention to the formation of black diasporic communities across the Atlantic in the nineteenth century that created a transnational black identity.[252] Gilroy argues against 'insiderism' which uses national ethnic fixity and instead, proposes for fluid identities. Gilroy writes that the Black Atlantic can be defined "through [a] desire to transcend both the structures of the nation state and the constraints of ethnicity and national particularity."[253] And this is clearly evident in the writings of David Walker, where we see a desire to transcend the boundary of any one single national identity, and a simultaneous disclaimer that he be not limited to a transatlantic space of the United States and Africa, for Walker transgressively conjures up Haiti and England as possible homes; for the African American, identity was in a state of constant disarray. [254] Such spaces exist at the interstices of national-ethnic identity, citizenship and racial affiliations.

The presence of the diasporic imagination need not necessarily be specific to the black American, as the antebellum period in America saw a large number of European immigrants entering the United States who were integrated within the United States and given full citizenship rights, but retained desires and memories of the past. Matthew Jacobson argues that the identity of these new immigrant communities (referring to the Polish, Jewish and Irish communities) was intertwined within a "diasporic imagination: which he defines as that "sense of undying membership in, and unyielding obligation to, a distant national community."[255] Despite their

---

[252] Paul Gilroy, *The Black Atlantic: Modernity and Double Consciousness* (London: Verso, 1993).

[253] Ibid., p. 19.

[254] This is an underlying note in David Walker's writings: "Is there not land in America, or 'corn enough in Egypt?' Why should they send us into a far country to die? See the thousands of foreigners emigrating to America every year: and if there be ground sufficient for them to cultivate, and bread for them to eat, why would they wish to send the first *tillers* of the land away? ... this land which we have watered with our *tears* and our *blood*, is now our *mother country*, and we are well satisfied to stay." p. 60.

[255] Matthew Jacobson, *Special Sorrows: The Diasporic Imagination of Irish, Polish, and Jewish*

cultural allegiance to a distant land, all whites were granted citizenship in the Naturalization Law of 1789.[256] The privilege of whiteness was not automatically conferred onto whites, but violently struggled for; the new immigrants – Teutons, Slav, Hebrew, Celt, Alpine – were never positioned in a homogeneous identity of whiteness and instead, what emerges is how contradictory "racial identities [came] to coexist at the same moment in the same body in unstable combinations."[257]

The diasporic condition, either as a result of being imperial British citizens living in the colonies, or of being slaves and immigrants, is a psychical by-product of various geo-political conditions. Jacqueline Mc Leod writes about the "international dimensions" in the histories and narratives of the black diasporic community[258] and what they share, she argues, is a common set of experiences of slavery and racism and socio-economic disenfranchisement. On a similar note, Stuart Hall writes that diaspora "does not refer to those scattered tribes whose identity can only be secured in relationship to some sacred homeland to which they must at all cost return, even if it means pushing other people into the sea"[259] and infact, diaspora identities "are those which are constantly producing and reproducing themselves anew, through transformation and difference."[260] The process of creating a new identity of imperial citizens happened as a result of the geographical translocation that accompanied colonization. For the British citizen in colonial India, imperial-diasporic citizenship was made

---

Immigrants in the United States (Berkeley: University of California Press, 2002), p. 10.

[256] Dispelling the myth that America was founded on racial inclusion, Jacobson proposes that whiteness and its privileges had been "among the central organizers of the political life of the republic" drawing attention to how "national subjectivity" and "national belonging" were both "inflected by racial conception of peoplehood, self possession, firmness for self government and collective destiny." p. 21.

[257] Jacobson, *Whiteness of a Different Color: European Immigrants and the Alchemy of Race* (Cambridge: Harvard University Press, 1999), p. 142.

[258] Jacqueline Mc Leod, *Crossing Boundaries: Comparative History of Black People in Diaspora* (Bloomington: Indiana University Press, 1999).

[259] Stuart Hall, p. 235.

[260] Ibid., p. 235.

possible through the consumption of not only texts that made their way across continents from England to the colonies but also through the establishment of the different socio-cultural realms within the city. The realm of print and newspapers formed a large part of the texts that were consumed and examining them allows us to understand how they aided in establishing and perpetuating a notion of imperial diasporic citizenship.

The first newspapers in India: English newspapers in Calcutta. Newspapers and the making of history.

The newspapers that are regarded as the first newspapers in India were printed by the British and meant for an English readership. The communications circuit of readers, writers and printers that emerged in Calcutta towards the end of the eighteenth century was defined by the British and their interests as the newspaper trade was carried out by printers who arrived from England. This explains the sophistication of the structure and format of the newspapers. These newspapers played an important function in acting as instruments in the social production of information to the English readers settled in India. Global and local news was made meaningful to them as they were linked with the imperial interests of the British State, and imaginatively participated in all that happened in Britain. In most ways, print made it possible for the readers to define themselves as imperial citizens. This notion of a diasporic imperial citizenship was possible as a result of the to-and-fro movement of texts and newspapers.

In *Imagined Communities*, Benedict Anderson argues that print capital in eighteenth century Europe played a seminal role in establishing the modern day nation-state.[261] New changes in print capital enabled the readers to comprehend and "think" of the world in a state of "simultaneity". He argues that two literary genres in eighteenth century Europe made this possible—the newspapers and the novel—neither of which could have emerged had it not been for print capitalism. According to Anderson, the newspapers were connected to the market and, in the process, became an extreme form of the book, but of "ephemeral

---

[261] Benedict Anderson, *Imagined Communities. Reflections on the Origin and Spread of Nationalism* (London: Verso, 1993).

popularity".[262] There was a communication that existed between one reader and millions of others of "whose existence" he was confident, yet of "whose identity" he did not have the "slightest notion."[263] The connection between differently positioned readers, consuming the same text, allowed for an imagined community to come into being. Anderson had in mind readers who were residing in a contiguous space and not seas or cultures across. The English readers in Calcutta, despite being continents away from England, considered themselves part of the continuity of Britain. The public realm that emerged within the reading domain of the English community in Bengal was a socio-political one, where print emerged and allowed the readers, on a daily basis, to identify with the political and social happenings of the empire and the metropole of London. Through this act of reading about Continental and American wars and treaties, the English readers, despite being geographically miles away from the center of power, defined themselves as imperialists.

A large section of the newspapers that were printed in Bengal chronicled news from Europe that was six months old. The Empire was formed in the imagination of the English readers through these narratives. For example, in the *Calcutta Chronicle*, on May 29, 1792,[264] there are summaries from other British newspapers of the previous year: the *Gazetteer*, Dec. 15, the *General Evening Post* Dec. 3, and the *Morning Post*. Dec. 14 (fig.8). The British readers in Bengal were kept informed of the wars that were waged across the globe, and of news from the different colonies. Extracts from state papers also featured in the newspapers; an instance is evident in the news of the "Secret Convention entered on the 5th of August, 1795, at Berlin, between His Majesty the King of Prussia and the French Republic" that was published in the *Calcutta Gazette* on February 6, 1800 (fig.9). Foreign news and their analyses were prominent; the *Supplement to the*

---

[262] Ibid., p. 34.

[263] Ibid., pp. 34-35.

[264] *Calcutta Chronicle*, 29 May (1792): 1.

Figure 8: Summaries from other newspapers.

IMPERIAL PRINT IN COLONIAL CALCUTTA (1780-1820).

Figure 9: Extracts from state papers.

Calcutta Gazette, on June 9, 1796 (fig.10) chronicled the wars on the Continent, alongside "Remarks on the Apparent Circumstances of the War, in the fourth week of October, 1795." As the news was old, it performed a function akin to a pseudo-historical narrative, reminding the readers of their role in global affairs and giving meaning and coherence to their identities as imperialists—those residing in the colonies were reminded that they were part of the Empire. In some ways, the newspapers were akin to novels but, as Anderson says, of an "ephemeral," nature. The English were portrayed as winners in all the accounts of war. These were akin to the periodicals in eighteenth century England where colonial events were narrated in such a manner so as to cast the British as superior and morally right, thus cultivating a sense of legitimacy in the processes of Empire formation.

The eighteenth century newspaper and journal was made out of different literary forms, and was a hybrid of sorts, a mixture of fiction and news. The periodical of the eighteenth century was an undefined, shapeless pastiche made out of different genres from different writers. Journalistic essays and poetry were included. Barbara Benedict writes that it was a mélange of "fact, fiction, literature and gossip" whereby literature was indistinguishable from news.[265] Past events when retold in the newspapers often read like a story. For the reader, situated in Calcutta, a notion of the Empire was created through the narratives in the newspapers that described victories that were fought, both local and global, using dominant tropes and motifs of war and exoticity. The newspapers featured recent news that narrated wars that had happened within India, and concerned the British; events that did not involve the British were not reported. An apt instance is the official correspondence between Cornwallis, a governor General of India (1786-1793) and the British government. Cornwallis was involved in a major war that the British fought against one of the ruling kings of South India, Tipu Sultan.

---

[265] Anderson, *Imagined Communities*, p. 10.

Figure 10: News on war on the continent.

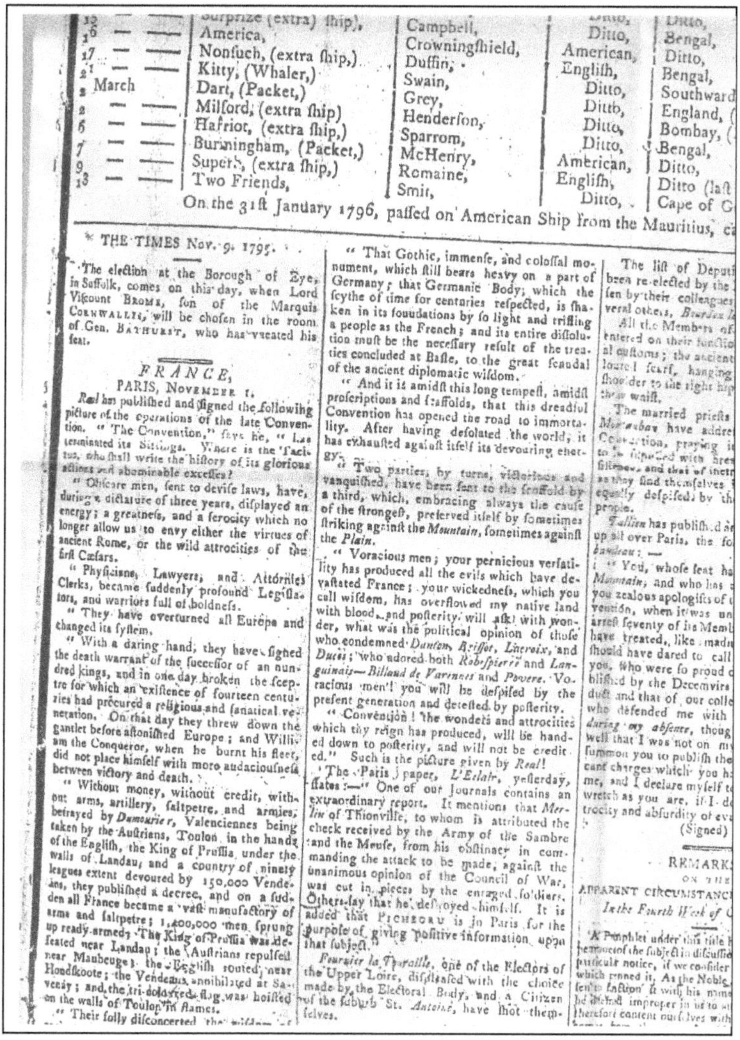

A letter that Cornwallis had written to the secretary of State on October 5, 1791, was printed in an Indian newspaper about six months later (fig. 11). The war was described as a major victory that clinched south India. He wrote:

> .... [various branches of business] obliged me to confine myself to a very concise statement of the principal occurrences, in my letter to the East India Company; but, by the means of that letter, and the copies of my correspondence with the residents at the Courts of Hyderabad and Poonah, and of my late letters to the Governor of Fort St. George, which will no doubt be transmitted to you from the India-House, you will have it in your power to convey to His Majesty a general knowledge of the present situation of our affairs in this country; and you will have the satisfaction to observe, not only that our success has already been considerable, ...
>
> Our success at Bangalore has tended to establish, in the general opinion of the natives, the superiority of the British arms; and it has, in particular, made an impression upon the minds of our allies ...[266]

The official treaty that was signed between Cornwallis and Tipu Sultan was published in the newspapers, allowing the English readers to actively participate in the political processes that were in operation (fig. 12).[267] The victory was portrayed as the final defeat of India .

---

[266] *Calcutta Chronicle.* 24 April (1792): 1-2.

[267] *Calcutta Chronicle,* 29 May (1792): 4.

Figure 11: Extract of letter written by Cornwallis.

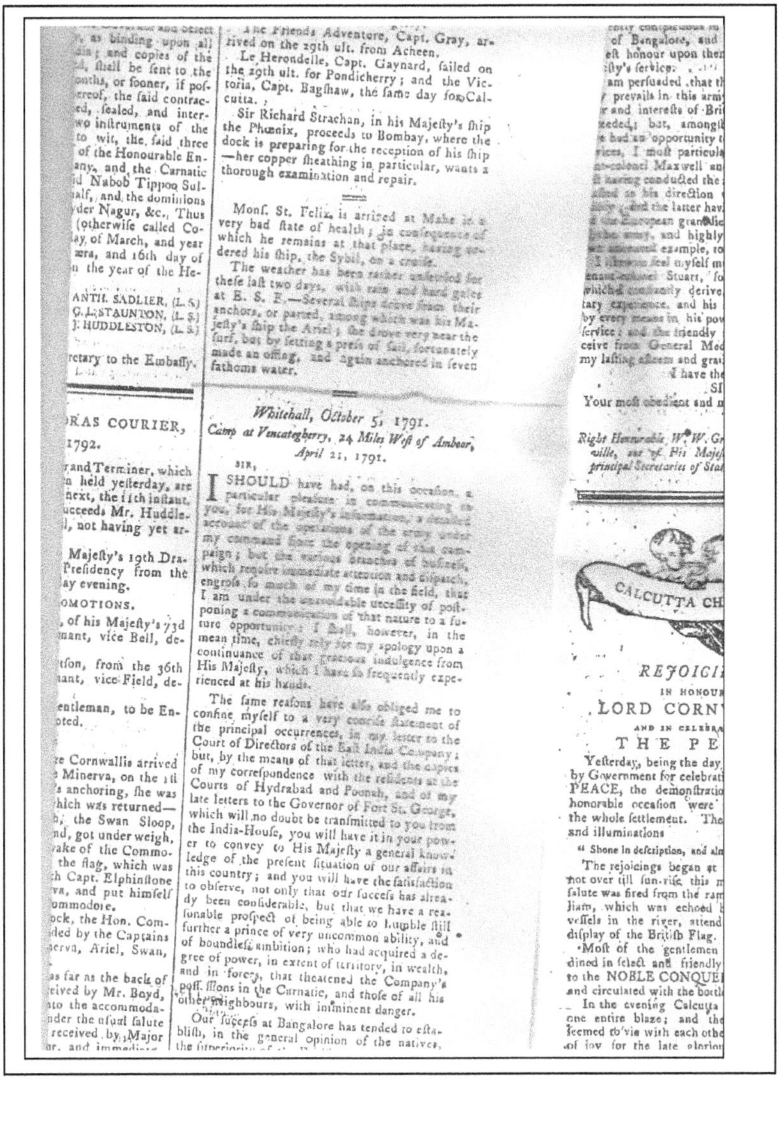

Figure 12: Treaty between Tipu Sultan and the EIC.

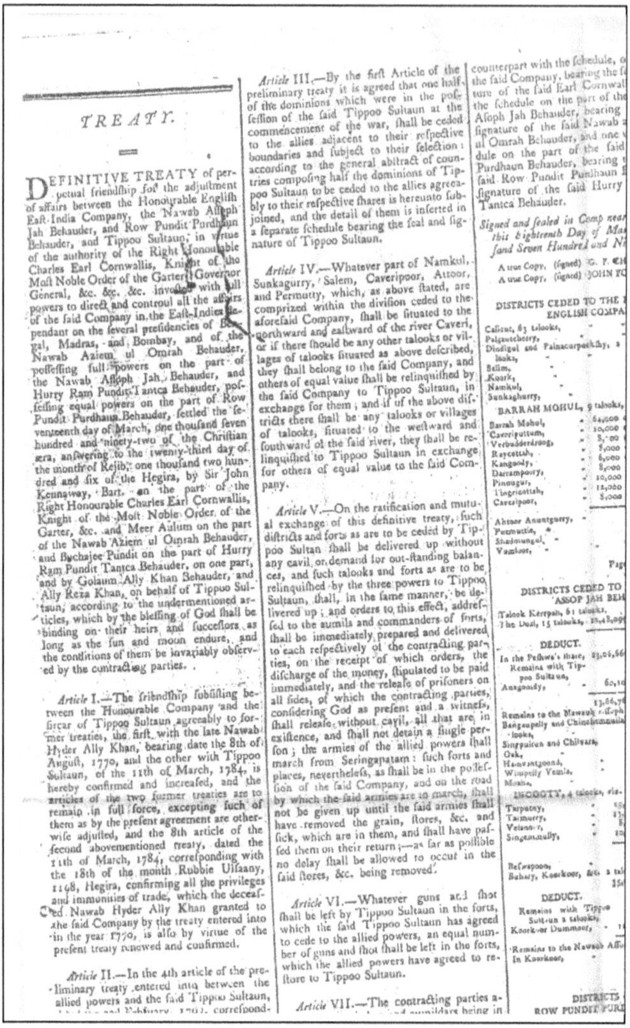

TREATY.

DEFINITIVE TREATY of perpetual friendſhip for the adjuſtment of affairs between the Honourable Engliſh Eaſt India Company, the Nawab Aſoph Jah Behauder, and Row Pundit Purdhaun Behauder, and Tippoo Sultaun, in virtue of the authority of the Right Honourable Charles Earl Cornwallis, Knight of the Moſt Noble Order of the Garter, Governor General, &c. &c. &c. inveſted with full powers to direct and controul all the affairs of the ſaid Company in the Eaſt-Indies dependant on the ſeveral preſidencies of Bengal, Madras, and Bombay, and of the Nawab Aziem ul Omrah Behauder, poſſeſſing full powers on the part of the Nawab Aſoph Jah Behauder, and Hurry Ram Pundit Tantca Behauder, poſſeſſing equal powers on the part of Row Pundit Purdhaun Behauder, ſettled the ſeventeenth day of March, one thouſand ſeven hundred and ninety-two of the Chriſtian æra, anſwering to the twenty-third day of the month of Rejib, one thouſand two hundred and ſix of the Hegira, by Sir John Kennaway, Bart. on the part of the Right Honourable Charles Earl Cornwallis, Knight of the Moſt Noble Order of the Garter, &c. and Meer Aulum on the part of the Nawab Aziem ul Omrah Behauder, and Buchajee Pundit on the part of Hurry Ram Pundit Tantca Behauder, on one part, and by Golaum Ally Khan Behauder, and Ally Reza Khan, on behalf of Tippoo Sultaun, according to the undermentioned articles, which by the bleſſing of God ſhall be binding on their heirs and ſucceſſors as long as the ſun and moon endure, and the conditions of them be invariably obſerved by the contracting parties.

Article I.—The friendſhip ſubſiſting between the Honourable Company and the ſircar of Tippoo Sultaun agreeably to former treaties, the firſt with the late Nawab Hyder Ally Khan, bearing date the 8th of Auguſt, 1770, and the other with Tippoo Sultaun, of the 11th of March, 1784, is hereby confirmed and increaſed, and the articles of the two former treaties are to remain in full force, excepting ſuch of them as by the preſent agreement are otherwiſe adjuſted, and the 8th article of the ſecond abovementioned treaty, dated the 11th of March, 1784, correſponding with the 18th of the month Rubbie Uſſaany, 1198, Hegira, confirming all the privileges and immunities of trade, which the deceaſed Nawab Hyder Ally Khan granted to the ſaid Company by the treaty entered into in the year 1770, is alſo by virtue of the preſent treaty renewed and confirmed.

Article II.—In the 4th article of the preliminary treaty entered into between the allied powers and the ſaid Tippoo Sultaun, ... February, 1792, correſpond-

Article III.—By the firſt Article of the preliminary treaty it is agreed that one half of the dominions which were in the poſſeſſion of the ſaid Tippoo Sultaun at the commencement of the war, ſhall be ceded to the allies adjacent to their reſpective boundaries and ſubject to their ſelection: according to the general abſtract of countries compoſing half the dominions of Tippoo Sultaun to be ceded to the allies agreeably to their reſpective ſhares is hereunto ſubjoined, and the detail of them is inſerted in a ſeparate ſchedule bearing the ſeal and ſignature of Tippoo Sultaun.

Article IV.—Whatever part of Namkul, Sunkagurry, Salem, Caveripoor, Attoor, and Permutty, which, as above ſtated, are comprized within the diviſion ceded to the aforeſaid Company, ſhall be ſituated to the northward and eaſtward of the river Caveri, or if there ſhould be any other talooks or villages of talooks ſituated as above deſcribed, they ſhall belong to the ſaid Company, and others of equal value ſhall be relinquiſhed by the ſaid Company to Tippoo Sultaun, in exchange for them; and if of the above diſtricts there ſhall be any talooks or villages of talooks, ſituated to the weſtward and ſouthward of the ſaid river, they ſhall be relinquiſhed to Tippoo Sultaun in exchange for others of equal value to the ſaid Company.

Article V.—On the ratification and mutual exchange of this definitive treaty, ſuch diſtricts and forts as are to be ceded by Tippoo Sultan ſhall be delivered up without any cavil or demand for out-ſtanding balances, and ſuch talooks and forts as are to be relinquiſhed by the three powers to Tippoo Sultaun, ſhall, in the ſame manner, be delivered up; and orders to this effect, addreſſed to the aumils and commanders of forts, ſhall be immediately prepared and delivered to each reſpectively of the contracting parties, on the receipt of which orders, the diſcharge of the money, ſtipulated to be paid immediately, and the releaſe of priſoners on all ſides, of which the contracting parties, conſidering God as preſent and a witneſs, ſhall releaſe without cavil, all that are in exiſtence, and ſhall not detain a ſingle perſon; the armies of the allied powers ſhall march from Seringapatam: ſuch forts and places, nevertheleſs, as ſhall be in the poſſeſſion of the ſaid Company, and on the road by which the ſaid armies are to march, ſhall not be given up until the ſaid armies ſhall have removed the grain, ſtores, &c. and ſick, which are in them, and ſhall have paſſed them on their return;—as far as poſſible no delay ſhall be allowed to occur in the ſaid ſtores, &c. being removed.

Article VI.—Whatever guns and ſhot ſhall be left by Tippoo Sultaun in the forts, which the ſaid Tippoo Sultaun has agreed to cede to the allied powers, an equal number of guns and ſhot ſhall be left in the forts, which the allied powers have agreed to reſtore to Tippoo Sultaun.

Article VII.—The contracting parties a- ... aumildars being in

counterpart with the ſchedule, o... the ſaid Company, bearing the ſ... ture of the ſaid Earl Cornwal... the ſchedule on the part of the Aſoph Jah Behauder, bearing ... ſignature of the ſaid Nawab ... ul Omrah Behauder, and one ... dule on the part of the ſaid Purdhaun Behauder, bearing ... ſaid Row Pundit Purdhaun ... ſignature of the ſaid Hurry Tantca Behauder.

Signed and ſealed in Camp near ... this Eighteenth Day of Ma... ſand Seven Hundred and Ni...

A true Copy. (ſigned) G. F. CH...
A true Copy. (ſigned) JOHN FO...

DISTRICTS CEDED TO THE ... ENGLISH COMPA...

Caliout, 63 talooks,
Palgautcherry,
Dindigul and Palnacurpoohſhy, ... talooks,
Selim,
Koark,
Namkul,
Sunkaghurry,

BARRAH MOHUL, 9 talooks,

Barrah Mohul,	64,000
Caveriputtum,	5,000
Verbudderdroog,	5,000
Raycottah,	6,000
Kangoody,	8,000
Darrampoury,	10,000
Pinnugur,	12,000
Tingricottah,	5,000
Careipoor,	

Ahtoor Anantgurry,
Purmuttie,
Shadmungul,
Vamloor,

Pag...

DISTRICTS CEDED TO ... ASSOP JAH BEH...

Talook Kerpah, 61 talooks,
The Dual, 15 talooks, 10,48,00...

DEDUCT.

In the Peſhwa's ſhare, 13,06,66...
Remains with Tippoo Sultaun,
Anagoondy, 60,10...
13,66,7...

Remains to the Nawaub Aſoph...
Bangoupelly and Chinchemnaila... looks,
Singpuiten and Chilvara,
Oak,
Hanumuntgoond,
Wimpelly Vemla,
Moaha,

INCOOTY, 4 talooks, viz.
Tarpatay,
Taimurry,
Velanoor,
Singemnully,

Beſwapoor,
Buhary, Koorkoor, &c. 3 tal... 15...

DEDUCT.

Remains with Tippoo Sultaun 2 talooks,
Koorkoor Dummoor, ...

Remains to the Nawaub Aſſ...
In Koorkoor,

DISTRICTS ...
ROW PUNDIT PURD...

Figure 13: Public entry of the captured princes.

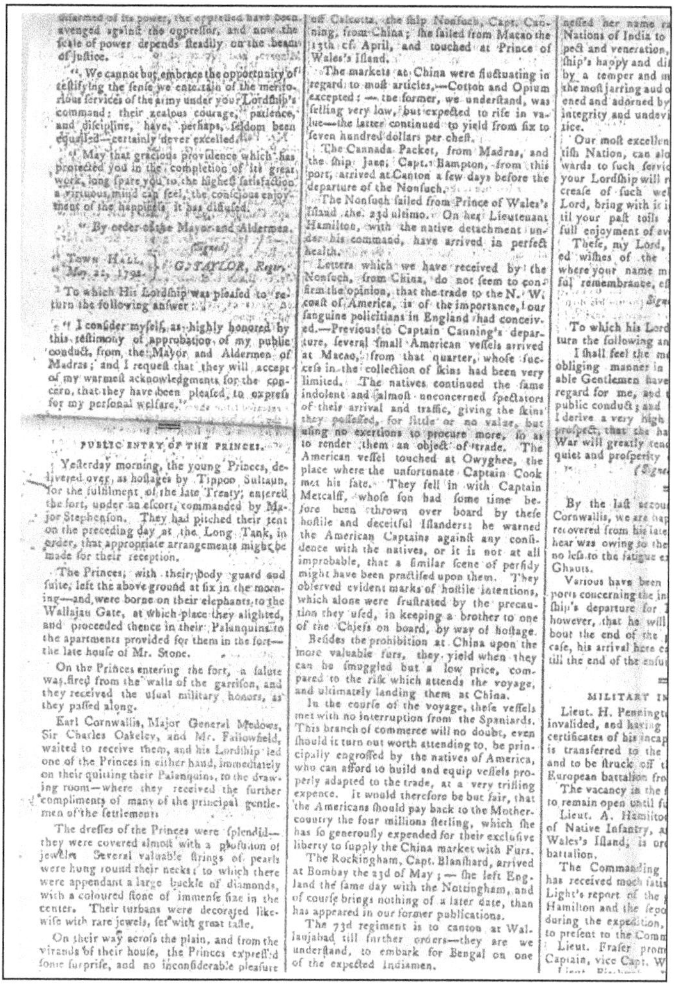

disarmed of its power, the oppressed have been avenged against the oppressor, and now the scale of power depends steadily on the beam of Justice.

"We cannot but embrace the opportunity of testifying the sense we entertain of the meritorious services of the army under your Lordship's command: their zealous courage, patience, and discipline, have, perhaps, seldom been equalled—certainly never excelled.

"May that gracious providence which has protected you in the completion of its great work, long spare you to the highest satisfaction a virtuous mind can feel, the conscious enjoyment of the happiness it has diffused.

"By order of the Mayor and Aldermen.

(Signed)

"Town Hall, "May 21, 1792. } G. TAYLOR, Regr."

To which His Lordship was pleased to return the following answer:

"I consider myself as highly honored by this testimony of approbation of my public conduct, from the Mayor and Aldermen of Madras; and I request that they will accept of my warmest acknowledgments for the concern, that they have been pleased to express for my personal welfare."

PUBLIC ENTRY OF THE PRINCES.

Yesterday morning, the young Princes, delivered over, as hostages by Tippoo Sultaun, for the fulfilment of the late Treaty; entered the fort, under an escort, commanded by Major Stephenson. They had pitched their tent on the preceding day at the Long Tank, in order, that appropriate arrangements might be made for their reception.

The Princes, with their body guard and suite, left the above ground at six in the morning—and were borne on their elephants to the Wallajau Gate, at which place they alighted, and proceeded thence in their Palanquins to the apartments provided for them in the fort—the late house of Mr. Stone.

On the Princes entering the fort, a salute was fired from the walls of the garrison, and they received the usual military honors, as they passed along.

Earl Cornwallis, Major General Medows, Sir Charles Oakeley, and Mr. Fallowfield, waited to receive them, and his Lordship led one of the Princes in either hand, immediately on their quitting their Palanquins, to the drawing room—where they received the further compliments of many of the principal gentlemen of the settlement.

The dresses of the Princes were splendid—they were covered almost with a profusion of jewels. Several valuable strings of pearls were hung round their necks; to which there were appendant a large buckle of diamonds, with a coloured stone of immense size in the center. Their turbans were decorated likewise with rare jewels, set with great taste.

On their way across the plain, and from the virandа of their house, the Princes expressed some surprise, and no inconsiderable pleasure

off Calcutta, the ship Nonsuch, Capt. Canning, from China; she sailed from Macao the 13th of April, and touched at Prince of Wales's Island.

The markets at China were fluctuating in regard to most articles,—Cotton and Opium excepted; — the former, we understand, was selling very low, but expected to rise in value—the latter continued to yield from six to seven hundred dollars per chest.

The Cannada Packet, from Madras, and the ship Jane, Capt. Bampton, from this port, arrived at Canton a few days before the departure of the Nonsuch.

The Nonsuch sailed from Prince of Wales's Island the 23d ultimo. On her Lieutenant Hamilton, with the native detachment under his command, have arrived in perfect health.

Letters which we have received by the Nonsuch, from China, do not seem to confirm the opinion, that the trade to the N. W. coast of America, is of the importance, our sanguine politicians in England had conceived.—Previous to Captain Canning's departure, several small American vessels arrived at Macao, from that quarter, whose success in the collection of skins had been very limited. The natives continued the same indolent and almost unconcerned spectators of their arrival and traffic, giving the skins they possessed, for little or no value, but using no exertions to procure more, so as to render them an object of trade. The American vessel touched at Owyghee, the place where the unfortunate Captain Cook met his fate. They fell in with Captain Metcalff, whose son had some time before been thrown over board by these hostile and deceitful Islanders: he warned the American Captains against any confidence with the natives, or it is not at all improbable, that a similar scene of perfidy might have been practised upon them. They observed evident marks of hostile intentions, which alone were frustrated by the precaution they used, in keeping a brother to one of the Chiefs on board, by way of hostage.

Besides the prohibition at China upon the more valuable furs, they yield when they can be smuggled but a low price, compared to the risk which attends the voyage, and ultimately landing them at China.

In the course of the voyage, these vessels met with no interruption from the Spaniards. This branch of commerce will no doubt, even should it turn out worth attending to, be principally engrossed by the natives of America, who can afford to build and equip vessels properly adapted to the trade, at a very trifling expence. It would therefore be but fair, that the Americans should pay back to the Mother-country the four millions sterling, which she has so generously expended for their exclusive liberty to supply the China market with Furs.

The Rockingham, Capt. Blanshard, arrived at Bombay the 23d of May; — she left England the same day with the Nottingham, and of course brings nothing of a later date, than has appeared in our former publications.

The 73d regiment is to canton at Wallaujabad till further orders—they are we understand, to embark for Bengal on one of the expected Indiamen.

nessed her name ra
Nations of India to
pect and veneration,
ship's happy and di
by a temper and m
the most jarring and o
ened and adorned by
integrity and undevi
tice.

Our most excellen
tish Nation, can al
wards to such servic
your Lordship will r
crease of such wel
Lord, bring with it i
til your past toils
full enjoyment of ev

These, my Lord,
ed wishes of the
where your name m
ful remembrance, ef

Sign

To which his Lord
turn the following an

I shall feel the m
obliging manner in
able Gentlemen have
regard for me, and
public conduct; and
I derive a very high
prospect, that the ha
War will greatly ten
quiet and prosperity

(Sign

By the last accou
Cornwallis, we are hap
recovered from his late
hear was owing to the
no less to the fatigue e
Ghauts.

Various have been
ports concerning the in
ship's departure for
however, that he will
bout the end of the
case, his arrival here c
till the end of the ensu

MILITARY IN

Lieut. H. Penningt
invalided, and having
certificates of his incap
is transferred to the
and to be struck off t
European battalion fro

The vacancy in the
to remain open until fu

Lieut. A. Hamilto
of Native Infantry, a
Wales's Island, is or
battalion.

The Commanding
has received much satis
Light's report of the
Hamilton and the sepo
during the expedition,
to present to the Comm

Lieut. Fraser prom
Captain, vice Capt. W

The sons of the defeated king were taken as captive hostages, and this capture was described as the possession of the wealth of India. Their public entry was described in extravagant terms (fig. 13):

> [The] dresses of the Princes were splendid – they were covered almost with a profusion of jewels. Several valuable strings of pearls were hung round their necks; to which there were appendant a large buckle of diamonds, with a colored stone of immense fire in the center. Their turbans were decorated likewise with rare jewels, set with great taste. … The attendance of the princes may be said to be not only numerous but splendid of its kind.[268]

News of the war against Tipu Sultan was a regular feature in 1792. The news from the *Madras Courier*, from March 15, 1792, was published in the *Calcutta Chronicle*, on April 10th, 1792: "[the newspaper] is laying before the public the following detail of [war] which comes from good authority." Newspapers made comprehensive events that were taking place and involved the Britishers, making clear to them the power of the British army. In 1792, when peace was declared, there was an article in the *Calcutta Chronicle*, with details of the war, and the subsequent treaty that was signed: " The late Peace with Tippu is undoubtedly as advantageous as honorable to the British Government; but it will derive greater glory when contrasted with the Peace of 1784, when we accepted rather than dictated; it serves to show how much our power and superiority has increased since that period, as it has enabled us to prescribe and insist upon a compliance with our own terms, at the walls of our enemy's capital."[269] The British were portrayed as legitimate rulers of India, and the Indians as the enemy. As Ian Atherton writes on the role of history and newspapers:

> It was a seventeenth century commonplace that history could teach useful lessons. … Gentlemen were adviced to study history for

---

[268] *Calcutta Chronicle*. 26 June (1792): 2.

[269] *Calcutta Chronicle*, 24 April (1792).

delight and profit. Civil or political history was considered to be none other than an accurate report of past and present facts and events. Reading contemporary history – the news – could, therefore, be as profitable as reading ancient history.[270]

The narrative of history in the newspapers represented India in need of being ruled by the British, and this was intrinsic to establishing a British identity in the colonies, enabling a diasporic notion of imperial citizenship. Even if there was dissent among the British, since escape to the colonies was particularly attractive to those with non-standard beliefs, including Dissenters, they all would have participated in agreeing that India needed to be ruled. Those in the colonies retained many of the characteristics of being a member of the ruling class.

Conclusion:

Despite the fact that the realm of early print culture only catered to the needs of the English residents, it would be too simplistic to blow away this as being too minor an episode in terms of cultural transformation. We do have to keep in mind that firstly, this realm was going to subsequently hegemonize Indian society, and as a consequence, would serve as a prototype for all future printing ventures. This particular form of cultural engagement is best seen as an example of cultural hegemony, where a politically subordinate group emulates and replicates something from a dominant group, and in this case it would be the manner in which the natives learnt about print culture. In the *Prison Notebooks*, Antonio Gramsci poses the issue of how and why subordinate groups seem to consent to their own domination; in other words, when and under what circumstances do people consent to be ruled by a dominant group (or a set of institutions).[271] The realm of culture was one means (rather than simply economic or military) whereby control of the dominant group was gained

---

[270] Ian Atherton, pp. 45-46.

[271] Antonio Gramsci, *Selections from the Prison Notebooks*. Translated and edited by Quintin Hoare and Geoffrey Nowell Smith. (New York: International Publishers, 1971), p.12.

by the "seemingly spontaneous consent given by the great masses of the population to the general direction imposed on social life by the dominant fundamental group."[272] Cultural hegemony is a relationship between the powerful and the less powerful groups in society. There were many aspects of British culture and technology that were imitated by the subordinate groups and willingly so. Within a few years, there were numerous newspapers being published by the Britishers, and the natives would soon learn about print culture and replicate this realm of letters.

In the last two decades of the eighteenth century, with the publication of numerous newspapers and books, a sub public republic of letters was formed that was inflected with notions of diaspora and imperialism. Empire of different kinds was in the minds of the English people across the globe. P.J. Marshall writes that the death of the American empire and the birth of the new Indian one occurred at the same time period between 1750 and 1783.[273] He writes that in 1765, the "British EIC was allowed the grant of the Bengal diwani- which was to be the basis of the new empire; in the same year, the weakness of American rule in North America was made evident in the resistance to the Stamp Act" and fifteen years or so later, "Britain was engaged in a war in north America against the local population, supported by the French" while in India, the "EIC and royal forces were fighting against a formidable coalition of Indian powers, also supported by French intervention."[274] Such discourses of empire were dominant both within England and in the colonies. The movement of print and the numerous acts of reading in the colonies influenced how the Britishers viewed themselves as diasporic imperial citizens. Undoubtedly, in India, they were aided in this process by the East India Company, which allowed newspapers to be distributed that did not need postage.

---

[272] Ibid., p. 12.

[273] P.J. Marshall, *The Making and Unmaking of Empires. Britain, India and America c. 1750-1783* (New York: Oxford University Press, 2005).

[274] Ibid., pp. 1-2.

5 CHEESE, WINE AND COLONIAL CALCUTTA: THE MAKING OF AN IMEPRIAL SOCIAL IDENTITY.

Did those Britishers who traveled to Calcutta towards the end of the eighteenth century arrive at a city that was extremely different from what they had left behind? In many ways, the dirt and squalor and the surrounding chaos of native life existed alongside the "white" city of Calcutta where there were beautiful, palatial houses and this was in some ways akin to what London was in the eighteenth century. By 1716, London was the largest European city and it was changing from a "compact traditional city to a rambling heterogeneous metropolis."[275] There was rapid migration, about 8,000 annually, of young people and women who were needed as servants and workers for burgeoning industries, and these migrants settled in densely packed neighborhoods "marked by open sewers, decaying rubbish, virulent diseases and overflowing graveyards."[276] The streets were filled with the vulnerable part of the population, begging for a living and on the border of poverty. As Sophie Gee argues, that a "glut of waste matter fills the pages of eighteenth-century literature – not just in minority texts but in canonical works such as *Paradise Lost, The Tale of a Tub*,

---

[275] *Walking the Streets of Eighteenth- century London, John Gay's Trivia (1716)*, eds. Clare Brant and Susan E Whyman, "Introduction." (New York: Oxford University Press, 2007), p. 4.

[276] Ibid., p. 4.

"A Modest Proposal," and *A Journal of the Plague Year*."[277] She goes on to write that this waste is "nothing if not memorable: Milton's infernal dregs, Swift's odious excrements, Pope's pissing contexts, Defoe's corpses."[278] At that time, this waste was supposed to be ignored but English writers were quite explicit in how waste was described in their literary works – "[d]ung, guts, and mud, dead dogs and turnip tops, sweep through the pages of eighteenth-century writing."[279] Maybe, in reality, it was not all that difficult for the Britishers to live in Calcutta, making us suspect their ramblings on how terrible life was in the colonial city. The following rant about hygiene and drinking water in a letter to the editor of a newspaper is truthful – undoubtedly, but while reading it, we do have to keep in mind that the conditions that they had left behind were really not that different .

> As I was Jogging along in my Palanqueen yesterday, I could not avoid observing without a kind of secret concern for the health of several of my tender and delicate Friends, a String of Paria Dogs without an Ounce of Hair on some of them and in the last stage of the Meange plunge in and refresh themselves very comfortably in the great Tank – …
>
> The great increase of Filth in it must likewise add to its impurity and contribute not a little to give it that Raw disagreeable smell which is very perceptible upon a Comparative trial with other Waters.[280]

Ship loads of people arrived in Calcutta and they rebuilt a city and a social life that replicated what had been left behind in England; a republic of letters was formed and newspapers comprised a large part of this realm.

---

[277] Sophie Gee, *Making Waste, Leftovers and the Eighteenth-Century Imagination* (Princeton: Princeton UP, 2009), pp. 2-3. In *Making Waste*, the first book about refuse and its place in Enlightenment literature and culture, Sophie Gee examines the meaning of waste at the moment when the early modern world was turning modern. Bernard Mandeville, praising English prosperity in *The Fable of the Bees*, told Londoners to treasure the dunghills in the streets, the running drains, animals, and crowds of beggars as daily reminders of London's wealth. p. 2-3.

[278] Ibid., p.3.

[279] Ibid., p. 2-3.

[280] *Bengal Gazette*, April 15th-22nd (1780): 2-3.

Reading these texts give us a better understanding of the nature of their social life. There was an underlying premise that even if Calcutta was a colonial city inhabited with heathen natives, it was almost like living in a far away, newly established town which was beset with difficulties but was in the process of being made livable.

I. Eighteenth century print culture in England and its role in determining social behavior: The intrinsic element of print and social life.

The socio-cultural relevance of newspapers in Calcutta becomes clear if we consider how reading was important in the every day lives of people in eighteenth century England. Those who traveled to India brought this habit of print, making the history of print during this time period of India also the history of print in eighteenth century England. One cannot describe how print culture evolved and developed in the Indian context without an understanding of how print became a consumer product and a profit making industry in England. Eighteenth century England saw the professionalisation of literature. Earlier in the century, in his *Dictionary* (1755), Samuel Johnson had defined literature as "learning, [a] skill in letters," and by the end of the eighteenth century, the notion of literature had acquired a different meaning: it meant a material product and profession. Barbara Benedict argues that this change in how the literary profession was defined reflects key alterations in the literary trade; from a loosely knit guild-based trade, the eighteenth century saw the emergence and growth of a profit-seeking print industry.[281] Such a growth was accompanied by the transformation of dilettante gentleman-writers into professional authors who wrote for money. This was made possible because of the "systematization of the entire process of making and selling books."[282] Readers, printers and sellers worked in conjunction to transform the entire trade into a "ubiquitous consumer product" and a profit making

---

[281] Barbara Benedict. *Readers, Writers, Reviewers and the Professionalization of Literature* (Cambridge: Cambridge University Press, 2006).

[282] Ibid., p. 3.

business. A national reading public emerged which was not only from the gentry and the moneyed, but cut across all classes. The readers accepted their roles as participants in a print-induced public culture.[283] A major concern for the readers of this period was that they read not only for entertainment and pleasure but for moral improvement. Popular print culture in the early eighteenth century was a "central institution for defining and disseminating genteel, bourgeois cultural standards."[284] Newspapers and periodicals, the most ephemeral of printed texts, played a seminal role in defining social manners and customs.

The best example would be seen in the periodicals that were published by Richard Steele and Joseph Addison, *The Tatler* and *The Spectator*, in London between 1709 and 1714. These periodicals were very influential and aimed towards reforming the ethical, moral and social manners of the mostly urban, middle class who comprised an emerging class of readers developing bourgeois standards which, Peter Stallybrass and Allon White argue, were carved out through negotiating between "high" elite culture and "low" popular culture.[285] The periodicals were subscribed to mostly by this class which emerged from Britain's growing professional bureaucracy, and its commercial and financial classes. Professions like clerks, tradesmen, bankers, stock company directors and insurance financiers emerged to play an important role in the nation's commercial and social life. According to Kathryn Shevelow, such periodicals were able to mediate between the elite and the non-elites:

> Indeed the periodicals often act as agents for the transmission of "genteel" codes of conduct, thus aligning themselves with values explicitly associated with the upper classes. Yet, they addressed readers represented as being in need of such instructions in manners. In fact, though literate and often upwardly mobile, a good segment of the

---

[283] Ibid., pp. 3-4.

[284] Erin Mackie, "Introduction", in *The Commerce of Everyday Life: Selection from the Tatler and the Spectator*, ed. Erin Mackie (London: Palgrave Macmillan, 1998), p. 14.

[285] Peter Stallybrass and Allon White, *The Politics and Poetics of Transgression* (Ithaca: Cornell University Press, 1985).

intended audience for the popular periodicals, and indeed some of their editors, were and perceived themselves to be marginal to many of the practices of upper-class culture.[286]

All spheres of social life were addressed, including the professional, the domestic and the public. Such periodicals were in keeping with the general ideology of that time, exemplified in institutions like the Society for the Reformation of Manners and Morals, an organization that was actively involved in correcting the morals of that time period, concentrating mostly on the lower classes. Unlike methods of coercion and public exposure, the periodicals used strategies of participation and persuasion.[287] The success of such periodicals reflects the rise of a growing public that chose to read, and had the recreational luxury to be able to do so. Thus, by this time, the earlier model of literary patronage, where the aristocracy provided support to the authors, had given way to a purely commercial mode of operation.

If print was central in establishing a sense of the "public," coffee houses played no less an important role in creating a space which was, by the seventeenth century, intrinsic to the social life of the city. This space, Mackie argues, was central in enabling public discussions to be initiated and conducted. The network of coffeehouses and presses established a new sense of the "public": a space where private individuals came together to debate and negotiate matters of public concern. Thus, the bourgeois public sphere came into being, through the popular periodical press, becoming a realm of power. What I have drawn upon above is the reciprocity between print culture and certain social characteristics, where in eighteenth century England the rise of a middle class was accompanied by socio-economic and political changes; readers, printers and sellers worked in conjunction to transform the entire book trade into a "ubiquitous consumer product" and a profit making business.[288] In order to make sense of how the newspapers

---

[286] Kathryn Shevelow, *Women and Print Culture. The Construction of Femininity in the Early Periodical* (London and New York: Routledge, 1989), pp. 2-3.

[287] Mackie, *Commerce of Everyday Life*, pp. 4-5.

[288] Benedict, *Readers, Writers*, pp. 3-4.

emerged in Calcutta covered a wide array of subjects, from social satire to poems, news, advertisements, it would be easy if we considered the English parts of this new colony as another suburb of London.

Print and the emergence of a white city in Calcutta

Print, like many other aspects of eighteenth century Western society, was carried across to Calcutta. When discussing the nature and need of these transferences, it is necessary to understand the relevance and importance of print in the everyday lives of the British community that lived in Calcutta in the last two decades of the eighteenth century. The city became a repository of many things that were British, and was able to attract a wide array of people from every spectrum of society, rich and poor. Many who came were younger sons with no taste for the ministry and little prospect in England. India was a dumping ground for surplus males of the upper and middle classes who then had to make their fortunes as a matter of survival. If the elder son died they would be recalled to inherit, otherwise it was understood that they had to make their own way. The East, with its tales of easily obtainable unfathomable wealth, was the destination for many from the influential and rich families of England. A city was therefore built that catered to this large civilian population and the latter half of the eighteenth century saw the emergence of a miniature, Westernised city in Calcutta, with all the accoutrements and trappings of Western social habits, unlike the first Calcutta, before it was destroyed by Sirajuddaulah in 1756, which was a much more 'Eastern' city of palaces. Early British 'nabobs' were also much more Indianised than sahibs were later to be. Calcutta was rebuilt in a more Western mode by Clive, in keeping with the socio-civic changes that were taking place in eighteenth century British towns; for example, a recent study of British towns in the middle of the century has revealed that there was an "explosion in the demand for and provision of high status leisure."[289] Facilities for enjoyment, like those that existed in an English county town or in a popular resort came into existence in increasing profusion in the white town of Calcutta.[290]

---

[289] Peter Borsay, *The English Urban Renaissance: Culture and Society in the Provincial Town, 1660-1770* (Oxford: Oxford University Press, 1989), p. 117.

[290] P.J. Marshall. "The White Town of Calcutta under the Rule of the East India Company," *Modern Asian Studies* 34.2 (May): 307-331, 324.

IMPERIAL PRINT IN COLONIAL CALCUTTA (1780-1820).

At the end of the eighteenth century, the white population in Calcutta was quite small. In fact, part of the population was a migrant one and sailors comprised a large number. Often they stayed behind and joined the work force as there were ample job opportunities for poor white men. By the mid eighteenth century, there were European domestic servants, artisans and shopkeepers.[291] Builders, tailors, coachmakers, watchmakers, carvers set up their businesses employing Indian craftsmen; dancing and music teachers held classes for members of the rich community and Calcutta was known as a "settlement dominated by wealthy men who lived high."[292]

> The white elite of Calcutta prided themselves on having created in India an environment in which the best of contemporary British institutions were faithfully reproduced. ... White Calcutta under the Company was a remarkably British place. ... Its development was largely unplanned and its main services, such as drainage, roads and police, were of a low standard. But it had individual buildings of considerable ambition ... and its wealthy citizens enjoyed many amenities: books, theatre, music and learned societies.[293]

The city developed in a haphazard manner. The municipal services of the city which were provided by the Company were not in good shape. European architects designed houses that were built in grand, classical styles and not suited for the climate.[294] Churches, schools and orphanages were also built. The prospects of making a fortune were very bright. Banking and trading houses were set up.[295] Apart from those who were directly

---

[291] Ibid., pp. 309-310.

[292] Ibid., p. 312.

[293] Ibid., p. 328.

[294] Ibid., p. 316.

[295] Ibid., pp. 310-318.

employed by the East India Company, there grew a class of rich white elites who were involved in different capacities with the numerous civic institutions that cropped up: "partners in the private banks, insurance companies and the ubiquitous agency houses, ... which managed shipping, indigo factories and a wide range of [trading] activities."[296] By 1769, the East India Company had started to implement British laws. With the establishment of the Supreme Court in 1774 that dealt with litigation involving both the Europeans and Indians, lawyers were able to reap enormous profits.

By the end of the eighteenth century, many socio-institutional and commercial changes had taken place in Calcutta. The warp and woof of the social existence of the city was dependent on print and its absence was considered an impediment in carrying out their day-to-day socio-civic businesses. Print was needed in order to conduct legal transactions; shopkeepers and traders needed to print advertisements and catalogues in order to sell their goods. Moreover, the British administration needed printed forms and stationery to document its work. Most of the printed material comprised non-literary texts. In order for the printing trade to sustain itself, the presses were involved in the mundane job of printing stationery, handbills, advertisements, catalogues, legal and mercantile blank forms, calendars and almanacs, registers and lists of the employees of the Company and of the European residents of Calcutta. The English community engaged with all the mundane aspects of their everyday lives through print. Thomas Watley, a printer, advertised what would be typically sold from a printer's shop: "Blank bonds, powers of attorney, letters of attorney, respondentia bonds, bills of lading, bills of exchange, printed wills, large and small, policies of insurance, with and without the arbitration clause, and of all descriptions, assignments for the disposal of Officers' privileges, handsome ruled paper for music."[297] Such advertisements would have targeted the residents of the white town.[298]

---

[296] Ibid., p. 313.

[297] *Calcutta Gazette,* October 18, 1792, XVIII.

[298] Pre-1800, all these socio-civic and legal forms of communication and transaction would have been undertaken through handwritten texts. Is it possible, therefore, to argue that when printed, mechanically reproduced texts replaced handwritten texts, an epistemic shift took place.

IMPERIAL PRINT IN COLONIAL CALCUTTA (1780-1820).

Newspapers comprised a significant bulk of the locally printed material and catered to the small English population in Calcutta. In *Printing in Calcutta to 1800*, Graham Shaw documents the number of presses that were in operation till 1800; from 1780 to 1790, there were between 3 and 5 presses continually in operation, and from 1791 to 1799, between seven and ten active in each year. The presses were mostly concerned with the printing of newspapers, and the increase reflects the opening of newspaper offices in Calcutta in 1791-2. The printing press of the East India Company, the Honourable Company's Press, was the most prolific printing press in Calcutta before 1800. Out of the forty printers, before 1800, only six were not associated with the printing of newspapers; "Lotteries crowd on lotteries, and newspapers on newspapers, but the projectors do not seem to consider where the money to support them is to come from."[299] Statistics reveal that in the last twenty years of the eighteenth century in Calcutta, twenty four weekly newspapers and monthly magazines were published.

Why were there, though, so many newspapers? More newspapers meant more advertisements as a large section of the newspapers was filled with them and they were an important source of income for the owners. Many servants of the Company invested in presses and in printing ventures, hoping for fast returns. One investor, Mr. Stocqueler, wrote that he sold his newspaper, *The Englishman,* in 1842 for 13,000 pounds, having purchased it for 1,800 pounds eight years previously.[300] Huge profits were possible because of the high rate of subscription and the income that was generated from advertisements. But, more often than not, newspaper ventures failed. Apart from this economic reason of profit, we also have to take into account the fact that this illogical equation between the number of readers and the available kinds of print can partially be explained if we consider the nature of print culture in eighteenth century Calcutta. Certain characteristics of print culture that we find in Calcutta are also evident in the nature of print in Georgian England. The disproportionate spurt of the growth of newspapers in Calcutta is emblematic of the commercialization of print

---

[299] *Calcutta Chronicle.* Jan 1, 1793, 7, 363, 2.

[300] Mrinal Kanti Chanda, *The History of the English Press in Bengal* (Calcutta: K.P. Bagchi, 1988), pp. 394-397.

culture in Georgian England, where by 1695, with the lapse of the Licensing Acts in England—meaning that that the government could not monitor publications—printing presses grew in an unprecedented manner. Some of the fundamental ideas surrounding the realm of print culture in Georgian England spilled onto the metropole of Calcutta.

Newspaper advertising and consumerism.

A large section of the newspapers that were printed in Calcutta were filled with advertisements, because without advertisements in newspapers, goods that were brought from Europe could not be publicly made known to the residents. The men could not do without claret and cheeses, and the women could not survive without stockings and hats. The relationship between traders, the European residents of Bengal and print culture is an intrinsic one for goods that were imported and advertised through print, and sold to the English residents. This was the function of print advertisements, and a public notice set up in 1768 in a commercial area of Calcutta, by one William Bolts, addressed to the "Public", draws -attention to the importance of print technology: "Mr Bolts takes this method of informing the public that the want of a printing press in this city being of great disadvantage in business, and making it extremely difficult to communicate such intelligence to the community as is of the utmost importance to every British subject."[301] And even if the newspaper had little circulation and subscription, advertisements made it economically possible for the newspaper to be printed. Newspaper publishers were fully cognizant of this fact and took advantage of the consumer fetishism displayed by the British. All newspapers had an alternative title; the full title of the *Bengal Gazette* was the *Bengal Gazette or Calcutta General Advertiser*; likewise the *India Gazette* was also subtitled *India Gazette, or Calcutta Public Advertiser*.

These social habits of consumption made it possible for the rich and the educated English to live in India. Those who lived in Calcutta had similar habits of consumption and they were bound to the metropole of London through these social habits. Advertisements in newspapers can be seen as a growth, synonymous with the growth of a consumer society. The

---

[301] Quoted in Nair, *Calcutta Press* (Calcutta: Firma KLM, 1987), p. 1.

index of the growth of consumerism parallels the growth of newspaper advertisements. Within a span of a hundred years, England had grown to become a consumer society, as a result of it its colonial expansions. James Walvin argues that the social and personal habits that were developed by the British was a result of the "specific course of British imperial and commercial history."[302] As European traders came in contact with distant regions, they remade these regions to "serve their broader self interest" and plants and commodities were transmuted into "major instruments of profit, public taste and global expansion." The centre of fashion was London, where one could see the "most lavish, obvious signs of material consumption." The humblest of British people could enjoy the tropical pleasures of coffee, chocolate and tea, as a result of the aggressiveness of the empire where the "colonial outposts" of "trading companies, plantation settlements, military bases and the extraordinary long reach of the Royal Navy" made a global empire possible.[303] The public imagination of such a consumer oriented society was defined through habits of consumption, commodities, things and tastes that were common to all and cut across all classes of people. But what is of importance is that these habits of consumption made it possible for the nation to imagine itself as a consumer oriented society. Advertisements in newspapers play an important role within this social context, for it was through advertisements that the consumer-readers were aware of the range of goods that were available. Advertising thus played a potent role in making it possible for all the citizens to fully be congnizant of the range of things.

The correlation between advertising and consumerism is transparent. The index of the growth of consumerism parallels the growth of newspaper advertisements. Advertising thus played an important role in making it possible for all the citizens to be aware of what they could consume. The emergence of advertising in England is symptomatic of a burgeoning consumer oriented society. Within a hundred years, by the end of the eighteenth century, newspaper advertising columns had grown

---

[302] James Walvin, *Fruits of Empire: Exotic Produce and British Taste. 1660—1880* (New York: New York University Press, 1997).

[303] Ibid., pp. 194, x-xiii, 173.

dramatically, a trend in keeping with the rapid growth of consumerism in England.³⁰⁴ A newspaperman, Nathaniel Mist, commented in 1725 on the function of newspaper advertising, and its role in connecting people who were otherwise strangers to each other:

> ... it is certain, that in a great and populous City like this, where the Inhabitants of one End of the Town are Strangers to the Trade and Way of Living of those of the other, many Things which prove of singular Use and Benefit could never be known to the World by any other Means but this of advertising ...³⁰⁵

In a large city, where most were strangers to each other, people could be connected through things by imaginatively participating in the lifestyle of others. Material exchange and consumption, in other words, allowed for participation in an imagined, consumer oriented community. Within a hundred years, by the end of the eighteenth century, newspaper advertising columns had grown dramatically, a trend in keeping with the rapid growth of consumerism in England, becoming a space for commercial exchange. According to T.R. Nevett, in a survey on the growth in advertising between 1800 to 1848, the "clearest trend revealed by the survey" was the "growth of consumer goods advertising."³⁰⁶ Newspaper advertisements can be seen as an inevitable offshoot of a burgeoning commercial culture.

Advertising, in its detailed particularization of things, as a literary technique was also evident in many of the novels of the late seventeenth and eighteenth century, where this genre developed the language of close particularization., According to Jill Campbell, detailed particularized "description in the public realm of print, a page of newspaper advertisements" revealed that the "needs or wants of individuals – their incompleteness as private selves" could be resolved"³⁰⁷ through material

---

³⁰⁴ According to Terry R. Nevett, in a survey on the growth of advertising between 1800 to 1848, the clearest trend revealed was the "growth of consumer goods advertising"; see *Advertising in Britain: A History* (London: Heinemann, 1982), pp. 35-36.

³⁰⁵ *Mist's Weekly Journal*, 22 May, 1725; quoted in Jeremy Black, *The English Press in the Eighteenth Century* (London: Croom Helm, 1987), pp. 51-52.

³⁰⁶ Nevett, pp. 35-36.

³⁰⁷ Jill Campbell, "Domestic Intelligence. Newspaper Advertising and the Eighteenth

things. Formal realism evident in the novels presumed that the breach between the individual and the larger community could be healed by careful reference to particularized material objects."[308] The growth of the novel and of newspaper advertising were simultaneous occurrences, and both emerged out of the social changes of that time, namely, the rapid dissemination of print culture and the emphasis on empirical observation. Campbell, in her examination of the novels of this time, states that newspaper advertising often appear directly within a narrative of the novel and *Belinda*, for example, is unlike any of the others of the epistolary genre. References to luxury commodities are an intrinsic characteristics of the plot; "the imported bird, exotic plants, cosmetics, floral essences, foreign wines and sauces, fashionable gowns, jewelry, fast horses, fancy chariots, novelty lamps, and cabinets with special locks" suggest that the discourse of advertising and the products it promotes were essential to social and domestic happiness, and needed to bring together the individuals of an atomized society.[309] In the eighteenth century, the "specific concrete references that were to bind the private individual to the larger social world became increasingly branded with product names"; thus, one could participate in the larger imagined community through commercial exchange.[310] These characteristics of a burgeoning consumer oriented society were transferred onto the colonies, making it easy for the Britishers to live in a far away land.

Print and advertising: making consumer culture possible in Calcutta. Advertisements that were plenty in the early newspapers in Calcutta reflect the consumerist lifestyle of the British residents who lived there towards the end of the eighteenth century. These habits of consumption were definitive of the identity of the Britishers. Advertisements would appear that would proclaim the sale of goods from ships that had arrived from England (fig.

Century Novel," *The Yale Journal of Criticism* 15(2): 251-291; 254. p. 252.

[308] Ibid., p. 253.
[309] Ibid., 279.
[310] Ibid., p. 254.

14):³¹¹ claret, red port, brandy, Jamaica rum and other varieties of alcohol, ham, pickled tongues, cheeses, salad oils, olives, raisins, currants, almonds, milk chocolate, confectionary, looking glasses, glassware, floor cloths, ladies and gentlemen's silk and cotton stockings, hats, cloth and cashmere, waistcoats shapes, boat cloaks, leather breeches and gloves, silk and cotton gloves, Irish linen, French cambric, Manchester goods of different sorts, books, stationary, perfumery, rifle guns, spare locks, gun powder and shot. Another advertisement stated that goods that were imported from Dublin were to be sold by auction: Four hawsers, sixteen coils of small rope, a quantity of patent blocks, a sextant, a case of artillery, mathematical instruments, a theodolite in a mahogany case, twenty kegs of paints, one hundred pounds of chocolates, fifty pots of spruce, two sets of china ware, fifty pieces of white handkerchiefs, two bureaus, a harpsichord, some buggy and phaeton harness, a roasting jack, seventeen cases of Holland's gin, a pipe of Madeira, a quantity of Chittagong Red Wood. British-ness in the colonies was defined through the capacity to consume commodities and objects.

Such kinds of advertisements were quite intrinsic in the every day lives of an Englishman by the eighteenth century, which is why Joseph Addison wrote in quite a tongue and cheek fashion, as early as 1710, in an essay in *The Tatler* that "If a Man has Pains in his Head, Cholicks in his Bowls, or Spots in his Clothes, he may here [referring to advertisements] meet with proper Cures and Remedies."³¹² Moreover, when advertisements were first written, they would have had to be stylistically different from regular prose and Addison also draws attention to their linguistic and stylistic characteristics: "The great Art in writing Advertisements, is the finding out a proper Method to catch the Reader's Eye; without which a good Thing may pass over unobserved"; therefore many stylistic techniques were made use of: "Asterisks and Hands were formerly of great Use for this purpose. Of late years, the N.B. has been much in Fashion; as also little Cuts and Figures…"³¹³ The linguistic and stylistic features of these eighteenth century advertisements that were printed in England were replicated in the

---

³¹¹ *Calcutta Chronicle*, 3 April (1792): 3.

³¹² Joseph Addison, *The Tatler* (Glasgow: Printed by Robert Urie, 1754), p. 190.

³¹³ Ibid., p. 190.

newspapers that emerged in Calcutta.

Figure 14: Advertisements in newspapers.

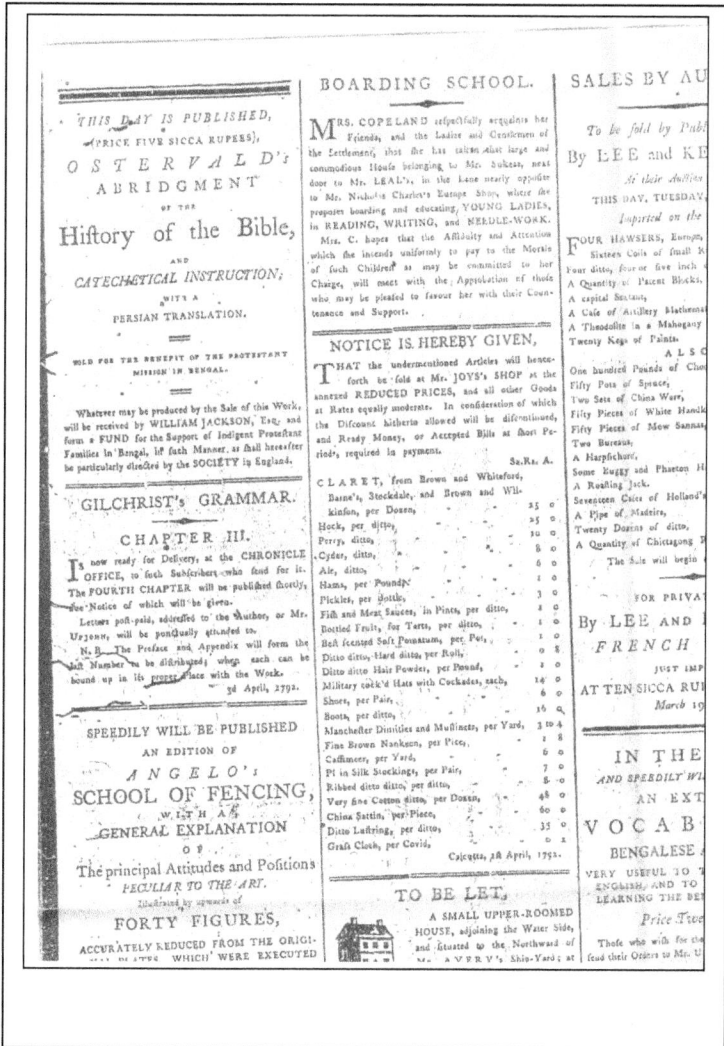

Many aspects of social life were addressed in the advertisements, and reading them gives us a clearer picture of how certain features of British life were transferred to the colonies and faithfully replicated. For a closer glimpse of the social life that emerged towards the end of the eighteenth century, H.E. Busteed's *Echoes of Old Calcutta, Reminiscences of the days of Warren Hastings, Francis, and Impey* is a useful text, with colorful descriptions:[314] how women dressed in the latest fashion, the marriages that took place, the enormous houses that were maintained with numerous servants (one's status was signified through the number of servants that were kept), the elaborate meals served, the hectic social life with dances and card games.[315] The emergence of such a social realm, quite distinct from how the natives lived, made it possible for the newly arrived Englishmen to settle down and rule the colonies.

a) Clothes and Fashion and lifestyle.

There was a wide assortment of working class and middle class Englishmen who traveled to Calcutta, and the advertisements reveal the nature of their work as bakers, boarding-school teachers, dance masters, carpenters, etc. In an advertisement in the *Calcutta Chronicle*, there was a notice of one "Mrs. Mann [who] begs leave to inform the ladies of the settlement that she has taken the house lately occupied by Mr. Allardice and immediately opposite Messrs. Steuart Coach Makers where she has now exposed for Sale an Assortment of milinary and Haberdashery on Commission."[316] No doubt, Mrs. Mann would have kept the residents abreast with the latest sartorial changes that were taking place in England for it was important for women to dress well; "[n]o care or skill is left unexerted to render the appearance easy and graceful, a necessary circumstance ... as gentleman in the course of their morning excursions continually drop in."[317] Of all the social activities, dancing was the "chief enjoyment" to which "Calcutta society ...

---

[314] H.E. Busteed's *Echoes from Old Calcutta, Reminiscences of the days of Warren Hastings, Francis, and Impey* (Calcutta: Rupa and Co., 2005).

[315] In particular, see Ibid., pp. 153-168.

[316] *Calcutta Chronicle*, Nov. 4th (1793): 4.

[317] Quoted in Busteed, pp. 174-175.

devoted itself" and [m]inuets and country dances were most in fashion."[318] An advertisement for dance lessons reads as follows: "Mr. BELVEDERE, the Dancing Master begs leave to acquaint the Ladies and Gentlemen of this Settlement and the public in general that he propose Opening a Dancing School for instructing Ladies and Gentlemen in the French, English and Spanish Dances , at one Gold Mohur per. Month, …none but People of Character will be admitted and decorum observed and Care will be taken that no offence shall be offered."[319] By screening who was being admitted to his classes, or by pretending to be cautious, Mr. Belvedere was ensuring that he was able to attract those who could afford the fees. A diary entry from this time period reads as follows:

> Saturday, March 9. Why, there was a ball at Colonel Gallier's, and the French women dancing cotillions as if they had not another hour to live. Mrs. Clavering was there and the Misses and the General and Bibby Johnson, and Miss Ashe, and Miss Howe, who lives with Lady Impey and is going to marry Dr. Campbell, who has fewer hair and more years than I have. There was he capering about and gallanting the lady and exercising her fan; she is not above sixteen.[320]

Many young women, like the above mentioned Miss Ashe and Miss Howe, would have been present in Calcutta, hoping to attract wealthy husbands, and boarding houses for such young women were opened. One Mrs. Copeland put out an advertisement for a boarding School for young women: "Mrs. Copeland respectfully acquaints her friends and the Ladies and Gentlemen of the Settlement, that she has taken that large and commodious house … where she proposes boarding and educating young ladies, in reading, writing, and needle work."[321] Pockets of imperial, colonial life were present in Calcutta, and the implication was that the city was but a

---

[318] Busteed, pp. 208-209.

[319] *Bengal Gazette*, April 15-22nd (1780): 2-3.

[320] Busteed, p. 181.

[321] *Bengal Gazette*, April 15th-22nd (1780): 2-3.

distant suburb of the center.

There were carpenters who catered to the needs of the newly settled Britishers, and who needed European furniture for their day to day living (despite the fact that furniture would have been brought over in ships): "Wanted a European Carpenter who understands wheel and Cabinet Work – to engage for a Term."[322] Food also was an important part of this settler, diasporic community; an account in *Echoes from Old Calcutta* describes the usual menu as "Two o' clock was the usual hour for dinner; Mrs. Fay gives an ordinary day's bill of fare for this meal for herself and husband, viz. soup, a roast fowl, curry and rice, a mutton pie, a fore-quarter of lamb, a rice pudding, tarts, very good cheese, excellent Madeira."[323] One Mr. Oldham advertised himself as a baker: "Mr. Oldham BEGS leave to acquaint the Ladies and Gentlemen of the settlement that He continues as usual to bake Bread and all sorts of Sweet-cakes for breakfast, Also the best sort of Biscuit, fit for the use of Ladies, and Gentlemen who travel, by Land, or sea."[324] All in all, the Britishers were able to live in Calcutta as a result of this elaborate social life that was established.

b) Servants: natives and Africans.

Interestingly enough, in *Echoes from Old Calcutta*, there is mention of native indentured labourers and also African servants who worked for the Britishers;[325] from "the earliest days of the English settlement in Bengal servants appear to have been a fertile source of worry"[326] and it was not unusual for "one hundred and ten servants to wait upon a family of four people."[327] When native servants left service, it became news in the settlement, and well advertised. When Mr. Oldham's *sircar* absconded with money, a notice was circulated in the newspaper, announcing a reward for 150 rupees: "WHEREAS ONE Rada Churn Doss of John Bazaar a Sircar

---

[322] *Bengal Gazette*, April 15th-22nd (1780): 2-3.

[323] Busteed, p. 175.

[324] *Bengal Gazette*, Dec. 23rd-30th (1780).

[325] Busteed, pp. 196-198.

[326] Ibid., p. 185.

[327] Ibid., p. 184.

of Mr. Oldham in Calcutta for many years, did on Tuesday [receive money but] has not since been heard of."[328] There was also a description of the man: "N.B. He was a thin spare Man about 5 Foot 6 Inches, Black Face and Pock Marked, 32 years Old, and is the Son of Taukoor Doss who was a Weighman to the Hon'ble Company, and has lived at the West end of the John Bazaar for many years."[329] The absence of this man must have been public news as there is an accompanying note which clarifies this: "Mr. OLDHAM BEGS leave to acquaint the Gentlemen of the Settlement, and the Public in General that the different Reports which has been circulated about Calcutta, for some days past relating to the Body of his Sircar, being found in a Chest in the New Fort, he believes it entirely groundless, and without any foundation…. Nor has he received any intelligence of him as yet."[330] Through these public notices, we get a glimpse of how the realm of indispensable native servants functioned in the imperial domestic circles.

In the early years of settlement, around the last two decades of the eighteenth century, African slaves were present in Calcutta, and there are references in the advertisements which corroborate this.[331] Subsequently, we do not hear about them and slavery was discontinued as the Slave Trade Act was passed in the British Parliament in 1807. African slaves were known as Coffree; one advertisement read: "STRAYED FROM the house of Mr. Robert Duncan in the China Bazaar. On Thursday last a Coffree Boy about 12 years Old, named Friday whoever brings back the same, shall receive the Reward of one Gold Mohur."[332] There was a large element of indignity attached to how black slaves were perceived by the Britishers and the following advertisement for black women who were to marry black slaves makes that clear:[333]

Wanted

---

[328] *Bengal Gazette*, Jan 20-27th (1781): 2-3.

[329] *Bengal Gazette*, Jan.20th-27th (1781): 2-3

[330] *Bengal Gazette*, Jan.20th-27th (1781): 2-3.

[331] For more on this, see H.E. Busteed's *Echoes from Old Calcutta*, pp. 194-197.

[332] *Bengal Gazette*, Jan20-27th (1781): 2-3.

[333] *Bengal Gazette*, Sept. 8th-15th (1781): 1.

BY a Gentleman now in Calcutta, three very handsome AFRICAN
LADIES of the true fable hue, (by the Vulgar) commonly called
Coffriesses.
They must not be younger than fourteen years each
Nor Older than twenty, or twenty five
They must be well grown Girls of their Age.
Strait Limbed, and strait Eyed.
And have a rational use of all their faculties
The better if a little squeamish
But beware of spot or blemish
They will be joined in the holy banes of Wedlock, to three
Gentlemen of their own Colour, Cast, and Country.

As the Master of those African Gentlemen would not wish to have
them disappointed, he hopes no Ladies will apply, but those who
are really and truly spinsters, for it would be a very disagreeable
circumstance to have their passions would up to the highest pitch
of wild desire, and then to have the banes forbidden in right of a
prior claim. – No matter whether by a Mogul from the East, or a
Hottentot from the West. – For in[sic] either circumstance it would
be equally distressing.

The presence of African slaves would have been insignificant and the above
episode an isolated incident. It is important to note that the Britishers did
not intervene in the personal lives of the natives, unlike their involvement
in the affairs of the African slaves, as the above advertisement reveals.

c) Sailing ships.

Food items, goods, books and people traveled across and so did everything
English which made it possible for the Britishers live. Not surprisingly,
news of sailing ships were important and regular features in the newspapers.
Ships moving between nations, "crossing borders in modern machines,"
were "micro systems of linguistic and political hybridity."[334] The western
artistic imagination of the eighteenth century was replete with icons of the

---

[334] Paul Gilroy, p. 12.

ship, or the slave ship; "ships were the living means by which the points within that Atlantic world were joined."[335] Ships brought news, via old newspapers, and carried goods, and were the most important means of link between the colonies and the metropole (fig.15). An advertisement would read as the following, and the details must have been of importance, and some relevance, to those who were reading it: The "Chichester, Captain Blake, sailed on Sunday last for Madras. ... The French ship Solitude, Captain Realey, arrived in the river on Tuesday last from Madras. ... The Northumberland Indiaman ... has been detained until further orders. ... A Geneose ship arrived in the river on Saturday from Europe... " [Intelligence of] public consequence received from Europe by the above ship is that England, Holland, and Prussia, had at last effected a mediation between the Empress of Russia and the Porte. ... The Swan sloop of war, commanded by Captain Elphinstone, arrived in Madras Roads from Europe on the 11th... The Hawke, Captain Pennel, arrived in England the 19th of September, with the news of the capture of Bangalore.[336] There would be a list of ships and the dates of arrival and departure, making traveling around the globe an easy affair. The English readers, geographically situated in Calcutta, would have found this interesting, as England was a maritime power. Therefore, the interest in certain news items was specific to that time period, and subsequently loses meaning.

d) Rivalry between individual printers and the EIC.

Not all residents agreed to the policies of the East India Company, and James Hicky's *Bengal Gazette* was quite critical of the EIC. The proprietor of a newspaper had to be in the good books of the East India Company for otherwise he could be deported or imprisoned as happened with James Hicky. Hicky would address the Public with his grievances:

> To the Public. Mr. Hicky, begs leave to inform ... that the most cowardly ... method has been made use of to prevent the sale of his Newspaper, by procuring an Order from the Council, to

---

[335] Ibid., p. 16.
[336] *Calcutta Chronicle*, April 3rd (1792): 2.

Figure 15: Sailing ships.

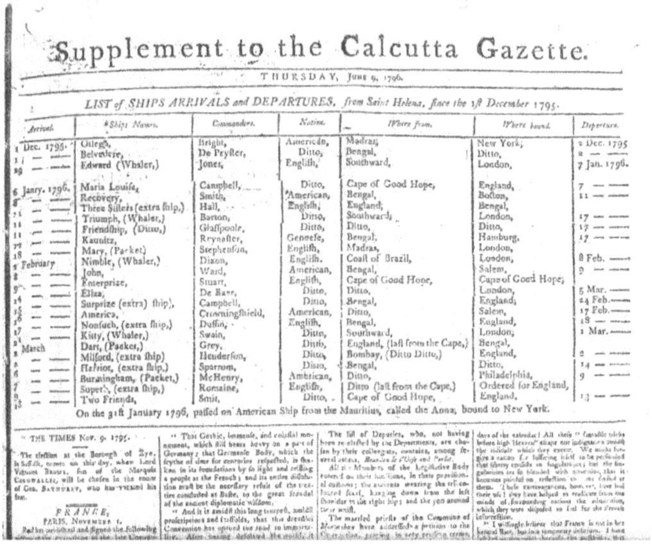

Supplement to the Calcutta Gazette.

THURSDAY, June 9, 1796.

LIST of SHIPS ARRIVALS and DEPARTURES, from Saint Helena, since the 1st December 1795.

Arrival.	Ships Names.	Commanders.	Nation.	Where from.	Where bound.	Departure.
1 Dec. 1795.	Otlego,	Bright,	American,	Madras;	New York;	2 Dec. 1795
11 — —	Belvedere,	De Peyster,	Ditto,	Bengal,	Ditto,	2 — —
29 — —	Edward (Whaler,)	Jones,	English,	Southward,	London,	7 Jan. 1796.
6 Janry. 1796.	Maria Louisa,	Campbell,	Ditto,	Cape of Good Hope,	England,	7 — —
8 — —	Recovery,	Smith,	American,	Bengal,	Boston,	11 — —
11 — —	Three Sisters (extra ship,)	Hall,	English,	England;	Bengal,	
11 — —	Triumph, (Whaler,)	Barton,	Ditto,	Southward;	London,	17 — —
11 — —	Friendship, (Ditto,)	Glasspoole,	Ditto,	Ditto,	Ditto,	17 — —
12 — —	Kaunitz,	Reynaster,	Genoese,	Bengal,	Hamburg.	17 — —
18 — —	Mary, (Packet)	Stephenson,	English,	Madras,	London,	
1 February	Nimble, (Whaler,)	Dixon,	English.	Coast of Brazil,	London,	8 Feb. —
8 — —	John,	Ward,	American,	Bengal,	Salem,	9 — —
9 — —	Enterprize,	Stuart,	English,	Cape of Good Hope,	Cape of Good Hope;	
14 — —	Eliza,	De Barr,	Ditto,	Ditto,	London,	5 Mar. —
15 — —	Surprize (extra) ship),	Campbell,	Ditto,	Bengal,	England;	24 Feb. —
16 — —	America,	Crowningshield,	American,	Ditto,	Salem,	17 Feb. —
17 — —	Nonsuch, (extra ship,)	Duffin,	English,	Bengal,	England,	18 — —
21 — —	Kitty, (Whaler,)	Swain,	Ditto,	Southward,	London;	1 Mar. —
March	Dart, (Packet,)	Grey,	Ditto,	England, (last from the Cape,)	Bengal,	
2 — —	Milford, (extra ship)	Henderson,	Ditto,	Bombay, (Ditto Ditto,)	England,	2 — —
5 — —	Hafriot, (extra ship,)	Sparrom,	Ditto,	Bengal,	Ditto,	14 — —
6 — —	Burmingham, (Packet,)	McHenry,	American,	Ditto,	Philadelphia,	9 — —
7 — —	Superb, (extra ship,)	Romaine,	English,	Ditto (last from the Cape,)	Ordered for England,	
13 — —	Two Friends,	Smit,	Ditto,	Cape of Good Hope,	England,	13 — —

On the 31st January 1796, passed on American Ship from the Mauritius, called the Anna, bound to New York.

THE TIMES Nov. 9. 1795.

FRANCE,

PARIS, November 1.

prevent their going by the Post,[337] by this step all Mr. Hicky's subscribers on the coast and at the subordinate settlements will be disappointed, and obligated either to take the *New India Gazette* or to go without any. ...

However he will soon let them see that he is not to be intimidated by such trifles, for before he will cringe, or fawn, to any of his oppressors, was the whole sale of his Paper to be stopped, He wou'd compose Ballads and sell them thro' the streets of Calcutta as Homer did.

And let them see that he is a Freemason of the first City in the British Empire, and free of the Printers and Stationers Company and that he has a power to print a Newspaper that no East India Company not the King their Master can wrest out of his hands. ...[338]

The newspaper industry was not a mere offshoot of the government and was censored subsequently, drawing protests from a large number of natives also.

Book advertising and print

No eighteenth-century book in England emerged from the printer without "pages of advertisements, printed or pasted onto the back," thus allowing for print to promote print.[339] Consumer fetishism was not limited to the use of material things, and a similar desire is evident in how printed texts were published and consumed in Calcutta. The advertisements in the newspapers allow us to gauge the nature of the communication network between author, reader, printer, and publisher that was evident in Calcutta. The newspapers and books that were printed in Calcutta, based on subscription readership, ensured the printers a sense of economic viability. This model of subscription publication was a system in use in eighteenth century England. Till the seventeenth century, there had been censorship in

---

[337] A rival newspaper, the *India Gazette* was distributed free of postage.

[338] *Bengal Gazette*, 18th-25th Nov. (1780): 53.

[339] Barbara Benedict, p. 7.

England, allowing the government control and surveillance of the kinds of books that were printed, and the number of books that could be printed. With the lapse of the Licensing Act in 1695, a free sphere of print culture evolved, without systematic government intervention. John Brewer describes the emergence of this realm of eighteenth century printers and publishers.[340] In 1689, the world of printing was limited to a few sections of London in St. Paul's Churchyard and Paternoster Row, dominated by a powerful trade guild, and was a community where everyone knew everybody else. But a hundred years later, the publishing industry had grown and in 1785, John Pendred wrote the first guide to English publishing which covered the provinces: *The London and Country Printers, Booksellers and Stationers Vade Mecum*. What "had begun as a London trade had become a national business."[341] The rise of the periodical press made it possible for the professional writer to emerge, and have a career based solely on writing. Commercial publishing meant the bookseller had the upper hand in determining what kinds of books were to be printed, displayed, and were sales-worthy. Subscription made it possible for the inevitable commercial viability in the market place, and the independence of the author as it implied a certain amount of sales, which covered production and distribution costs. The eighteenth century saw subscription publication emerge, bringing together the interests of the author, patron and bookseller. The subscriber had become the patron—which in the earlier centuries was the role played by the Court or wealthy individuals. This model was followed by the printers and writers in Calcutta, and ensured some degree of economic independence for emergent writers.

With the emergence of subscription readership the relationship between the author, reader and printer changed. Newspapers played a role in disseminating news about new publishing ventures, becoming a medium though which new printing enterprises were advertised and therefore, it was through print that a desire for more print was created and sustained. For example, an advertisement for a new weekly publication, the *Chittagong*

---

[340] John Brewer, "Authors, Publishers and the Making of Literary Culture," in *The Book History Reader,* ed. David Finkelstein and Alistair McCleery (London and New York: Routledge, 2002).

[341] Ibid., p. 244.

Herald, was announced in the following manner in the *Calcutta Chronicle* (fig. 16): "Three gentlemen have stepped forward in support of this agreeable 'Publication' and look forward to entertain their 'small settlement' every Sunday." A poem was enclosed, addressed to the Public: "Ye gentlemen and ladies all, / Who live at Chittagong, / On you the Herald means to call / Each Sunday, with a song;" and the poem ends with a few lines from the printer, "Great-Sir, I beg you'll tell the town, / My types are very few; / My press is old and broken down, / With scarce a single screw."[342] By informing the readers of new literary and journalistic ventures, and also by often making requests for monetary advances, a subscription-based readership was formed.

It is fascinating to examine the nature of the books that were printed and sold by the printers in Calcutta; advertisements reveal the specific nature of what was being printed (fig. 17).[343] *History of the Bible and Catechetical Instruction with a Persian Translation, Sold for the Benefit of the Protestant Mission in Bengal.* Grammar books were written in volumes: "Gilchrist's *Grammar*, Chapter III, is now ready for Delivery, at the Chronicle Office, to such Subscribers who send for it. The Fourth Chapter will be published shortly, due Notice will be given." The printers served as book-sellers, and there was an absence of a separate establishment for books to be published. There were advertisements for books that were to be published, and waited for buyers; "Speedily will be published an edition of *Angelo's School of Fencing, with a General Explanation of the Principal Attitudes and Positions Peculiar to the Art.* [it is only on request] – Those gentlemen who are inclined to favor the publication will be pleased to signify their intentions to Mr. Upjohn." Often, these proposals would be in addition to lengthy descriptions of the text that was to be printed (fig.18):[344] "Proposals for Publishing by Subscription, *The Musical Olio, or Chearful Companion: Being A Collection of Songs, sung at The Anacreontick Society, The Beef-Steak Club, and Several Other Convivial Meetings*; by Dibdin and Others. The Work to be printed on English Foolscap, with a beautiful Type; to consist of One Hundred and

---

[342] *Calcutta Chronicle*, March 13 (1792): 4.

[343] *Calcutta Chronicle*, April 3 (1792): 3.

[344] *Calcutta Chronicle*, Nov. 6 (1792).

Figure 16: Advertisements for a new publication.

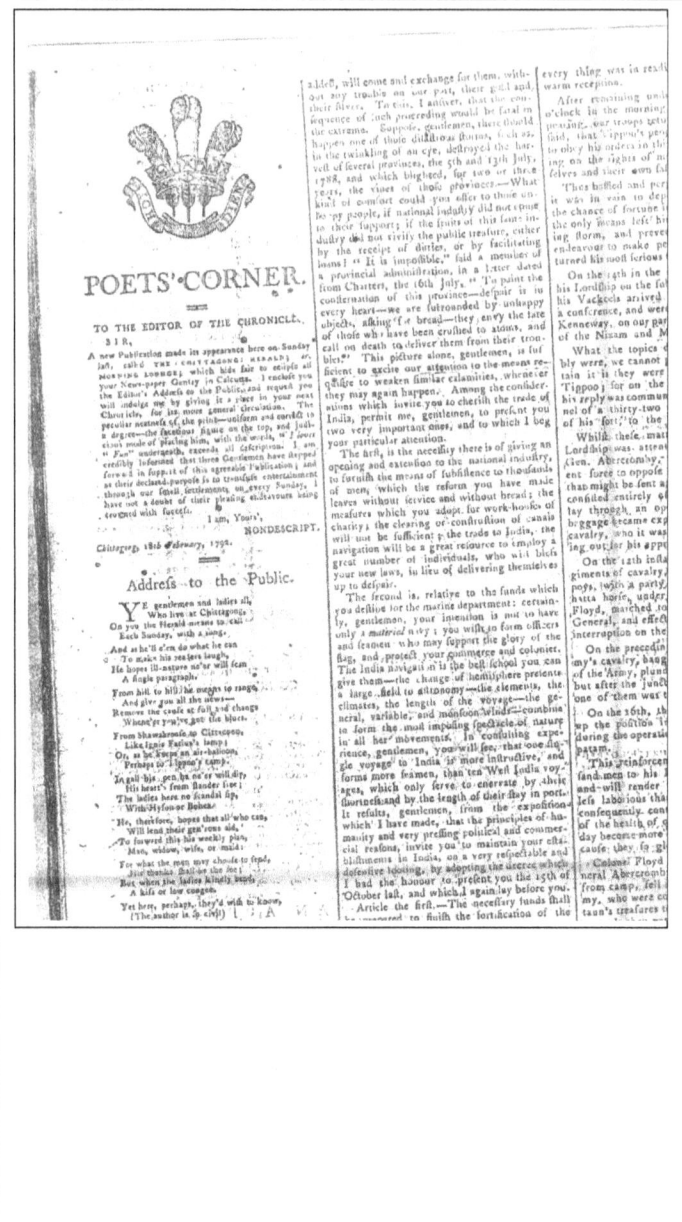

IMPERIAL PRINT IN COLONIAL CALCUTTA (1780-1820).

Figure 17: Advertisements of printed books.

Figure 18: Advertisements of books that were to be printed.

Fifty Pages, and to contain near Two Hundred Songs,—When Fifty copies are subscribed for, the Work will be put to Press. And it is the Compiler's Intention to Print off no more than are really subscribed for. Gentlemen wishing to become Subscribers to the above Work will be pleased to make known their intentions to Mr. A. B. Bone, at the Circulating Library."
Vocabulary books were printed (fig.19):[345] "In the press, and speedily will be published, an extensive Vocabulary, Bengalese and English, Very Useful to teach the natives English, and to assist Beginners in learning the Bengal language. Those who wish for the work, are requested to send their orders to Mr. Upjohn." Books in translation were also printed:
"The Following Books, translated from the Persian. May be had on application to Mr. Upjohn at the Printing Office: *Narrative of Transactions in Bengal, Memoirs of Abdulkurreem, Pundnameh – Persian and English, Epitome of Mohammaden Law and The Compendium of Revenue Accounting.*" It is not surprising that printing offices served as booksellers: "for sale, at the printing office, *The Happy Prescription, Comedy in Rhyme. The Two Connoisseurs,*" and another advertisement said, "*New Publication. Lately Published. Dissertation concerning the Landed Property of Bengal.*" There were also bilingual publications (fig. 20): "*The Tootinameh,* now in the press, is a collection of Persian Tales, written expressly for the improvement of young students; and the English part is by a gentleman whose publications have been well received, both here and in Europe, to render into English such subjects as the present, with any degree of success is no pleasant or easy task on account of accommodating the sense to a different idiom so as to preserve the spirit of the original and at the same time avoid the ridiculous extremes of stupidity or bombast."[346] The reading public knew about books that were printed from manuscripts: an advertisement stated "Lately published, a correct and elegant edition of *The Works of Hafez,* from a most accurate and valuable copy."[347] Thus, the realm of printed texts—of grammar books, translations, poems—that emerged in the last two decades of the eighteenth century in Calcutta catered to the needs of the Britishers.

---

[345] *Calcutta Chronicle,* April 3 (1792): 3.

[346] *Calcutta Chronicle,* May 8 (1792): 2.

[347] *Calcutta Chronicle,* April 3 (1792): 3.

Figure 19: Advertisements of vocabulary and grammar books.

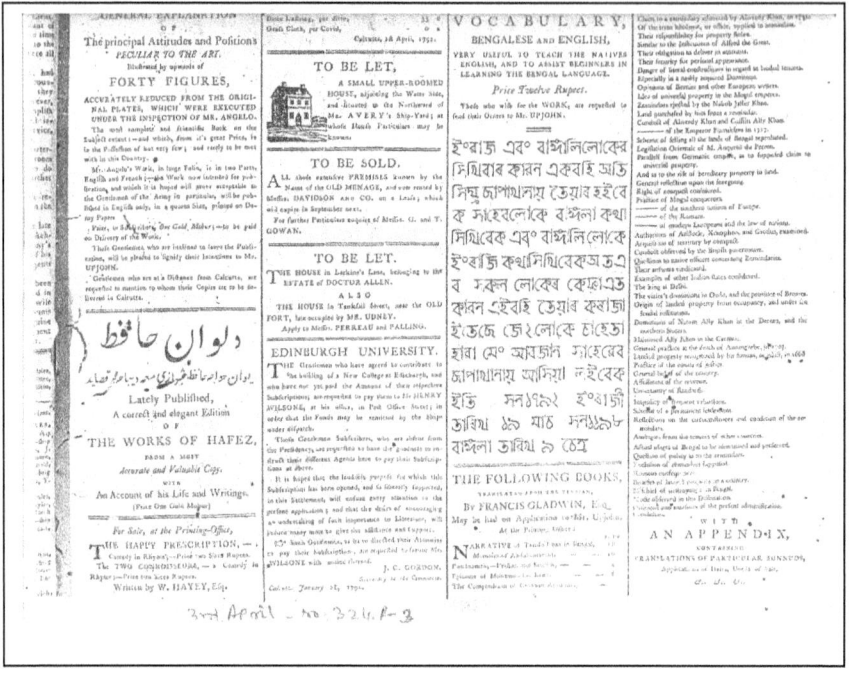

IMPERIAL PRINT IN COLONIAL CALCUTTA (1780-1820).

Figure 20: Advertisement of a bilingual translation.

Conclusion

There was no formal exchange of technology between the natives and the British. One can assume that close interaction with the British made it possible for the natives to emulate the habits of those in power. The native elite of Calcutta were willing to explore and adapt to the new things from the west and their desires were "much stronger than the willingness of Europeans to receive anything in return."[348] By a "mechanism which remains unexplained," architectural styles were imitated by the black town. P. J. Marshall writes that the Indian intelligentsia responded to the European civilization it encountered in a productive fashion. In fact, he argues that "private self indulgence by individual Europeans made a greater contribution to Indian awareness of the west than public policy."[349] The whites established a lavish, British lifestyle for themselves, leaving "abundant pickings for Indians who were minded to take advantage of their prodigality"; cultural habits were diffused in an accidental fashion. This fact is important to keep in mind as it partially explains how print culture was transferred into Calcutta. A high level of sophistication marked the nature of print within the white city of Calcutta, and the natives engaged with this notion of print culture. When we trace the beginnings of print culture in Calcutta, we have to go back to how print developed and was used by the whites who lived in Calcutta at the end of the eighteenth century.

Moreover, the press initiated a shift in the very nature of how texts were to be written, preserved and disseminated. It initiated a shift in the very method of writing, a shift that involved cultural habits —Indians would sit on the floor and write, unlike Europeans who used tables. Nathaniel Halhed describes it in the following manner: "As they have neither chairs nor tables, their posture in writing is very different from ours: they sit upon their heels, or sometimes upon their hams, while their left hand hold open serves as a desk whereon to lay the paper on which they write, which is kept in its place by the thumb: so that they never write on a large sheet of paper without folding it down to a very small surface."[350] Can

---

[348] Marshall, "White Town," p. 330.

[349] Ibid., pp. 329, 308.

[350] Nathaniel Brassey Halhed, *A Grammar of the Bengal Language*, p. 2.

we possibly argue that such a shift, which undoes the existing socio-cultural structure, implies a sense of power embodied in the printing press? A similar shift occurred in Europe, in the modern period, with the introduction of printing presses where diverse occupational groups worked with each other in the new workshops that were set up by the early printers. Elisabeth Eisenstein describes the numerous processes that were involved:

> The preparation of copy and illustrative material for printed editions led to a rearrangement of all book-making arts and routines. Not only did new skills, such as typefounding and presswork, involve veritable occupational mutations; but the production of printed books also gathered together in one place more traditional variegated skills. In the age of scribes, book-making had occurred under the diverse auspices represented by stationers and lay copyists in university towns; ... The advent of printing led to the creation of a new kind of shop structure; to a regrouping which entailed closer contacts among diversely skilled workers and encouraged new forms of cross-cultural interchange. ...
>
> Thus it is not uncommon to find former priests among early printers or former abbots serving as editors or correctors. University professors also often served in similar capacities and thus came into closer contact with metal workers and mechanics.[351]

When the printing presses were introduced in Bengal, the hierarchical status between the English and the Indians was maintained. The editors and the master printers were Europeans, many of whom were employed from England, while the compositors were Indians. We learn about the operation of printing presses by narratives that were written:

---

[351] Elizabeth Eisenstein, "Defining the Initial Shift: Some Features of Print Culture" in *The Book History Reader,* ed. David Finkelstein and Alistair McCleery (London and New York: Routledge, 2002), pp. 156-157.

> The Editor ... on reaching his office ... delivers to him (the head printer) such manuscripts, or extracts from other papers and periodicals, as are to constitute the contents of the journal for the day following. The printer then distributes this matter or copy ... to the compositors ... and the galley proof ... is then delivered to ... a reader, to examine and correct ... superintended by the head printer. The galley proofs ... are collected together late in the evening, when there appears no probability of more news, correspondence, or advertisements reaching the office ... Editor or his deputy then selects such portion of the matter ... as it is important.... From this, the subordinate printer proceeds to ... form a page of the paper. The pressmen cover the [iron frames] with ink by means of balls composed of sheep skins... a proof impression of the pages is then taken off and ... carefully read by the head printer and the Editor after which the printing of the whole impression commences.[352]

The printer would be European, and a big printing establishment would keep around eighty to a hundred compositors.

The communications circuit of the colonizers operated within a realm of power in its establishment of print technology. But what is of immense importance is that in the very process of establishing power, we can see power also being dissipated. At the initial stages, print was not meant for the natives, but the model of the press would eventually be replicated by the Indians. Mastery of the printing press was achieved by blacksmiths, for example, men from a socially lower hierarchy. (There is controversy if Panchanan was a blacksmith or a goldsmith; either way he would have been a low-caste.) Print democratized knowledge. This is not of much relevance for this chapter but explains how and why Indians were able to master print so incredibly fast. Fifty years later, in 1849, Michael

---

[352] J.H. Stoccqueler, "The Calcutta Press," in *Calcutta Quarterly Magazine and Review* 3(Oct.1833): 424-425.

Madhusudan Dutt was settled and married in Madras, and working towards establishing a poetic career. In a letter that he wrote to his friend, he informed him about his plans to publish a literary work, "The Captive Ladie," and his strategy of going about doing so:

> Now, my dear fellow, I have to ask a favour of you. I am publishing my book by subscription. There are few persons of whom I know; consequently, I cannot expect to cover the expenses of printing (very great in Madras), by what the book will fetch here. Can't get me a few subscribers? I am sure, if you try [you] will succeed. Two Rs. Per copy is the charge. Surely you will get, at least, 40 even from amongst our old school-friends. Let me know before the beginning of next month, the number of copies you want. I have a capital opportunity of sending them without incurring any expense whatever.[353]

It was quite audacious for Michael Dutt to dream of a poetic career without any private patronage and an absence of an English-reading native audience. How was he to create an audience, and sustain himself economically as a poet? His strategy was simple: to make use of subscription readership that would make the publishing venture economically feasible. This particular kind of a relationship between the reader, writer, and the publisher was new in the Indian context. In the eighteenth century, the English introduced certain aspects of the publishing industry within India, and in the process, changed the very nature of the literary profession. Subscription-based writing was one such instance. Native usage of print was an occurrence that took place post 1800; it was a matter of a few decades for the transference of print to take place—a mere matter of twenty or so years if we count the time from its inception to the time when the natives mastered the technology.

---

[353] Ghulam Murshid, ed. *Letters of Michael Madhusudan Dutt. The Heart of a Rebel Poet* (Delhi: Oxford University Press, 2007), p. 62.

6 HETEROGLOSSIC TEXTS: ENGLISH-NATIVE NEWSPAPERS IN COLONIAL CALCUTTA.

Between 1780 and 1800, many newspapers in Calcutta printed news in multiple languages side by side on the same sheet of paper (fig. 21). This was a moment in the history of newspapers in England and in India that had not happened before and was not replicated subsequently. Any reader of these beautiful multilingual sheets of paper would question as to why such newspapers went out of fashion in a few decades after they were printed. Not only had the new technology of print culture entered India with the Britishers but also, this technology, in the process of establishing itself within a colonial situation, underwent changes on how it was conceptualized. Colonization determined the nature of print culture which is why multilingual newspapers emerged in Calcutta and for a few moments in the history of print culture and of newspapers, there were such heteroglossic texts. The sheer new-ness of the visual text was and is mind-boggling in all respects – specially if we see how radical it was conceptually.

Is it possible that such a multilingual text could only happen in south Asia where a multilingual society exists. In some ways, and unwittingly so, the Britishers captured an aspect of Indian society within these printed texts and the sheer spirit of invention marks these newspapers. The possibilities of what could have been if newspapers had continued to be multilingual are not explored for it denotes an epistemic shift, thus answering a question: what happens when a technology that has its origins in a different social space enters a new geographical locale and

IMPERIAL PRINT IN COLONIAL CALCUTTA (1780-1820).

Figure 21: Multilingual texts.

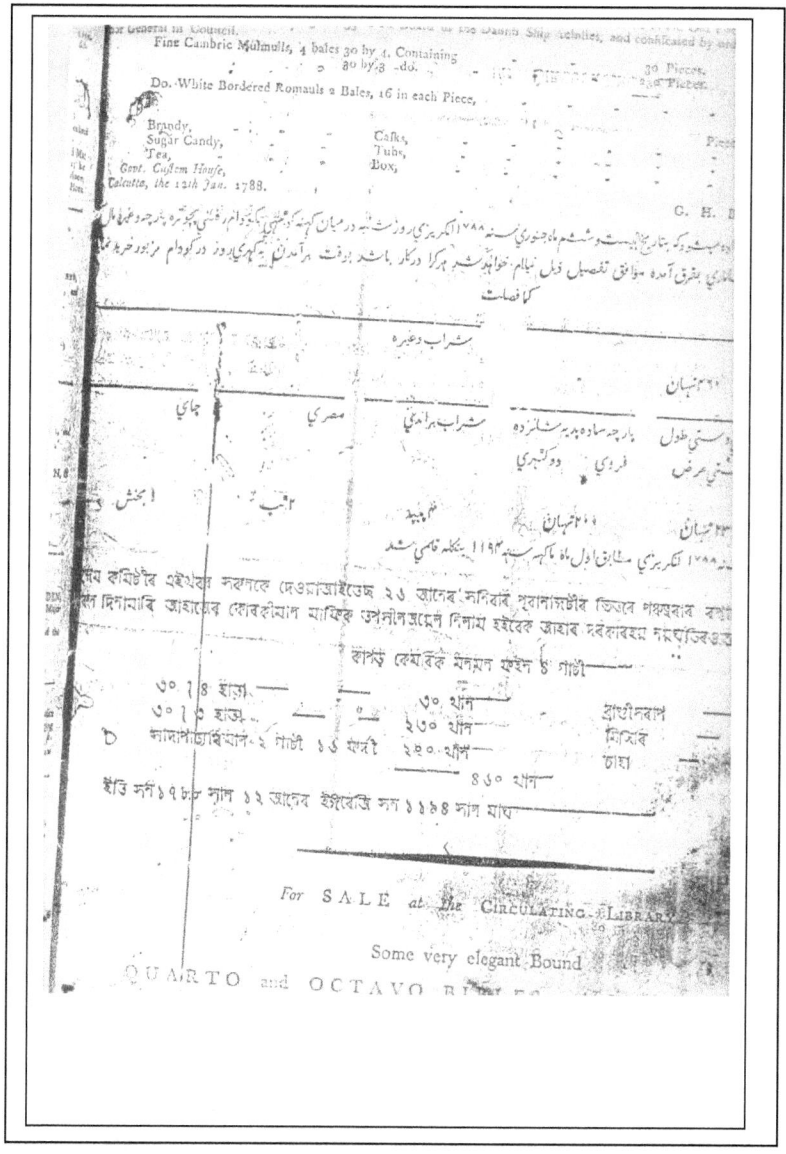

how does it change? The heteroglossic nature of Indian society was reflected in how these newspapers were formed; moreover, in some ways, the Britishers were attempting to portray and capture Indian society in these newspapers.

In the first half of the chapter, I look at the nature of multilingual newspapers and the need for such texts, and how they emerged. I argue that these texts, innocuously reflected the heterogeneity that existed in Indian society. In the second half, this linguistic heterogeneity was transferred on to the natives, and I look at the first literary writings in English, using the example of Henry Derozio. His writings reflect the heterogeneous space from within which they emerged and Derozio's acclaim, both local and global, was not replicated subsequently by natives in the following century, revealing a similar story of the multilingual newspaper.

Sahib involvement in native print. The need for heteroglossic print.

What remains a fuzzy unexplored area is whether the natives took up print culture easily enough or was there initial resistance at the advent of the new technology? The nature of print that entered south Asia had evolved since its beginnings three hundred years ago in the west. Even a hundred years ago, there was conflicting attitudes in England towards print technology. Manuscript culture was present even after 1710 and the Act of Queen Anne and it was considered a "competitive if not the dominant mode of transmitting and reading 'literary' and 'academic' materials."[354] This act of clinging on to an "outdated" technology of the fading aristocratic world of letter represented an authorial choice. But obviously enough, there were enormous epistemic shifts made as a result of print and Eisenstein writes about its revolutionary impact on how science was conceptualized:

> The advantages of issuing identical images bearing identical labels to scattered observers who could feed back information to publishers enabled astronomers, geographers, botanists, and zoologists to expand data pools far beyond all pervious limits – even those set by the exceptional resources of the long lasting

---

[354] "Social Authorship and the Advent of Print," p. 12.

IMPERIAL PRINT IN COLONIAL CALCUTTA (1780-1820).

Alexandrian Museum. ... The closed world of the ancients was opened; vast expanses of space (and later of time) previously associated with divine mysteries became subject to human calculation and exploration.[355]

As a result of print, knowledge could spread in faster methods than had been possible previously. In the western world, the shift that took place from a manuscript culture was a gradual but inevitable one, but we do not really such ambiguities in how print culture was perceived by the natives in Calcutta as the sophisticated social characteristics of late eighteenth century print were transferred on to the colony. In Bengal, the Britishers developed native fonts, which were subsequently made use of by the natives. But, did the availability of fonts make it easier for the natives to make the shift from manuscript to print culture? More importantly and is a question we should be asking at the present is whether native usage was impacted by the fact that the Britishers made use of native fonts? In what can but only be described as being ironical, the Britishers printed multilingual texts but these were subsequently used in a different context altogether by the natives. These texts that were initially printed by the Britishers for their own needs, incidentally represented the multilingual nature of Indian society.

The efforts that were taken to obtain and create fonts and types in Indian languages are little known facts. Many of the newspapers would be beautifully illustrated with Indian languages and a single page would have Urdu, and Bengali side by side. During the time period that I am referring to - between 1780 and 1820 - these newspapers were only read by the Britishers, which means that the Indian languages only had English readers. In 1830, a report in *The Friend of India* said that before this period, "the press had been confined to Europeans, and the only works in the native languages were printed at their expense and circulated gratis."[356] A question that needs to be answered is: why were there elaborate Indian prints in

---

[355] Eisenstein, pp. 256-257.

[356] "Art. V. - On the effect of the Native Press in India," *The Friend of India*. Quarterly Series (No. 1): 130-154, p. 133.

newspapers that would not necessarily be read by all the English readers of the newspapers?

The larger argument that was used to legitimate British colonization was that it was needed to do good for the natives; this explains to a great extent many of the socio-cultural and technological exchanges that took place between the Britishers and the natives. The relationship is best described in the following manner:

> Britain possesses the means of improvement and instruction beyond most nations in Europe. India on the contrary is ignorant and wretched, while a bounteous Providence is pouring forth upon her almost every blessing which can render a country happy. But it is to Britain alone that she can look for instruction and relief. Did other nations posses the means of imparting them in the fullest manner, the opportunity is denied them. How could any other nation interfere so as to gain the confidence of India? It is to Britain alone that Providence has committed this pleasing task, and in a more full and ample manner than has ever been done to any nation at any former period.[357]

The reason that was used to justify the need for colonization was that the Indians needed the Britishers for "improvement and instruction" because as a nation, Britain alone could provide them with the required education as the other nations "lacked" the means of imparting them. Moreover, during the early years of British presence, the task of colonization was seen as a "pleasing" one which would enable the Indians to "gain the[ir] confidence." It would be a meaningful enterprise if we allowed ourselves to view print culture as part of the process of "instruction" accompanying empire and colonization. This implies that we have to consider print as functioning against manuscript culture and regard it as it was considered by the Britishers: a vast systemic and civilizational improvement.

---

[357] Ibid., p. 135.

During the initial years of colonization, India was seen as a part of Britain.[358] It would be rather simplistic and naïve if we were to interpret this phase of colonization of Bengal as operating within absolute binaries of ruler and ruled. It was important to keep the new British citizens in the colonies happy, and learning the languages made that possible through better communication. In a review of Halhed's grammar book in 1783, a similar concern was articulated:

> Our settlements in the East form deservedly one of the greatest objects of national concern. Populous and rich, our chief attention should be fixed on making them happy and secure....
> ...without an easy and general intercourse with the natives, through the medium of language, no system of regulation, which the wisdom of man may frame, can promise any solid, rational, or permanent establishment of authority and power.
> ... we shall confine our observations to strictures on the history and the usefulness of a language of very high antiquity, spoken by millions of industrious Briitsh subjects, and of great importance, in various lights, towards the proper management of the commercial, military, and revenue departments of Bengal.[359]

The review draws attention to certain fundamental assumptions within which empire was established and these make for interesting speculation; the Bengali language was an example of "novelty, as well as of utility" and therefore, it was brought to public attention. What is equally fascinating is that the reviewer normalizes the publication of such a grammar book and even recommends it to the English reader; he writes that the book presented the readers with "elements of a language hitherto disregarded,

---

[358] The loss of the thirteen American colonies is said to have brought to an end the first British empire based on the Atlantic Ocean, and occurred at a time period between 1750 and 1783 which also saw the "first waves of Indian conquests made by the EIC." The British EIC was given the grant of the Bengal diwani in 1765 and in fifteen years, Britain was engaged in a war in North America against the local population. (P. J. Marshall, *The Making and Unmaking of Empires*, p. 1)

[359] "A Review of 'A Grammar of the Bengal Language.'" In *The English Review* (1783): 1-2.

and almost unknown in Europe."³⁶⁰ In some way, this act of being able to codify a native language and transfer it to print technology is seen as an act of British cultural superiority: "Another gentleman employs the extraordinary efforts of a singular and persevering genius in the fabrication of types of a very novel and difficult construction: whilst we find a Governor General, (unlike every description of public men in Britain) amidst all the busy scenes of war and state affairs, cultivating the arts of peace."³⁶¹ There is little documented evidence as to whether the natives were critical of how print evolved in Calcutta and the British government's attempts to cultivate such a realm could thus be seen as an act of "peace".

It was not only that print technology symbolized the British colonizers desire to promote the arts of peace but there were some necessary practical reasons to why such heteroglossic texts were printed and circulated amongst the white community. Francis Gladwin, wrote in a letter in 1784 to the Board of Directors of the EIC as to why a newspaper like *The Calcutta gazette, or Oriental Advertiser* was needed; "[to start a gazette] as it might be made Useful to the Junior part of the Company's Servants by the insertion of Extracts from the most approved Persian Authors; in the original Character with English Translations, and thus facilitate their Improvement in that Language, the study of which has been so frequently recommended to them by the Court of Directors."³⁶² In the preface to the *Asiatik Miscellany*, Gladwin wrote that it would be an enterprising endeavor to print Persian works alongside English translations:

> And though this part of the Work may, at first sight, seem particularly designed for those who study the Persian language, and will undoubtedly be of singular use to them, it is yet by no means on their account alone, that the extracts appear in that form. The translations will, we trust, be always matter of curiosity and entertainment to English readers also, who in seeing them accompanied by their respective originals, will have no reason to be satisfied, that what is presented to them as a specimen of eastern

---

³⁶⁰ Ibid., p. 12.

³⁶¹ Ibid., p. 12.

³⁶² Quoted in *A History of the Calcutta Press*, Nair, p. 110.

history or composition, is neither spurious nor disguised by borrowed ornament, but is genuine, pure and unadulterated.[363]

British superiority was evident in that print could erase the impure and adulterated parts of a manuscript language. The natives must have accepted this assumption for we find scant criticism against the emergence of native types and print.

Theories of Utilitarianism: can colonization make the natives happy?

India, as a colony, was viewed as a precious possession and such a view is articulated quite strongly in a text like *The Annals of the College of Fort William*,[364] which was written in the early nineteenth century and symptomises some of the basic principles underlying empire formation: the empire should be maintained with the "spirit of enterprise and boldness which acquired it" but it should not "be administered as a temporary and precarious acquisition -- as an Empire conquered by prosperous adventure, and extended by fortunate accident, of which the tenure is as uncertain as the original conquest and successive extension were extraordinary"; the colony would be considered "as a sacred trust, and a permanent succession."[365] Notwithstanding such a view about the colony, there is still no direct reason as to why there was a need to invest so much intellectual resources into India and what determined the underlying principles behind colonization? But we do find that there are abstract concepts of goodness and happiness that recur over and over again in a text like *The Annals of the College of Fort William*, which nudge us towards assuming, that at least, during the initial years of empire building in India, British imperialism did desire to portray itself as something more than mere brute power. The assumption that the act of colonization would lead to the happiness of the natives is clearly an utilitarian one and is best summarized in John Stuart Mill's definition of Utilitarianism when he described it as that "creed which accepts as the foundation of morals, Utility, or the Greatest Happiness

---

[363] Quoted in Ibid., pp. 116-117.

[364] *The Annals of the College of Fort William.*

[365] Ibid., p. xi.

Principle, holds that actions are right in proportion as they tend to promote happiness, wrong as they tend to produce the reverse of happiness."[366] In the "Introduction" to the *Annals*, which mostly puts forward a rationale of the newly established College of Fort William, the English readers are told that the "general happiness and prosperity of the country" depended on the "conduct" of the civil servants of the EIC, and they would be unable to engage in communication unless they were conversant with the "Native languages" and the laws and customs of the land.[367] It was the "sacred duty, true interest, honour and policy of the British nation" that compelled the British government to rule for the "prosperity and happiness" of the people of India.[368] In a similar manner, it was argued that the English would preserve Indian culture in a more comprehensive fashion than had been, and therefore the need to preserve manuscripts was that it would eventually lead to the happiness of the Indians:

> The preservation and augmentation of the Collection of Eastern Manuscripts, afford the only means of arresting the progressive destruction of Oriental learning. Since the dismemberment of the Muslim, those works have been dispersed over India, and have been exposed to the injuries and hazards of time, accident and neglect. It is worthy of the ambition of this great Empire to employ every effort of its influence in preserving from destruction and decay, these valuable records of Oriental history, Science and Religion.[369]

By engaging with the natives and by teaching them, the Indian subjects would also have a more favourable view of the British rulers. There would diffuse among them "a spirit of civilization and an improved sense of those genuine principles of morality and virtue," that would promote their happiness and establish a stable British empire.[370]

---

[366] Stuart Mill, *Utilitarianism* (London: Longmans, Green, Reader and Dyer, 1871), pp. 9-10.

[367] *Annals*, p. iii-iv.

[368] Ibid., p. xv.

[369] Ibid., p. 114.

[370] Ibid., p. 115

The civil servants were not the "agents of a commercial concern" but were the "ministers and officers of a Powerful Sovereign."[371] Their education in the College of Fort William would help them to discharge their duties in a manner that would allow them to "honour" the "British name in India" and would lead to the "prosperity and happiness" of the "Native subjects."[372] They would learn to perform the duty of ruling "the extensive and valuable dominions" the nation had acquired in India, for by discharging this duty, depended the "prosperity and permanency" of the Empire.[373] The education of the civil servants would not be exclusively "European or Indian" but would involve the combined principles of Asian and European policy and government." Their education would be of a mixed nature, the "foundation" laid in England and "the superstructure systematically completed in India."[374] The College of Fort William was meant to teach the civil servants so that they could understand the existing laws and regulations, thus "enabling" them to discharge their duty.[375] Good administration would eventually create happy subjects:

> The due administration of just laws within these flourishing and populous provinces, is not only the foundation of the happiness of millions of people, but the main pillar of the vast fabric of the British Empire in Asia; the mainspring of our Empire is situated here…
> … the excellence of the general spirit of these laws is attested by the noblest proof of just, wise, and honest government; by the restoration of happiness, tranquility, and security, to an oppressed and suffering people, and by the revival of agriculture, commerce, manufacture, and general opulence in a declining and impoverished country.[376]

---

[371] Ibid. p. iv.

[372] Ibid., p. v.

[373] Ibid., p.19.

[374] Ibid., p. xii.

[375] Ibid., p. 92.

[376] Ibid., pp. 93-94.

The fundamental premise was that the natives would welcome British presence and would want to be ruled and such an explanation partially explains the enormous flow of culture and technology into India. It is within this Utilitarian interpretative model that we can understand the enormous efforts taken to not only create native fonts, but also the need to set up the institution of print culture in an elaborate manner.

Involving people and technology: the processes behind the creation of native font.

In a succinct commentary on how it took centuries for print to develop in the west, unlike the rapid manner in how it evolved in Calcutta, Halhed, in *The Grammar of the Bengal Language*, summarizes the efforts taken by Charles Wilkins to perfect the native types:

> With a rapidity unknown in Europe, he surmounted all the obstacles which necessarily clog the first rudiments of a difficult art, as well as the disadvantages of solitary experiment; and has thus singly on the first effort exhibited his work in a state of perfection which in every part of the world has appeared to require the united the united improvements of different projectors, and the gradual polish of successive ages.[377]

When the East India Company government established its printing press, Wilkins was its first head. But as we look closely at the nitty gritty details of the workings of the Srirampur Mission Press, one realizes that natives were active participants in the process of how technology was exchanged; Joshua Marshman, while describing Panchanan's efforts, wrote: "[with his] assistance we created a letter foundry, and although he is dead now, he had so full communicated his art to a number of others, that they carry forward the work of type casting, and even of cutting the matrices with a degree of accuracy which would not disgrace European artists."[378] Largely due to the

---

[377] Halhed, pp. xxiii-xxiv.

[378] From Sisir Kumar Das' *Sahibs and munshis: an account of the College of Fort William* (Calcutta: Orion Publications, 1978), p. 96.

efforts of William Carey, there was interaction between the Srirampur Mission press and the College of Fort William and many of the books written by the scholars of the college were printed in this press. Carey appointed many good scribes in different languages. The Bengali letters were engraved on the basis of a sample prepared by Kali Kumar Ray, the Bengali copyist of the College. Kali Kumar Ray must have been a scribe. What is interesting is that both natives and Englishmen were involved in the process of making types, therefore making the evolution of Indian print a collaborative venture.[379]

Panchanan taught the art of cutting types to Manohar, who was to become his son in law. Marshman described Manohar as "an expert and elegant workman who was subsequently employed for forty years at the Srirampur Press and to whose exertions and instructions Bengal is indebted for the various beautiful fonts of the Bengali, Nagree, Persian, Arabic and other characters which have been gradually introduced into the different printing establishments."[380] Over a span of around thirty years, between 1801-1830, the Srirampur Mission press printed books in over fifty languages.

A lot of intellectual labor went into the process of making types and perfecting the font. John Gilchrist made some changes to the printing of the Perso-Arabic scripts. In 1802, he wrote to the College Council: "as the types and printing materials which Mr. Gladwin presented to College are probably the best now to be procured, I request you will state to College my wish to take charge of, and employ them for the good of my department here, in the works I am about to publish in Hindoostanee language."[381] He

---

[379] *Annals:* "Many learned Natives are now attached to the Institution, who have been invited to Fort William by my special authority from different parts of Asia. ... The sudden dismission of the learned Natives attached to the College would therefore be an act of manifest injustice on the grounds already stated; it would also be an act of the most flagrant impolicy; nor would it be consistent either with the interest or the honour of the Company in India, ...pp. l-li.

[380] From *Sahibs and munshis*, p. 97.

[381] Ibid., p. 98.

also promised to return the types when needed to the College Council and thus was started the Hindoostane Press. Till then, there were some presses in operation: the Chronicle Press, Stuart and Cooper Press, Ferris and Greenway Press, and the Hurkaru Press. On 20th June, Gilchirst wrote to the College Council that he had made major improvements in 'Oriental typography' on the "European principle of separating words by spaces and joining the letters of each vocable, as much as possible." Lumsden subsequently made changes to Gilchrist's innovations. In 1805, he presented plans of improving the existing types in Persian and for establishing a new press. He also wanted a new set Persian types to be made by the best artists in Calcutta, under the guidance of Sheikh Kutb Ali, the Persian writing master at the College. He argued that "the letters of the Persian alphabet are joined together in such a manner as to render the frequent use of Logographic types indispensably necessary to the accurate execution of any literary work that may be printed in the Persian character."[382] The types that were used by the College were meant to "imitate more nearly the written character" and it was hoped that the printed texts would vie with "manuscripts in beauty and cheapness" even as they surpassed manuscripts in "accuracy."[383] The types were executed under the immediate supervision of natives attached to the College.[384]

It is not surprising that there are detailed discussions on the painstaking efforts taken to create the new types of Indian languages, and the sheer beauty of these native mechanical fonts. The emphasis was on the mechanical superiority of print versus handwritten manuscripts and to understand the logic of this argument, one needs to remember that by the end of the eighteenth century, when the socio-cultural characteristics of print were carried alongside the technology of print itself, print culture was seen at the apex of the communication circuit in Europe. Print technology in Europe during the fifteenth and sixteenth centuries reflected the larger social shift that was taking place whereby handicraft productions were giving way to mechanical processes and scribes were being replaced.[385] For

---

[382] Ibid., p. 99.

[383] *Annals*, p. 210.

[384] Ibid., p. 211.

[385] Eisenstein, 1979: 50-51, 54-55; McLuhan, 1994: 174.

this change to occur, a fundamental shift had to take place where printed books were construed as more credible than manuscripts; printers thus started to champion the superior accuracy and credibility of books in comparison to manuscripts at the beginning of the sixteenth century.[386] There was nothing intrinsic to the trustworthiness of books, and in fact, Adrian Johns argues that when printed books were first published in the early modern period, textual corruptions multiplied but this time period also saw the social constructedness of printed texts as being fixed and credible in comparison to handwritten texts.[387]

Within the colonial context in Calcutta, when we look closely at the debates and rationale raised on how the realm of print was to emerge, the concerns were not merely with replacing a manuscript culture, but there was an equally strong emphasis on how beautiful the natives types were. Halhed, in the "Introduction" to the *Grammar of the Bengal Language* wrote on the mechanical aspects of the fonts:

> The public curiosity must be strongly excited by the beautiful characters which are displayed in the following work: and although my attempt may be deemed incompleat or unworthy of notice, the book itself will always bear an intrinsic value, from its containing as extraordinary an influence of mechanic abilities as has perhaps ever appeared. That the Bengal letter is very difficult to be imitated in steel will readily be allowed by every person who shall examine the intricacies of the strokes, the unequal length and size of the characters, and the variety of their positions and combinations. It was no easy task to procure a writer accurate enough to prepare an alphabet of a similar and proportionate body throughout, and with that symmetrical exactness which is necessary to the regularity and neatness of a fount.[388]

The element of beauty involved in the creation of the types in Indian languages is a factor that has never been considered in how print was

---

[386] Johns, 1998, p. 5.

[387] Ibid., p.31.

[388] Halhed, p. xxiii.

construed in Europe. In many ways, such a perspective compels us to be more nuanced in how empire worked in the colonial context, legitimizing the need to invest time, labour, money and people in establishing a realm of print.

Bakhtin: making sense of heteroglossia.

The heteroglossic newspaper that emerged, thus, was a pastiche of sorts – and in this particular context, more so as a single news item was printed in multiple languages simultaneously on the same page. This heteroglossic text reveals a particular moment in the initial moments of colonial presence in Calcutta, and in many ways, reflects the multilingual nature of Indian society. To understand this phenomenon more comprehensively, Mikhail Bakhtin's notion of heteroglossia in a novel is quite pertinent.[389] Bakhtin writes that at any given moment of its evolution, language is stratified" into linguistic dialects but also into "languages that are socio-ideological: languages of social groups" and therefore, "literary language [used in novels] itself is only one of these heteroglot languages."[390] Language, therefore, is a reflection of society. In describing the heteroglossic novel, he writes at lengths about the nature of heteroglot languages:

> The novel as a whole is a phenomenon multiform in style and variform in speech and voice. In it the investigator is confronted with several heterogeneous stylistic unities, often located on different linguistic levels and subject to different stylistic controls. ...[T]hese heterogeneous stylistic unities, upon entering the novel, combine to form a structured artistic system, and are subordinated to the higher stylistic unity of the work as a whole, a unity that

---

[389] Mikhail Bakhtin, *The Dialogic Imagination*, edited by Michael Holquist (Austin: University of Texas Press, 2004). He describes it: "Heteroglossia, once incorporated into the novel ... is another's speech in another's language, serving to express authorial intentions but in a refracted way. Such speech constitutes a special type of double-voiced discourse. It serves two speakers at the same time and expresses simultaneously two different intentions... And all the while these two voices are dialogically interrelated, they... know about each other... it is as if they actually hold a conversation with each other." p. 324.

[390] Ibid., p. 272.

> cannot be identified with any single one of the unities subordinated to it.
>
> The novel orchestrates all its themes, the totality of the world of objects and ideas depicted and expressed in it, by means of the social diversity of speech types and by the differing individual voices that flourish under such conditions.[391]

Bakhtin urges us to go beyond the usual interpretative models of "linguistic and stylistic thought" that are used to understand the questions regarding the "philosophy of discourse."[392] There is an equation that he draws between society and language, and argues that that we must understand that the "life and behavior of discourse" reflects and emerges from a "contradictory and multi languaged world."[393] He goes on to write:

> The living utterance, having taken meaning and shape at a particular historical moment in a socially specific environment, cannot fail to brush up against thousands of living dialogic threads, woven by socio-ideological consciousness around the given object of an utterance; it cannot fail to become an active participant in social dialogue.[394]

It is reductive to look at language outside its social matrix and for Bakhtin, at any "given historical moment of verbal-ideological life," each generation has its own language, and therefore, "at any given moment, languages of various epochs and periods of socio-ideological life cohabit with one another."[395] The heteroglot nature of language represents the "co-existence of socio-ideological contradictions between the present and the past, between differing epochs of the past, between different socio-ideological groups in the present."[396] This coexistence of different linguistic styles and

---

[391] Ibid., pp. 261-263.

[392] Ibid., p. 275.

[393] Ibid., p. 275.

[394] Ibid., p. 276.

[395] Ibid., p. 290-291.

[396] Ibid., p. 291.

languages is an example of hybridization; which is a mixture of two social languages within the limits of a single utterance.[397]

The multilingual newspaper allowed the convergence of multiple languages that had and existed in different social moments in the history of India: English was the language of the new British rulers, while Persian had been used earlier and Bengali was the language in use by the inhabitants of Bengal. The hegemonic present of colonial rule, the native present and the immediate past all featured in this heteroglot text, creating the illusion of linguistic parity while in reality that was not the case. Examining the reasons as to why such a multilingual text would exist does give us an opportunity to understand the heterogeneous nature of Indian society.

Acts of Reading. Towards a new approach.

How did an English reader situated in Calcutta read these newspapers which printed news in languages that were not really known to them? The act of reading in this instance was informed by the fact that the reader was situated in a multilingual colonial city of which they were the rulers and this geographical situation needs to be imagined as we, located in the present, reread these newspapers and arrive at new interpretative models. Robert Darnton writes that reading has a "history" and that it is not the "always and everywhere the same."[398] He goes on to say:

> We may think of it as a straightforward process of lifting information from a page; but if we consider it further, we would agree that information must be sifted, sorted, and interpreted. ... As our ancestors lived in different mental worlds, they must have read differently, and the history of reading could be as complex as the history of thinking. ...[reading] is an activity involving a peculiar relation – on the one hand the reader, on the other the text. ...

---

[397] Ibid., p. 358.

[398] Robert Darnton, "Towards a History of Reading," in *The Kiss of Lamourette. Reflections in Cultural History* (New York: Norton, 1990), pp. 154-187; p. 187.

> Think how often reading has changed the course of history –
> Luther's reading of Paul, Marx's reading of Hegel, Mao's reading of
> Marx.[399]

For us, reading about how the multilingual texts could be read by the Britishers make us wonder about the initial moments of colonial presence in Calcutta. Did these moments differ from the nature of how print emerged in other colonial situations and a good point of comparison would be on how print emerged in colonial America. In "Print and Everyday Life in the Eighteenth Century," Patricia Crain writes that one of the ambiguities in eighteenth century print in America was that while print was seen as essential to the development of the public sphere, it [mostly works of fiction] was also viewed as a "medium of deception and seduction."[400] In the initial moments of colonial presence in America, there was engagement with the languages of the native Americans; John Eliot translated the Bible into Massachusetts in 1663; this is an extinct Algonquian language spoken in what is presently southeastern Massachusetts. Devotional literature and some legal publications were also printed in this language. The native Americans in southeastern Massachusetts were converts to Christianity and lived in their settlements and were mostly self-governed but their relation with the English was overseen by colonial authorities. The efforts taken to learn the languages of the native Americans were minimal, in comparison to how it had taken place in the Indian context.

The readers of the multilingual text that emerged in colonial Calcutta in the last two decades of the eighteenth century were Britishers, both locally and globally. The capacity to capture native fonts onto paper and display it alongside English within a newspaper asserted British

---

[399] Ibid., p. 187.

[400] Patricia Crain, "Print and Everyday Life in the Eighteenth Century" in *Perspectives on American Book History*, eds. Scott E. Casper, Joanne D. Chaison, and Jeffrey D.Groves (Amherst, MA: University of Massachusetts Press, 2002), pp. 47-78; p. 74.

superiority. Colonization was not only a geo-political affair and in fact, the socio-cultural component was equally important. What was essentially a societal state of affairs was transferred onto print and the heterogeneity of Indian society was seamlessly reflected on such a multilingual text.

Creating a heterogeneous literary space: native mastery of English.

The realm of early nineteenth century print culture in Calcutta was a heterogeneous space: Europeans printing books for themselves for reasons of politics, administration, aesthetics, proselytization and natives learning about this realm through close interaction. The picture that emerges is one of constant activity where natives and colonizer engaged with print in a heteroglossic manner.[401] A similar perspective allow us to state that when we try to draw a picture of the early years of English literary writings in Calcutta, and the use of print by these writers, we are compelled to make certain assumptions in the absence of any concrete anecdotes of what was happening. My specific focus in this section is on Henry Derozio who was writing in the early years of the nineteenth century and is considered as the first Indian poet writing in English.[402] Here, I argue that he was able to engage with print and English literary conventions with reasonable sophistication that was not possible for most natives at that time, because of his social and racial positional -- more *sahib* than native. It is due to the efforts of writers like Derozio that natives subsequently engaged with the realm of English literature. Derozio was an outsider of sorts and despite that was able to consider the English literary tradition as his own. This would have encouraged newly anglicized young natives to do the same.

---

[401] Such an inclusive perspective in the socio-literary history of print is argued for by Robert Darnton in his essay, "The Forgotten Middlemen of Literature," where Robert Darnton argues that the communication circuit does not necessarily only include books; some "unfamiliar figures" have to be added -- like the "rag pickers, papermakers, typesetters, wagon drivers, booksellers, and even readers." Darnton argues that our knowledge of literary history has to be more inclusive and we would take into account the everyday lives of men and women "who had a way with words." In *The Kiss of Lamourette. Reflections in Cultural History* (New York: Norton, 1990).

[402] All works of Derozio are cited from the following collection, *Derozio, Poet of India. The Definitive Edition.* edited by Rosinka Chaudhuri (Calcutta: Oxford University Press, 2008).

Derozio is considered as the first Indian to write English poetry. This is a bit random - was he Indian after all? As an East Indian, Derozio identified himself as an Indian, yet he was culturally and racially more *sahib* than native Indian. There are numerous poems and essays in the literary journals that were printed in the last two decades of the eighteenth century and early years of the nineteenth century. They were all written in India, for an Indian readership, but for a readership that was mostly British and lived in India for reasons of work. The institution of print was Indian, except the readership. This sphere of print was replicated and learnt by the natives. This is the context which we have to use in order to understand Derozio. We also have to keep in mind that English literature was going to influence all spheres of Indian literature. Pierre Bourdieu[403] aptly describes this phenomenon of "cultural production" where English literary writings would dominate the native scenario as the "site of struggle" when what was at "stake" was the power to "impose the dominant definition of the writer" and in the process "delimit the population of those entitled to take part in the struggle to define the writer";[404] Derozio was participating in and defining what would become the dominant definition of literature in India. Henry Derozio published his first collection called *Poems* in 1827; the Baptist Mission Press was his publishing house. The same press published one of Rammohun Roy's initial works in 1819, *A Second Conference Between an Advocate and an Opponent on the Practice of Burning Widows Alive*. Everybody in the domain of English print knew each other. It was, after all, a small realm of print.

White settlers? – and thus the need for multilingual texts.

We will never know for sure if the multilingual newspaper, in some way, indicates the Britishers desire to engage with India to a greater extent than was needed, but there is reason to believe so as in the early decades of the nineteenth century, there were debates regarding the possibility of

---

[403] Pierre Bourdieu, "The Field of Cultural Production," in *The Book History Reader*, eds. David Finkelstein and Alistair McCleery (New York: Routledge, 2002), pp. 77-99.

[404] Ibid., pp. 77-79.

Europeans settling in India which would have given them the impetus to learn native languages. We know that there was a dialogue regarding this issue as Rammohun Roy wrote a tract titled, "Remarks on Settlement in India by Europeans"[405] where he describes these debates: "Much has been said and written by persons in the employ of the Hon. East India Company and others on the subject of the settlement of Europeans in India, and many various opinions have been expressed as to the advantages and disadvantages which might attend such a political measure." Rammohun Roy was a cultural mediator for the Britishers, explaining Indian customs to the rulers, and the theme of European settlement features in Rammohun's writings. That Rammohun did deal with such a social issue is surprising but indicates that it must have been under consideration to a certain degree, and draws attention to the heterogeneity of Indian society.

Rammohun begins his analysis in by locating his own position as an employee of the East India Company and then goes on to cite reasons as to why it was needed for Europeans to settle in India; all the reasons would benefit the natives. He writes:

> European settlers in India will introduce the knowledge they possess; ...[there would be] free and extensive communication with the various classes of the native inhabitants; ...the European inhabitants the European settlers would gradually deliver the minds from the superstitions and prejudice; ... the settlers being more on par with the rulers of the country, and aware of the rights belonging to the subjects of a liberal Government, ... would obtain ... many necessary improvements in the [local] laws and judicial system; -- the ... support of the European settlers would ... afford to the natives protection against the impositions and oppression of their landlords and other superiors; ... the European settlers, from motives of benevolence, public spirit and fellow-feeling towards their native neighbors, would establish schools and other seminaries of education for the cultivation of the English language throughout the country, and for the diffusion of a knowledge of European arts and sciences.

---

[405] Rammohun Roy, "Remarks on Settlement in India by Europeans." in *The English Works of Raja Rammohun Roy. Part III,* (eds.) Kalidasa Nag and Debajyoti Burman (Calcutta, Sadharon Brahmo Samaj), pp. 79-86.

For Rammohun, European knowledge would greatly benefit the Indians. He writes that an invasion could be avoided if "supported by a large body of European inhabitants; --- [and] a connection [would be formed] between Great Britain and India." If a separation did take place, then there still would exist a large group of "respectable settlers (consisting of Europeans and their descendants, professing Christianity, and speaking the English language in common with the bulk of the people, as well as possessed of superior knowledge, scientific, mechanical, and political)" which "would bring that vast Empire in the east to a level with other large Christian countries in Europe." The settlers and their descendants would enlighten and civilize the surrounding nations of Asia.[406] Rammohun was supremely confident that certain aspects of western civilization would become intrinsic to India, in the same manner as had Islamic civilization prior to this.

Derozio was one such descendant of European settlers; he was more European than Indian, and yet he identified himself as being a non-native Indian rather than an European. He was conscious of the formation of the new group of East Indians, a body whose numbers were daily increasing. He wrote:

> They are a body, and yet they are not a body. This involves a paradox. But it is cleared up when we remark that they are a body, inasmuch as their numbers are great and are becoming greater daily; and they are not a body, inasmuch as they do not seem to belong to each other. Most of them, at least the better portion, are anxious for their weal, but each individual is as anxious to effect this in his own way. One will not concede to the other. Every man is jealous of his neighbour, although every man will be glad to ameliorate the condition of his countrymen. ... Let them unite, let them bring themselves together, form associations and societies, learn the sentiments of each other, find out their own value, and ascertain what they are capable of effecting, then, and not till then, will they be enabled to improve their condition. There was the East

---

[406] Ibid., pp. 81-83

Indian Dinner Club, but it fell. And what was the cause of this? Nothing less than the baneful want of unison in feeling. ...[407]

Derozio was concerned that many East Indians sent their children to England for reasons of education; and no "parent (how patriotic soever he might be) would educate his children in India merely to try the experiment of improving the tone of the education here thereby." He goes on to write: "The man who has the welfare of his countrymen at heart will endeavor to raise funds for their improvement, establish institutions for the same purpose"; he was born in India, and "proud to acknowledge" his country" but "even love of country" would not "hinder" him expressing what he believed to be right.[408] A whole new community was formed that gained access to all aspects of a pluralistic Indian civilization.

Not replicated subsequently.

The heteroglossic newspaper was a moment in the history of colonial print, initiating the start of a new period in literary writings. If we flip through the pages of literary journals and newspapers that emerged out of Calcutta in the early nineteenth century, we come across a plethora of poetry and literary essays in English. The writers were Englishmen or East Indians, residing in Calcutta. These writings cannot be considered as part of the English literary tradition of England; neither are they considered as Indian writings in English. These work are in fact lost to any literary tradition and it is important to consider retrieving them and include them to what is considered as Indian writings in English. The only exception to this group of writers is Derozio as he is considered as the first Indian writing in English. Even if his writings were meant for an English speaking readership -- local and global -- they operated within a realm of print that was established in Calcutta. I would state that it is because of him, as an East Indian trying to master the literary habits of the Britishers, that his native students in Hindu College were enabled to do the same. After all, Derozio was an outsider, like his native students.

---

[407] Derozio, "No. III: Education in India -- Lines to my Brother in Scotland," in *Derozio*, ed. Rosinka Chaudhury, pp. 88-89.

[408] Ibid., p. 89.

IMPERIAL PRINT IN COLONIAL CALCUTTA (1780-1820).

Within a few years, English educated young natives engaged with this realm of English literary print. Michael Madhusudan Dutt comes immediately to mind when we consider natives writings in English. Michael dashed off his poems to all the journals that he could; the literary journals that published his poems were the *Literary Gleaner*, the *Literary Gazette*, the *Bengal Herald*, the *Oriental Magazine*, and the *Comet*. Michael Dutt would try to retrace Derozio's steps in some ways. Michael was a brilliant student in the Hindu College; he was also an Anglophile, evident in some of his early poems in English:

I sigh for Albion's distant shore,
Its valleys green, its mountain high;
Tho' friends, relations, I have none
In that far clime, yet, oh! I sigh
to cross the vast Atlantic wave
For glory, or a nameless grave!

My father, mother, sister, all
Do love me and I love them too,
Yet oft the tear-drops rush and fall
From my sad eyes like winter's dew.
And, oh! I sigh for Albion's stand
As if she were my native-land!

In 1842, he sent a contribution to Bentley's Miscellany, with an accompanying letter to the editor:

> It is not without fear that I send you the accompanying productions of my juvenile Muse, as a contribution to your Periodical. The magnanimity with which you always encourage the aspirants to 'Literary Fame' induces me to commit myself to you. 'Fame,' sir, is not my object at present; for I am really conscious I do not deserve it; -- all that I require is Encouragement. I have a strong conviction that a Public like the British -- discerning, generous and magnanimous -- will not damp the spirit of a poor

foreigner. I am a Hindu, a native of Bengal -- and study English at the Hindu College in Calcutta. I am now in my eighteenth year --- 'a child' -- to use the language of a poet of your land, Cowley, 'in learning but not in age.'[409]

His poetry was not published, and eventually, he failed to become a writer in English, but he did become a great writer in Bengali. The story is this - Michael did not have access to the realm of print and literary advisors as did Derozio. Neither were the Britishers willing to accede literary value and space to the natives at this moment of time. There were many like Michael, Kasiprasad Ghosh and Soshee Chunder Dutt -- and their works are nearly forgotten.

Conclusion.

It is fitting that in conclusion, we also consider the other side of the picture of how native print that was made use of by the Britishers; by the early nineteenth century, missionaries had started to try to convert Hindus by distributing free pamphlets. Rammohun Roy wrote about this phenomenon in 1821 in *The Brahmanical Magazine or The Missionary and the Brahmun:*

> ... But during the last twenty years, a body of English gentlemen, who are called missionaries, have been publicly endeavoring, in several ways to convert Hindoos and Mussalmans of this country into Christianity. The first way is that of publishing and distributing among the natives various books, large and small, reviling both religions...
> if they were true missionaries, they would preach in countries like Turkey and Persia, ... In Bengal, where the English are the sole rulers, and where the mere name of Englishman is sufficient to frighten people, an encroachment upon the rights of her poor timid and humble inhabitants and upon their religion, cannot be viewed [as a justifiable act][410]

---

[409] "Letter. 4th Oct., 1842." in *A heart of a Rebel Poet. Letters of Michael Madhusudan Dutt,* ed. Ghulam Murshid (Calcutta: Oxford UP, 2004), p. 21.

[410] Rammohun Roy, *The Brahmanical Magazine*, p. 138.

In order to transmit the ideas of Christianity, knowledge of native languages was needed, alongside the complete establishment of native fonts. This was but one of the central reasons as to why there was so much immediate efforts taken by the Baptist missionaries to fund the formation of native fonts.

The initial moments of colonization were different in comparison to what happened subsequently. We do realize that the speedy manner in which native fonts supplemented English print made it possible for the shift to take place from a manuscript culture to a realm of print. The natives would catch on to what it meant to be a part of this new realm, thus democratizing the very nature of who had access to knowledge.

7 CONCLUSION: THE EMERGENCE OF A LARGER PRINT PUBLIC SPHERE.

My journey in this book describing the initial stages of print in Calcutta and the advent of English writings in India has also revealed that the world of print in its first few decades, though a reasonably small one, was quite multi-racial and diverse, involving both the Britishers and the natives. Printers arrived from England and set up printing houses. These presses were initially brought by the printers themselves, or were ordered from England once they settled in Calcutta.[411] Some learnt the trade in Calcutta itself, sensing business opportunities in establishing such institutions. They had to involve natives in their enterprises, and inevitably, natives learnt about print and set up their own presses. My analysis of printed texts in English has allowed me to look at the larger social structures from within which they emerged, keeping in mind the reasons for writing and also those who were involved as writers. Undoubtedly, English writings and the emergence of print technology were simultaneous occurrences.

The print induced public came into existence due to the efforts of these adventurous European printers who came and settled in Calcutta; some of them were quite anti-East India Company and vociferous about their opinions. It is due to the efforts of such printers that the technology and the culture of print were able to flourish. Eventually, these habits of

---

[411] Graham Shaw, *Printing in Calcutta to 1800, A description and checklist of printing in late 18th century Calcutta* (London: The Bibliographical Society, 1981), pp. 29-38.

IMPERIAL PRINT IN COLONIAL CALCUTTA (1780-1820).

print were picked up by the natives. The initial presence of the East India Company within Calcutta, and the gradual rise of an European city must have been of immense interest to most natives; the newness of the situation would have intrigued all segments of the local society.

There was nothing sacrosanct in this imperial print space, and the rabidly scurrilous journalism of James Hicky is ample evidence. His tabloid, the *Bengal Gazette*, was the first newspaper in India, and was lapped up by the English reading non native public for its scandalous reports of the officials of the EIC. He was sued as his 'news' was considered libel, and his newspaper was prohibited from being circulated through the Calcutta General Post Office. In defense he wrote to his reading public in 1780,

> To the Public. Mr. Hicky, begs leave to inform.. that the most cowardly … method has been made use of to prevent the sale of his Newspaper, by procuring an Order from the Council, to prevent their going by the Post, by this step all Mr. Hicky's subscribers on the coast and at the subordinate settlements will be disappointed, and obligated either to take the New India Gazette or to go without any.
> …
>
> However he will soon let them see that he is not to be intimidated by such trifles, for before he will cringe, or fawn, to any of his oppressors, was the whole sale of his Paper to be stopped, He wou'ld compose Ballads and sell them thro' the streets of Calcutta as Homer did.
>
> He has now but three things to loose [sic] his Honour, in the support of his Paper, his Liberty, and his Life, …
>
> And let them see that he is a Freemason of the first City in the British Empire, and free of the Printers and Stationers Company and that he has a power to print a Newspaper that no East India Company not the King their Master can wrest out of his hands.

...⁴¹²

Print could be used within the domain of the public to arouse sympathy, to censure institutions of power, and even spread slanderous rumours. Even as print was used by the Europeans, natives learnt every civil, social and scandalously dirty aspect of this new technology.

Beyond Postcolonial Theory.

What I have described above was one process of intellectual and technical exchange that allows us to understand the engagement between colonizer and colonized, English and native. Postcolonial theory can explain these engagements, and a lot of this theory operates from the premise that the colonialist, imperial project and its discourse inevitably and always makes use of specific fixed ideas to how the native "other" is to be defined: as "heathen, barbarian, chaos, violence".⁴¹³ For example, Homi Bhaba, in one of his seminal essays, "Signs Taken for Wonder," draws upon a narrative which describes natives being awe struck at the materiality of the printed book.⁴¹⁴ He argues that the book as used by the natives was a hybrid formation; the "effect of colonial power," he writes, is the "production of hybridisation rather than the noisy command of colonialist authority or silent repression of native tradition."⁴¹⁵ In other words, Bhaba suggests that the engagement between the colonial powers and the native always results in a hybrid formation. What exactly is this notion of the hybrid? In this book, where I examine the transference of print into India, I have tried to understand the extent to which it is a relevant and valid theoretical tool, allowing me to understand the interaction between native and colonizer. For the most, my empirical based archival research has revealed that the

---

⁴¹² *India Gazette*, 17th and 25th Nov., 1780, quoted in Thankappan Nair, *A History of the Calcutta Press* (Calcutta: Firma KLM, 1987), pp. 51-53.

⁴¹³ Homi Bhabha, "Sly Civility," in *The Location of Culture* (New York: Routledge, 1994), Reprint 2005, pp. 132-144, p. 143.

⁴¹⁴ Homi Bhabha, "Signs Taken for Wonders: questions of ambivalence and authority under a tree outside Delhi, May 1817" in *The Location of Culture*, pp. 145-174.

⁴¹⁵ Ibid., p. 160.

postcolonial notion of the hybrid is but pertinent in some instances, and has not been of much relevance in this context. My book explains that the emergence of print technology in the colonial context and its subsequent usage cannot be contained within the notion of the hybrid; the complexities involved in describing the changes of a heterogeneous culture, that is in itself with porous borders, has to be seen on a continuum of change.

Bibliography:

Bibliography

Primary Texts, located at the National Library, Kolkata.

Newspapers (1780-1815).

Hicky's Bengal Gazette or Calcutta General Advertiser.

The India Gazette.

The Calcutta Gazette.

The Bengal Journal.

The Asiatic Miscellany.

The Calcutta Chronicle and General Advertiser.

The Asiatic Mirror and Commercial Advertiser.

The World.

Reverend J. Long, *Volume 1. Selections from Unpublished Records of Government for the Years 1748-1767 inclusive. Relating mainly to the Social Condition of Bengal.* (Calcutta: Office of the Superintendent of Government Printing, 1869).

Secondary Texts.

Addison, Joseph. *The Tatler.* Glasgow: Printed by Robert Urie, 1754.

Altick, Richard Daniel. *The English Common Reader: A Social History of the Mass Reading Public, 1800-1900,* 2nd ed. Columbus: Ohio State UP, 1998.

Anderson, Benedict. *Imagined Communities: Reflections on the Origin and Spread of*

Nationalism. New York: Verso, 1991.

The Annals of the College of Fort William, from the Period of its Foundation. Arranged and Published by Thomas Roebuck, Calcutta, Printed by Philip Periera at the Hindoostanee Press, 1819.

Appadurai, Arjun. *Modernity at Large: Cultural Dimensions of Globalization.* Minneapolis: University of Minnesota Press, 1996.

"Art. V. - On the effect of the Native Press in India," *The Friend of India.* Quarterly Series (No. 1): 130-154, pp. 132-133.

Ashcroft, Bill, Gareth Griffiths and Helen Tiffin, eds. *The Post-colonial Studies Reader.* London: Routledge, 1995.

Atherton, Ian. "The Itch grown a Disease: Manuscript Transmission of news in the Seventeenth century" in *News, Newspaper and Society in Early Modern Britain*, ed. Joan Raymon London: Frank Cass, 1999. pp. 39-65.

Bakhtin, Mikhail. *The Dialogic Imagination*, edited by Michael Holquist. Austin: University of Texas Press, 2004.

Ballantyne, Tony. *Orientalism and Race: Aryanism in the British Empire.* New York: Palgrave, 2002.

Baron, Sabrina, Eric Lindquist and Eleanor Shevlin, eds. *Agent of Change: Print Culture Studies After Elizabeth L Eisenstein.* Amherst: University of Massachusets Press, 2007.

Benedict, Barbara. *Readers, Writers, Reviewers and the Professionalization of Literature*. Cambridge: Cambridge University Press, 2006.

Barrow, Ian. *Making History, Drawing Territory: British Mapping in India, c. 1756-1905*. New Delhi: Oxford University Press, 2003.

Bentinck, William. "Bentinck's Minute on the Press dated January 6, 1829" in *The Correspondences of Lord William Cavendish*, Vol. I. ed. C.H. Philips. Oxford: Oxford University Press, 1977.

Bhabha, Homi, ed. *Nation and Narration*. London: Routledge, 1990.

———. *The Location of Culture*. New York: Routledge, 1994.

Bhattacharya, Tithi. *Powers of Print*. New Delhi: Oxford University Press, 2007.

Bishop, L. "Book History". *The John Hopkins Guide to Literary Theory and Criticism*, ed. Michael Groden, Martin Kreiswirth, and Imre Szeman. 2nd Ed. Baltimore: John Hopkins UP, 2005, pp. 131-136.

Black, Jeremy. *The English Press in the Eighteenth Century*. London: Croom Helm, 1987.

Blackburn, Stuart. *Print, Folklore and Nationalism in Colonial South India*. New Delhi: Permanent Black, 2003.

Blackburn, Stuart, and Vasudha Dalmia, eds. *India's Literary History. Essays on the Nineteenth Century*. New Delhi: Permanent Black, 2004.

Blake, Norman. *Caxton and his World*. London: Andre Deutsch,1969.

Brown, Matthew. "The Thick Style: Steady Sellers, Textual Aesthetics, and Early Modern Devotional Reading." *PMLA*. Vol. 121(1): 67-86.

Borsay, Peter. *The English Urban Renaissance: Culture and Society in the Provincial Town, 1660-1770*. Oxford: Oxford University Press, 1989.

Bowen, H.V. *The Business of Empire: The East India Company and Imperial Britain, 1756-1833*. Cambridge: Cambridge University Press, 2006.

Buckingham, James Silk, ed. *Derozio's Poems, The Oriental Herald and Journal of General Literature*. Vol. XXII, July to September 1829, London: Hurst, Chance, 1829.

Burton, Antoinette. *At the Heart of Empire, Indians and the colonial encounter in Late-Victorian Britain*. Berkeley: University of California Press, 1998.

Busteed, H.E. *Echoes from Old Calcutta, Reminiscences of the days of Warren Hastings, Francis, and Impey*. Calcutta: Rupa and Co., 2005.

Campbell, Jill. "Domestic Intelligence. Newspaper Advertising and the Eighteenth Century Novel" *The Yale Journal of Criticism* 15(2): 251-291.

Chakravarty, Swapan, and Abhijit Gupta, eds. *Print Areas: Book History in India*. New Delhi: Permanent Black, 2004.

———. *Moveable Type*. New Delhi & Ranikhet: Permanent Black, 2008.

Chanda, Mrinal Kanti. *The History of the English Press in Bengal*. Calcutta: K.P. Bagchi, 1988.

Chatterjee, Rimi B. *Empires of the Mind: A History of Oxford University Press in India under the Raj*. New Delhi: Oxford University Press, 2006.

Chaudhury, Rosinka. *Gentleman Poets in Colonial Bengal. Emergent Nationalism and the Orientalist Project*. Calcutta: Seagull, 2002.

Chaudhuri, Sukanta, ed. *Calcutta: The Living City. Volume I: The Past*. Calcutta: Oxford University Press, 1990.

Christian, Barbara. *Black Feminist Criticism: Perspectives on black women writers*. Teachers College Press, 1985.

--------- "But What Do We Think We've Being Doing Anyway: The State of Black Feminist Criticism(s) or My Version of a Little Bit of History" in *New Black Feminist Criticism 1985-2000, Barbara Christian*, eds. Gloria Bowles, M. Giulia Febi and Arlene R. Keizer. Urbana: University of Illinois Press, 2007. pp. 5-19.

-------- *Black Women Novelists: The Development of a Tradition*. Westport, Connecticut: Greenwood Press, 1980.

Crain, Patricia. "Print and Everyday Life in the Eighteenth Century" in *Perspectives on American Book History*, eds. Scott E. Casper, Joanne D. Chaison, and Jeffrey D. Groves. Amherst, MA: University of Massachusetts Press, 2002. pp. 47-78.

Colebrooke, H.T. *Essays on the History, Literature and Religions of Ancient India*. New Delhi: Cosmo Publications, reprint 1977.

Collet, Sophia Dobson. *The Life and Letters of Raja Rammohun Roy*, ed. Dilip

Kumar Biswas and Prabhat Chandra Ganguli. Calcutta: Sadharon Brahmo Samaj, 1900. Reprint 1988.

Colley, Linda. *Britons: Forging the Nation, 1707-1837*. Yale: Yale University Press, 2005.

Darnton, Robert. "Literary Surveillance in the British Raj. The Contradictions of Liberal Imperialism." *Book History* 4(2001):133-176.

———. *The Kiss of Lamourette. Reflections in Cultural History*. New York: Norton, 1990.

Das, Sisir Kumar. *Sahibs and munshis: an account of the College of Fort William*. Calcutta: Orion Publications, 1978.

Dasgupta, Keya. "A City Away from Home: The Mapping of Calcutta" in *Texts of Power. Emerging Disciplines in Colonial Bengal*, ed. Partha Chatterjee. Minneapolis: University of Minneapolis Press, 1995.

Derozio, Poet of India: The Definitive Edition. ed. Rosinka Chaudhuri. New Delhi: Oxford University Press, 2008.

Dirk, Nicholas. ed. "Introduction," in *Colonialism and Culture*. Ann Arbor: University of Michigan Press, 1992.

Drummond, David. *The Weekly Examiner*, 15th August (1840): 280.

DuBois, William. *The Souls of Black Folks*. New York and London: Norton, 1999.

Duff, Alexander. *India and India Missions*. Edinburgh: Whittaker, 1839.

Earl of Northbrook. *The Teachings of Jesus Christ in His Own Words*. London, Sampson Low, 1990.

Edney, Matthew. *Mapping an Empire. The Geographical Construction of British India, 1765-1843*. Chicago: University of Chicago Press, 1999.

Eisenstein, Elizabeth. *The Printing Press as an Agent of Change*. Cambridge: Cambridge University Press, 1980.

Fanon, Frantz. *The Wretched of the Earth,* Reprint of *Les damnes de la terre*. New York: Grove, 1968.

———. *Black Skin, White Mask,* Reprint of *Peau noire, masques blancs*. London: Pluto Press, 1986.

Febvre, Lucien and Henri-Jean Martin. *The Coming of the Book. The Impact of Printing. 1450-1800*. London: NLB, 1976.

Finkelstein, David, and Alistair McCleery, eds. *The Book History Reader*. New York: Routledge, 2002.

Fort William-India House Correspondence, vol. IX, 1782-85, edited by B.A. Saletore, Delhi, 1959.

Foucault, Michel. *The History of Sexuality Vol. I*. New York: Vintage, 1990.

———. *Discipline and Punishment: The Birth of a Prison*. New York: Vintage, 1995.

Fraser, Nancy. *Unruly Practices: Power, Discourse, and Gender in Contemporary Social Theory*. Minneapolis: University of Minnesota Press, 1989.

———. *Justice Interruptus*. New York: Routledge, 1997.

Ghosh, Anindita. "An Uncertain 'Coming of the Book'; Early Print Cultures in Colonial India." *Book History* 6(2003):23-55.

Giddens, Anthony. *The Consequences of Modernity*. Cambridge: Polity, 1990.

Gilchrist, John. *A Dictionary of English and Hindoostanee*. Stuart and Cooper, n.d.

Gilroy, Paul. *The Black Atlantic: Modernity and Double Consciousness*. London: Verso, 1993.

Gramsci, Antonio. *Selections from the Prison Notebooks*. Translated and edited by Quintin Hoare and Geoffrey Nowell Smith. New York: International Publishers, 1971.

Greene, Jody. "Francis Kirkman's Counterfeit Authority: Autobiography, Subjectivity, Print." *PMLA* 121(1):17-32.

Habermas, Jurgen. *The Structural Transformation of the Public Sphere*, trans. Thomas Burger. Cambridge: MIT Press, 1989.

Halhed, Nathaniel. *A Grammar of the Bengal Language*. 1778. Reprint, ed. R. C. Alston. England: The Scolar Press, 1969.

Hall, Catherine. *White, Male and Middle Class: Explorations in Feminist History*. London: Routledge, 1992.

———. "Histories, Empires and the Post-Colonial Moment" in *The Post-Colonial Question: Common Skies, Divided Horizons*, ed. Iain Chambers and Lidia Curtis. New York: Routledge, 1996, pp. 65-77.

Harley, Brian. *The New Nature of Maps; Essays in the History of Cartography.* Baltimore: John Hopkins University Press, 2002.

Hogg, Richard and David Denison, eds. *A History of the English Language.* Cambridge: Cambridge University Press, 1992.

Jacobson, Matthew. *Special Sorrows: The Diasporic Imagination of Irish, Polish, and Jewish Immigrants in the United States.* Berkeley: University of California Press, 2002.

------ *Whiteness of a Different Color: European Immigrants and the Alchemy of Race.* Cambridge: Harvard University Press, 1999.

Jones, Adrian, *The Nature of the Book: Print and Knowledge in the Making.* Chicago: University of Chicago Press, 2000.

Jones, William. *The Collected Works of Sir William Jones. 3 Volumes.* New York: New York University Press, 1993.

Joshi, Priya. *In Another Country: Colonialism, Culture, and the English Novel in India.* New York: Columbia University Press, 2002.

———. "Quantative Method, Literary History," *Book History* 5(2002):263-274.

Joshi, V.C. and Rajat Ray. eds. *Rammohun Roy and the Process of Modernization in India.* Delhi, Vikas Publishing House, 1975.

Kāmala, Abu Henā Mostapha. *The Bengali Press and Literary Writing, 1818-31,* 1st edition. Dacca: University Press, 1977.

Kesavan, B.S. *The History of Printing and Publishing in India.* India: National Book Trust, 1984.

Kuiter, William. *The British in Bengal 1756-1773, a Society in Transition Seen through the Biography of a Rebel: William Bolts, 1739-1808.* Paris: Les Indes Savante, 2002.

Lehrer, Seth. "Epilogue: Falling Asleep over the History of the Book" *PMLA* 121 (1):229-234.

Lepore, Jill. "Literacy and Reading in Puritan New England." *Perspectives on American Book History,* ed. Scott Jasper, Joanne Chaison and Jeffrey Groves. Amherst: University of Massachusetts Press, 2002, pp. 17-46.

Majumdar, Jatindra Kumar. *Raja Rammohun Roy and Progressive Movements in India, A Selection of Records (1775-1845).* Calcutta: Art Press, 1941.

McDowell, Paula. "Defoe and the Contagion of the Oral: Modeling Media Shift in A Journal of the Plague Year." *PMLA* 121(1):87-106.

Mc Leod, Jacqueline. *Crossing Boundaries: Comparative History of Black People in Diaspora.* Bloomington: Indiana University Press, 1999.

Mukerjee, Meenakshi. *The Perishable Empire. Essays on Indian Writing in English.* New Delhi: Oxford University Press, 2002.

Muller, Max. *Biographical Essays.* London: C. Scribner's Sons, 1884.

Murshid, Ghulam. ed. *Letters of Michael Madhusudan Dutt: The Heart of a Rebel*

Poet. Delhi: Oxford University Press, 2007.

Naregal, Veena. *Language Politics, Elites and the Public Sphere: Western India under Colonialism*. London: Anthem Press, 2001.

Mackie, Erin. ed. *The Commerce of Everyday Life: Selections from the Tatler and the Spectator*. England: Palgrave Macmillan, 1998.

Marshall, P.J. "The White Town of Calcutta under the Rule of the East India Company." *Modern Asian Studies* 34.2(2000):307-331.

---------. *The Making and Unmaking of Empires. Britain, India and America c. 1750-1783*. New York: Oxford University Press, 2005.

Mehrotra, Arvind Krishna. *An Illustrated History of Indian Literature in English*. New Delhi: Permanent Black, 2008.

Mongia, Padmini. *Contemporary Postcolonial Theory: A Reader*. London: Arnold, 1996.

Nair, Thankappan. ed. *Calcutta in the Eighteenth Century*. Calcutta: KLM Firma, 1984.

---------. *A History of the Calcutta Press*. Calcutta: KLM Firma, 1987.

---------. ed. *Calcutta in the Nineteenth Century*. Calcutta: Firma KLM, 1999.

---------. *Hicky and His Gazette*. Calcutta: S.T. Books, 2001.

Nevett, T.R. *Advertising in Britain: A History*. London: Heineman, 1982.

Ogborn, Miles. *Indian Ink, Script and Print in the Making of the English East India Company*. Chicago, University of Chicago Press, 1997.

Outram, Dorinda. "Cross Cultural Encounters in the Enlightenment" in

The Enlightenment World, ed. Martin Fitzpatrick Peter Jones et al. New York: Routledge, 2004.

Pearson, Jacqueline. *Women's Reading in Britain, 1750-1835: A Dangerous Recreation*. Cambridge: Cambridge University Press, 1999.

Raj, Kapil. "Refashioning Civilities, Engineering Trust: William Jones, Indian Intermediaries and the Production of Reliable Legal Knowledge in Late Eighteenth century Bengal." *Studies in History* 17(2001):23-47.

"Review of Halhed's *Grammar of the Bengal Language*." in *The English Review, or, An Abstract of English and Foreign Literature* 1(1783):5-14.

"Review of *A Grammar of the Bengal Language*," *A New Review* 3(1783):156-157.

Robertson, Bruce Carlisle. *Raja Rammohun Roy: The Father of Modern India*. New Delhi: Oxford University Press, 1999.

Robertson, Emma. *Scenes and Characteristics of Hindostan*. London: William H. Allen and Co., 1835.

Rose, Jonathan. *The Intellectual Life of the British Working Classes*. New Haven: Yale University Press, 2001.

Said, Edward. *Orientalism*. New York: Vintage, 1979.

Sarkar, Sushoban Chandra. *Notes on the Bengal Renaissance*. Bombay: People's Publishing House, 1946.

Seal, Brajendranath. *Rammohun, the Universal Man*. Calcutta: Sadharon Brahmo Samaj, 1933.

Sen, D.C. *History of Bengali Language and Literature*. Calcutta: Calcutta University Press, 1911.

Shaw, Graham. *Printing in Calcutta to 1800: A Description and Checklist of Printing in Late 18th Century Calcutta*. London: The Bibliographical Society, 1981.

Shevelow, Kathryn. *Women and Print Culture. The Construction of Femininity in the Early Periodical*. London and New York: Routledge, 1989.

Sinha, Mrinalini. *Colonial Masculinity: The 'Manly Englishman' and the 'Effeminate Bengali' in the Late Nineteenth Century*. New York, St. Martin's Press, 1995.

Stallybrass, Peter and Allon White. *The Politics and Poetics of Transgression*. Ithaca: Cornell University Press, 1985.

Stark, Ulrike. *An Empire of Books: Naval Kishore Press and the Diffusion of the Printed Word in Colonial India*. New Delhi: Permanent Black, 2009.

Stocqueler, J.H. "The Calcutta Press," *Calcutta Quarterly Magazine and Review* 3(October 1833):424-425.

Black Public Sphere, The. ed. the Black Public Sphere Collective. Chicago: University of Chicago Press, 1995.

The English Works of Raja Rammohun Roy. Parts I - V. ed. Dr. Kalidas Nag and Debajyoti Burman. Calcutta: Sadharon Brahmo Samaj, 1948.

The Cabridge Companion to Foucault, ed. Gary Gutting. Cambridge: Cambridge University Press, 2006.

Vincent, David. *Literacy and Popular Culture: England 1750-1914*. Cambridge: Cambridge University Press, 1989.

Walker, David. "Our Wretchedness in Consequence of the Colonizing Plan" in *David Walker's Appeal to the Coloured Citizens of the World*, ed. Peter P. Hinks. University Park: Penn State Press, 2000. pp. 47-82.

Walking the Streets of Eighteenth- century London, John Gay's Trivia (1716), eds. Clare Brant and Susan E Whyman, "Introduction." New York: Oxford University Press, 2007.

Wall, Wendy. *The Imprint of Gender: Authority and Publication in the English Renaissance*. Ithaca, Cornell UP, 1993.

Walvin, James. *Fruits of Empire: Exotic Produce and British Taste. 1660 -1880*. New York: New York University Press, 1997.

Warner, Michael. *Letters of the Republic* (Harvard: Harvard University Press, 1990).

---- *Publics/ Counter Publics*. Cambridge: Zone Books, 2003.

Waters, Malcolm. *Globalization*. London and NY: Routledge, 2001.

Wilson, H. *Essays and Lectures on the Religions of the Hindus*. New Delhi: APS Reprint, 1976.

Wilson, Kathleen. "The Good, the Bad, and the Impotent: Imperialism and the Politics of Identity in Georgian England," in *The Consumption of Culture,* ed. Ann Bermingham and John Brewer. New York: Routledge, 1995, pp. 237-262.

———. *The Sense of the People, Politics, Culture and Imperialism. 1715-1785.* Cambridge: Cambridge University Press, 1995.

IMPERIAL PRINT IN COLONIAL CALCUTTA (1780-1820).

www.ingramcontent.com/pod-product-compliance
Lightning Source LLC
Chambersburg PA
CBHW071201160426
43196CB00011B/2149